Afterlife

Afterlife

THE STRANGE FATE OF
LITERARY REMAINS

DAVID WYATT

LOUISIANA STATE UNIVERSITY PRESS
BATON ROUGE

Published by Louisiana State University Press
lsupress.org

Copyright © 2025 by David Wyatt
All rights reserved. Except in the case of brief quotations used in articles or reviews, no part of this publication may be produced or transmitted in any format or by any means without written permission of Louisiana State University Press.

Designer: Kaelin Chappell Broaddus
Typefaces: Arno Pro, text; Lapture Display and Acumin Pro Wide, display

Cover image courtesy Martina Berg/Adobe Stock.

Library of Congress Cataloging-in-Publication Data

Names: Wyatt, David, 1948– author.
Title: Afterlife : the strange fate of literary remains / David Wyatt.
Description: Baton Rouge : Louisiana State University Press, 2025. | Includes bibliographical references and index.
Identifiers: LCCN 2024048627 (print) | LCCN 2024048628 (ebook) | ISBN 978-0-8071-8394-6 (cloth) | ISBN 978-0-8071-8403-5 (paperback) | ISBN 978-0-8071-8450-9 (epub) | ISBN 978-0-8071-8452-3 (pdf)
Subjects: LCSH: Posthumous books. | Unfinished books. | LCGFT: Literary criticism.
Classification: LCC PN56.P558 W93 2025 (print) | LCC PN56.P558 (ebook) | DDC 809—dc23/eng/20250131
LC record available at https://lccn.loc.gov/2024048627
LC ebook record available at https://lccn.loc.gov/2024048628

for Leslie Brisman

CONTENTS

ACKNOWLEDGMENTS ix

Introduction 1

ONE ♦ *King Lear* and the Hope of the Reader 13

TWO ♦ Wordsworth, the Loved One, and the Making of *The Prelude* 36

THREE ♦ Ending *Great Expectations* 57

FOUR ♦ Harriet Jacobs and the Ordeal of Reception 85

FIVE ♦ The Dickinson Wars 109

SIX ♦ Faulkner Revises: *Sartoris* and *Flags in the Dust* 126

SEVEN ♦ Plath and the Rabbit Catcher 147

EIGHT ♦ "Have Sure Tried": Hemingway's Unfaltering Career 168

NINE ♦ Ralph Ellison's Labor of Love 188

Afterword: Literature and Re-Dreaming 208

NOTES 215

BIBLIOGRAPHY 231

INDEX 245

ACKNOWLEDGMENTS

Howard Norman, my most faithful reader, has been with me every step of the way. He not only read and reread every sentence but gave me my first one. For this and countless other acts of friendship, I cannot thank him enough.

My Maryland colleague Bob Levine provided essential encouragement at the moment of setting out, and his work as an editor also set an inspiring standard. If you want to get something done, ask for help from a busy man.

Al Filreis came on board near the end and assisted me across the finish line. On his boundless enthusiasm, I am happy to continue to depend.

Jerry Kennedy opened the door for me at Louisiana State University Press, and his thoughtful response to my chapter on Hemingway made it a much better thing. At the press, James W. Long was a faithful shepherd of my manuscript through the production process, and Elizabeth Gratch smoothed out the rough edges with her peerless copyediting.

John Meredith Hill's lovely letter about teaching Plath's poems reminded me of how many of them deal with the anxiety of "whether there will be new poems arriving at the kitchen table after the dishes are done."

Over a decade ago, Ted Leinwand asked me to fill in for him in his Shakespeare course. Little did I know how much would result from that lecture on *King Lear*. When I set out to write about Shakespeare, Ted gave me the benefit of his eagle eye, and Sandy Mack also cheered me along. Nothing could have been more encouraging than his simple reply, "I think it works."

At *The Hopkins Review,* Dora Malech continues to support my work in a quarterly as scholarly as it is sexy. Permission to reprint "The Dickinson Wars" is gratefully acknowledged.

At *American Literary History,* Gordon Hutner refined my Hemingway chapter through a very fine sieve, and I thank him for permission to reprint "'Have Sure Tried': Hemingway's Unfaltering Career."

Thanks as well to HarperCollins for permission to quote Plath's "The Rabbit Catcher."

Thanks are due as well to the librarians at the Kennedy Library in Boston for all their good help with the Hemingway Collections and to the archivists in the Special Collections at Virginia for guiding me though the Faulkner and Noel Polk papers. Permission to quote from these holdings is gratefully acknowledged.

In dedicating my book to Leslie Brisman, I acknowledge the spirit of John Milton hovering over the entire project. My lifelong love of *Paradise Lost* was instilled in me by Leslie during my senior year at Yale, and I am happy to see that as of this writing he is still teaching there. It is also necessary for me to correct an error: in my published recollections of our time together, "The Last Spring at Yale," I recalled a meal served to me by Leslie that included pork. As Leslie keeps kosher, this could not have happened, and I want to apologize to Leslie and to his family for this unfortunate act of misremembering.

Afterlife

Introduction

Books have biographies. Some literary works pass into print with minimal editing or second thoughts; others take a long and winding road, even across centuries, before finding their way between covers. If you believe that "Publication – is the Auction / Of the Mind of Man," you will withhold all but a handful of your 1789 poems from the public during your lifetime. If you think of your five-act plays more as guides to production than as works meant for a reader's eye, you will give less attention to their post-performance life than you have given to the publication of your narrative poems. The reluctance and the diffidence turned out to have a fructifying effect, giving us the Dickinson and the Shakespeare industries. By contrast, if you have the energy and the time, you may attempt to foreclose any future messing with your novels and stories by revising them yourself, by gracing them with prefaces, and by bringing them out in a *New York Edition*. James was thereby able to give his work an "after-life," as F. W. Dupee calls it, while he was still alive.

This is a book about what happens to a body of work left unpublished or in some way unfinished at a writer's death. Some bookshelves, like Henry James's, discourage rearrangement because they have been fully rounded out and even reshaped by the author before the advent of "the distinguished thing." Others remain radically open-ended and have therefore lent themselves to posthumous editing. When Hemingway took his life in July 1961, for instance, he left behind at least five major unfinished projects, including a memoir of his early years in Paris, two thousand handwritten pages of a honeymoon novel, and a novelized account of his 1954 safari. Each of these three manuscripts eventually found its editor and so became, respectively, *A Moveable Feast* (1964), *The Garden of Eden* (1986), and *True at First Light* (1999).

There are many kinds of literary remains, with the thousands of handwritten and typed pages in the Hemingway archive being an extreme example of abundance. Dickinson left behind fascicles—handwritten pages tied together with string—and a curious kind of notation, one involving a romance with the dash, that has left scholars to wonder and to argue about the proper orthography for her lines. In Shakespeare's case, the quartos square off against the folios, as they pit first versions against later, perhaps more reliable ones. Given the vexed condition of so many beloved texts, it is perhaps not surprising that between the author and the published work falls the editor.

But editing turns out to be inseparable from error. Whoever edited act 1 of *Henry V* managed to introduce a crux of which careers are made. Mistress Quickly is remembering Falstaff as he nears his end: "A parted ev'n just between twelve and one, ev'n at the turning o' the tide—for after I saw him fumble with the sheets, and play with flowers, and smile upon his finger's end, I knew there was but one way. For his nose was as sharp as a pen, and a babbled of green fields" (2.3.11–16). How lovely it is, to imagine this great heart ending his life by invoking England's green and pleasant land. But the final phrase in the recollection was not the original phrase, as a footnote in *The Norton Shakespeare* reminds us. The folio text ends with the phrase *a Table of green fields*. Lewis Theobald provided "the justly admired emendation" in 1726, and the change has stood the test of time, with most scholars accepting the change as responding to what Samuel Johnson calls "the hope of the reader," the hope in this case being that Falstaff's final words might make a kind of beautiful sense.

While, in the following pages, I am more concerned with the practical decisions made by editors than with theories of "textual editing," it may be useful nevertheless to rehearse one of the major controversies about the ways in which literary works ought to be presented to the public.

In his 1950 article "The Rationale of Copy-Text," W. W. Greg attempted to refine the idea of a "copy-text," a concept originated by Ronald B. McKerrow in his edition of the works of Thomas Nashe. In the search for "some one text . . . as providing over-riding authority," McKerrow had argued for "using the earliest 'good' print as copy-text." Despite McKerrow's use of the word *good* in his definition of which copy-text to adopt, in deploying the adjective, he did not mean to invite editors to behave as *literary* critics: "We are not to regard the 'goodness' of a reading in and by itself, or to consider whether it appeals to our aesthetic sensibilities or not."

Despite McKerrow's strictures, Greg was careful to admit that it might not always be possible to secure "the guidance of some particular early text." How was one to adjudicate between the three extant texts of *King Lear*, for instance, when it was clear that the earliest of the published versions was in many ways corrupt? Greg went on to issue a warning against falling prey to "the tyranny of the copy-text." "Wherever there is more than one substantive text of comparable authority . . . the copy-text should be allowed no over-riding or even preponderant authority." Finally, "it is impossible to exclude individual judgement from editorial procedure." Even as he strove to lay down an authoritative way of proceeding, Greg found himself compelled to admit that the act of editing was sometimes a deeply subjective enterprise.

By the early 1960s, the McKerrow-Greg copy-text paradigm came nevertheless to dominate the world of scholarly editing in the United States. That story begins with Mark Twain.

In 1961, an executive at the recently reorganized Harper & Row proposed to bring out a new uniform edition of Twain's works—the last such edition dated back to 1899. The Twain industry was in chaos; the Library of Congress listed over twenty-six hundred variant publications of Twain's works. Scholars at the University of Iowa and, later, the University of California attempted to tackle the job of bringing respectable versions of Twain back into print.

Meanwhile, in 1963, the Modern Language Association (MLA)

established the Center for Editions of American Authors—the CEAA. The principles guiding editorial decisions at the center were laid down by Fredson Bowers, who argued that the McKerrow-Greg approach to scholarly editing now reigned supreme. Funding for the enterprise was sought from the Ford Foundation and, after its founding in 1965, from the National Endowment for the Humanities (NEH). Millions of dollars were disbursed by the CEAA to editorial projects located at universities around the country, resulting in highly labored editions of Melville, Hawthorne, Crane, and Twain. In 1976, the CEAA was renamed and replaced by the Center for Scholarly Editions (CSE). Still an arm of the MLA, the CSE no longer operated as a grant-making entity and existed instead to give a seal of approval after an edition had been inspected by a representative of the committee.

As the approved CEAA editions began to appear, they caught the attention of Lewis Mumford. In a 1968 article entitled "Emerson behind Barbed Wire," Mumford offered an acerbic review of the Belknap Press's edition of Emerson's journals. Focusing on the first of what became sixteen volumes, Mumford argued that "the present edition is an exhibition of current standards of American scholarship at its meticulous best *by* scholars and strictly *for* scholars." An odd principle of selection seemed to have been at work: some 130 pages of juvenilia had been included, along with a college theme book of 44 pages. The pages of the edition were graced with "twenty different diacritical marks," with hosts of strikethroughs and parentheses within parentheses. With a "mass of raw material" on display, Mumford concluded, "this edition leaves the major task of editing to the reader."

In a follow-up article called "The Fruits of the MLA," Edmund Wilson amplified the attack. Echoing Mumford's claim that the CEAA editions were burdened with a critical apparatus making them difficult to enjoy, Wilson quoted "someone in the academic world" as saying, about Bowers's edition of Whitman, "in editing *Leaves of Grass,* he had done everything for it but read it."

One of the more pungent critiques of the CEAA editions came from inside the project itself. In 1991, Hershel Parker published an article called "Textual Criticism and Hemingway." Written in a retrospective mood, the essay looks back at work done by "the editing factories set up around the country by the Center for Editions of American Authors." Then the associate editor of the Northwestern-Newberry edition of *The Writings of Herman Melville*, Parker had an intimate knowledge of the workings of one such factory. One of the "grounds of self-incrimination," Parker writes, was that "CEAA editors tended to separate editorial work from the study of the creative process.... Our superficial grasp of textual-editorial issues left us utterly unaware of the exciting, dangerous, and significant issues rising from that ambiguous terrain where textual and biographical evidence have aesthetic implications."

Parker and McKerrow each deploy the word *aesthetic*. In *A Rationale of Textual Criticism* (1989), G. Thomas Tanselle also uses the word: "It is often said that textual criticism is a fundamental branch of scholarship because the textual critic must provide an accurate text before the literary critic can profitably begin to analyze it. But any text that a textual critic produces is itself the product of literary criticism, reflecting a particular aesthetic position and thus a particular approach to what textual 'correctness' consists of." In each passage, the "aesthetic" seems to refer to the art of the text being edited. Just how the art of the text might be identified and then reconciled with "textual and biographical evidence" leaves us, in Parker's words, on "ambiguous terrain."

Whatever the limitations of the Melville project may have been, Parker stuck with it: he eventually became the general editor of the project and oversaw its completion, in fifteen volumes, in 2017. John Bryant, the editor of the Melville Society's journal, has described the result as "not just a set of books; it is a cultural icon." Several of the Northwestern-Newberry volumes have been leased by the Library of America (LOA) and praised by Cheryl Hurley, its former president, as "scrupulous and intelligent." And there lies an irony: the Library of America often became reliant upon the very editions against which it had been conceived as an alternative.

That conception owed a lot to Edmund Wilson. Wilson had long hoped to sponsor editions of American writers fashioned after the inexpensive but handsomely produced French Pléiades series, and he protested in a letter to the *New York Review of Books* that the MLA had diverted NEH funds from his cherished project and given them instead to the CEAA. A number of scholars, including Richard Poirier and Daniel Aaron, had also been working on a project like the one envisioned by Wilson, and after securing NEH funding in 1979, they were able to launch the Library of America. The enterprise advertises itself as championing "our nation's cultural heritage by publishing America's greatest writing in authoritative new editions." LOA volumes include a minimum of scholarly apparatus and are issued with sewn bindings and published on lightweight, acid-free paper. The first LOA authors to appear were Melville, Hawthorne, Whitman, and Stowe, and as the decades wore on, the project broadened its mandate to include titles such as *Crime Novels* and *Reporting Vietnam*. In his balanced overview of the controversy surrounding modern scholarly editing, Wayne Franklin comes to the conclusion that "the Library of America is probably the single most important publishing venture in the history of American literature."

But the Library of America project did not so much find a way to solve a problem as to reconfigure it: LOA volumes often simply converted CEAA editions into a more readable form. As for the CEAA/CSE volumes themselves, doubts remain. "I'm down on MLA editions," writes Robert Levine, the general editor of *The Norton Anthology of American Literature*. "They produce ahistorical texts that work on the fantasy that editors can and should recover initial authorial intention. They also work mistakenly with the idea that all editorial interventions corrupt a MS." But "times have changed," Levine argues in an article about editing Melville's novel *Pierre*, "and a number of scholars have become suspicious of MLA-approved editions that claim, somewhat mystically, to provide what the author intended, as if authors existed apart from the processes that helped to bring their writings into print (and as if textual editors could read their minds)." Norton now tends to adopt first printings, which, pre-1925, are in the public domain.

Those of us who teach literature at the college level are looking for editions that are reliable, readable, and affordable. In a graduate seminar, we might find it useful to bring in an MLA-approved edition, but otherwise, we will rely, as in the case of Faulkner, for instance, on the Random House paperbacks edited by Noel Polk. Polk has done something marvelous, in essence splitting the difference between the approaches taken by the CEAA and the LOA. He has scrupulously based his text on the manuscripts and typescripts held at the University of Virginia and elsewhere, and he has then produced an apparatus-free page with minimal textual notes confined to an appendix. (Polk also had no CEAA volumes on which to rely.) As he writes in *Children of the Dark House,* and this despite all the care taken, "none of the texts I have edited can be considered 'definitive'—whatever that means—by any of the general standards accepted over the years by followers of W. W. Greg and Fredson Bowers and promoted by the Modern Language Association's Center for Editions of American Authors (CEAA) and its successor, the Center for Scholarly Editions (CSE)."

These matters have been addressed with care in Jerome J. McGann's *A Critique of Modern Textual Criticism.* I, too, am concerned with what McGann calls "transmission histories," but only up to a point. In his foreword to the second edition of the *Critique,* D. C. Greetham suggests that McGann can appear to be proposing a kind of interminable work. As opposed to the "search for the single unitary utterance"—the definitive edition—"McGann offers instead versions, historically mediated texts, texts in infinite regress from their moment of composition, materialist texts that achieve meaning only through the continual negotiation with the institutions of their reception and transmission."

This is a worthy project, but it is not my own. In my all too brief chapters, I attempt, rather, to locate a single, recurring problem in the lifework of the author at hand—a limit of contraction, to use William Blake's phrase—and then to illuminate it by way of the posthumous editings to which that work has been subjected. In some cases, as with Faulkner and Ellison, I do a little editing myself, expressing preferences for one or another version of the surviving texts, while in others, as with Dickinson and Plath, I am content to detail a controversy. All of the works under review—as opposed to letters, diaries, or journals—and with the exception of Dickinson's poems, are "public" works, writings created for publication.

The following chapters attempt to explore editorial choices made by persons known or unknown. Each choice has serious consequences for the ways in which our great writers will survive into the future, although the choices made are themselves subject to revision. My anthology of survivals therefore celebrates the strange and unpredictable ways in which literature fights its way onto the page even as it continues to be made new.

In choosing to focus on textual changes made after the death of the author—on what happens in the *afterlife*—I am elevating certain editors to the role of cocreator, while others, depending on your point of view, may appear as impious deformers. There might well be no readable version of Hemingway's *The Garden of Eden* without the work of editor Tom Jenks, but perhaps, as Joan Didion has argued, there ought not to be any such novel at all. In a *New Yorker* article about posthumous Hemingway entitled "Last Words," she makes the conservative case: "The peculiarity of being a writer is that the entire enterprise involves the mortal humiliation of seeing one's own words in print. The risk of publication is the grave fact of life, and, even among writers less inclined than Hemingway to construe words as the manifest expression of personal honor, the notion that words one has not risked publishing should be open to 'continuing investigation' by 'serious students of literature' could not be calculated to kindle enthusiasm." Didion proceeds to question the purpose and value of publishing everything from *A Moveable Feast* to *The Dangerous Summer*. "You think something is in shape to be published or you don't," she concludes, "and Hemingway didn't."

In the final months of his life, as Hemingway continued work on his Paris memoir, he was open with his editor at Scribner's about his struggles with the book. "Have material arranged as chapters—they come to 18—and am working on the last one—No 19—also working on title. This is very difficult." The letter is dated February 6, 1961. While much of the book was by this point complete—Mary Hemingway's 1964 edition of *A Moveable Feast* was to contain eighteen chapters—Hemingway kept working on it. In a letter addressed to Scribner's and dated April 18, 1961, a letter never mailed and one that only came to light after Hemingway's death, he wondered whether the book could be published "without a final chapter." "I failed to complete the pieces," the letter began. "I am very sorry. It is not to be published the way it is now and it has no end."

So what would we rather have? A respectful concession to a husband's final wishes or a wife's persistence in bringing his work to light, however unfinished it might appear to be? While Didion feels confident in judging the morality of the wife's editorial act, the book Scribner's did shape into print in 1964 became perhaps the most beloved in the Hemingway canon, loved especially by readers who could not be deemed, in Didion's words, "serious students of literature."

"Concentrate on *scene*," Ralph Ellison wrote to himself, as he forged ahead on his second novel, and I have taken his advice. Shakespeare leads the way, and his example proves definitive. The love test that opens *King Lear* culminates in the killing scene that ends it, and all the scenes in between can come to seem hopelessly incidental. But Shakespeare means to show us that everything happening along the way also matters, even and including a scene "left out in all the common books," as Alexander Pope wrote, and one he restored in his 1726 collated edition of Shakespeare so as to show us how Cordelia finds "a better way."

Wordsworth wrestles with where to place his two "spots of time," but he knows they are central to his memory project and to the question of whom he loves. Dickens, not quite willing to grant Pip and Estella and Miss Havisham the forgiveness they seek, captures their dilemmas in "Tell Me" scenes. For Harriet Jacobs, the struggle against her rapacious master and her jealous mistress culminates in a whispering scene in which the cruelties of slavery position the Black woman, the white man, and the white woman on a desperate circuit of deceit and desire. Believing in the efficacy of the revisionary act but also half in love with the gallantry of the prank, Faulkner cannot resist opening his third novel with male hijinks that defer his project of reckoning with the costs and pleasures of revenge. In Hemingway, the late work turns upon bedroom scenes in which men confront or finesse patterns of betrayal haunting the career from its inception. In *Three Days before the Shooting . . .*, Ellison deploys a cascade of claiming scenes dramatizing a nation's failure to extend love to all of its children. Dickinson and Plath, working in compressed lyric spaces, repeatedly call up a scene in which an exalted speaker maps out the endless distances across which she might join with or liberate herself from an obscure object of desire.

As may be apparent from this swift summary, in the course of writing this book, I have found myself drawn to a recurring theme. In a word, to what I call "love." How was it that in each of my nine chapters this subject kept coming up? Given that *love* is a word I often invoked during my fifty years of college teaching, my attraction to it should have come as no surprise. Teaching, for me, was an act of "overpassing" to love, as Faulkner puts it, a sharing of a space in which, as those of us gathered together in a room attempted to make our way through a usually difficult text, we became like Quentin and Shreve in *Absalom, Absalom!* as they attempt to understand the romance between Henry Sutpen and Charles Bon:

> "And now," Shreve said, "we're going to talk about love." But he didn't need to say that either, any more than he needed to specify which he he meant by he, since neither of them had been thinking about anything else; all that had gone before just so much that had to be overpassed and none else present to overpass it but them, as someone always has to rake up the leaves before you can have the bonfire. That was why it did not matter to either of them which one did the talking, since it was not the talking alone which did it, performed and accomplished the overpassing, but some happy marriage of speaking and hearing wherein each before the demand, the requirement, forgave condoned and forgot the faulting of the other—faultings both in the creation of this shade whom they discussed (rather, existed in) and in the hearing and sifting and discarding the false and conserving what seemed true, or fit the preconceived—in order to overpass to love, where there might be paradox and inconsistency but nothing fault nor false. (261)

It seems impertinent to break this passage down, but the example set by Quentin and Shreve throughout Faulkner's novel argues otherwise. Reading—and this is what the two young men are doing, interpreting the stories that have come down to them—involves a "demand." The activity of reading is invoked in the passage by way of the metaphor of the leaves. Not only the leaves that fall in autumn—surely the primary intended referent—but the leaves (the pages) of a book. When I come to this passage in the course of teaching *Absalom*, I hold up my copy of the novel and then run my thumb across the leaves of the book. And then I say: "These are the leaves we have been asked to rake through and then to burn, as we consume Faulkner's story, and in the process its central mystifying character is consumed. *Absalom, Absalom!* is a Bon-fire."

Charles Bon is consumed because we want to know. In the pursuit of this knowledge, in a novel filled with the repeated question "But why?" where the central question is why did Henry Sutpen shoot Charles Bon, the students and the teacher in the room (Quentin and Shreve are conducting their seminar in a dorm room at Harvard) must consent, as the two freshmen do, to hear as well as to speak. If this goes well, it results in a "happy marriage" of minds. There will be "faultings" involved, all kinds of misreadings along the way. But these faultings are valuable because they reveal the price to be paid in the struggle to understand. Empathy will often "fall far short," to quote a phrase from Harriet Jacobs. It may always fall far short of perfect understanding, and the awareness of its having done so could be called empathy's gift. The felt exposure of the limits of any one person's capacities enjoins forgiveness—overpassing—rather than condemnation and becomes part of the meaning of the interpretative process. It takes love, then, to really get at the truth about, say, a character in a novel, a passionate act of attention that comes to rest not on certainty (Faulkner dismisses the word in chapter 4 of *Absalom*) but on a reading making room for paradox and inconsistency.

Posthumous editing itself requires an act of overpassing. Given the uncertainties involved in any such attempt, those doing this work are required to accept the inevitable faultings attendant upon the process of recovery. But I have also come to believe that a study of these outcomes can generate a surprising set of revaluations. It reveals the project of literature itself to be one of continuous creation. The myth of the solitary genius working alone gives way to a model of textual making as, often enough, a work of many hands. A longing for closure must learn to comport with an acceptance of openness. Revision moves to the center of the story, and the willingness of an author to revise a text is often mirrored in that text by characters who choose to amend their behavior.

Shakespeare, Wordsworth, Dickens, Jacobs, Dickinson, Faulkner, Plath, Hemingway, Ellison—these are my chosen nine. But I feel as if they had chosen me; their work will not leave me alone, and in part because it is *unfinished*. The new discoveries that keep being made, as in the trove of Hemingway manuscripts found in 2022 at Sloppy Joe's café, also call into question how and when an author's work is ever really "done."

These writers may have chosen me, but there is no reason to choose among them. I well remember the moment during a PhD oral exam when a student, assuming her task was to judge the authors on her list and even to dismiss some of them, provoked me to say, "But we're supposed to love it all!" "Well, maybe not *all*," a colleague replied. I accepted the need for his gentle correction, but what I said I would say again. It is a matter of upholding an ideal. I therefore begin by turning to a play in which much of the trouble comes out of an attempt to force a ranking of one's loves, with King Lear's question, "Which of you shall we say doth love us most?"

ONE

King Lear and the Hope of the Reader

Samuel Johnson rejected Shakespeare's ending. He confessed himself so "shocked by Cordelia's death, that I know not whether I ever endured to read again the last scenes of the play till I undertook to revise them as an editor." Johnson preferred the ending supplied by Nahum Tate's 1681 edition of *The History of King Lear*, in which Lear and Cordelia survive. Also "run through the whole" of Tate's *Lear* is "*a* Love *betwixt* Edgar *and* Cordelia." Tate's romance plot rendered "Cordelia's *Indifference and her Father's Passion in the first Scene probable*" and helped to explain Edgar's disguise as a way of staying close to the woman he loved. Thus, as Lear turns to Cordelia and asks her to speak in act 1, Tate gives her an aside:

> Cord. Now comes my Trial, how I am distrest,
> That must with cold speech tempt the chol'rick King
> Rather to leave me Dowerless, than condemn me
> To loath'd Embraces!

Cordelia will not speak as asked, that is, because by not doing so, she guarantees the loss of her dowery and thereby debars an unwanted marriage to Burgundy. She will save herself for Edgar, and Tate's *Lear* ends with these two good characters joined in marriage. Tate's work of amendment fittingly concludes with his Lear saying to his Cordelia, as he hands her to his Edgar, "I wrong'd Him too, but here's the fair Amends."

Tate described Shakespeare's *Lear* as "a Heap of Jewels, unstrung and unpolisht; yet so dazzling in their Disorder, that I soon perceiv'd I had seiz'd a Treasure." The audiences of some 150 years approved of many of Tate's changes, especially of his final reversals. Not until 1838 did William Charles Macready attempt to bring "the true text" of *King Lear* to the stage. But this *Lear,* as Charles Shattuck writes, was "only two-thirds Shakespeare." Lines were cut as unintelligible or obscene, the blinding of Gloucester was suppressed, and Macready almost eliminated the Fool until his stage manager convinced him that a woman might play the part. His production did allow for Lear's death but concluded not with two rhymed couplets but with Kent's

> He hates him
> That would upon the rack of this tough world
> Stretch him longer.

As Stanley Wells concludes, "The metamorphoses the text has undergone in performance" over the centuries underscore the "impossibility of regarding the play of *King Lear* as anything approaching a fixed entity."

In the preface to his edition of Shakespeare's plays, Johnson describes a writer who "always makes us anxious for the event." In Shakespeare, "one event is concatenated with another, and the conclusion follows by easy consequence" such that "the end of the play is the end of expectation." But in *Lear,* Johnson argues, and even though we "are hurried irresistibly along," Shakespeare has only "incidentally enforced" his "moral" when he "suffered the virtue of Cordelia to perish in a just cause, contrary to the natural ideas of justice, to the hope of the reader, and, what is yet more strange, to the faith of chronicles." Johnson concludes the line of argument as follows: "In the present case the publick has decided. Cordelia, from the time of Tate, has always retired with victory and felicity."

As even this brief foray into the performance and publication history of *King Lear* demonstrates, the hope of the reader of the play depends upon the taste and competence of an editor.

Coleridge might seem to be echoing Johnson when he claimed that the genius of Shakespeare is "expectation in preference to surprise." But the crux of the matter turns upon what a reader might be willing and able to expect. The hope of a Restoration or eighteenth-century reader had, by the time of Coleridge's remark, given way to the much more strenuous expectations of a Charles Lamb: "A happy ending! as if the living martyrdom that Lear had gone through, the flaying of his feelings alive, did not make a fair dismissal from the stage of life the only decorous thing for him."

As Frank Kermode reminds us, "*King Lear* is a fiction that inescapably involves an encounter with oneself, and the image of one's end." The many endings imposed upon *Lear* from Tate forward turn out to constitute, however, only one variable in the ongoing human encounter with the play. And the process of editorial "amendment," as Johnson styles it, was anticipated by Shakespeare himself. As the editors of *The Norton Shakespeare* admit, "the textual traces of *King Lear* have probably given scholars more cause for debate than any of Shakespeare's other works" (2314). This is because Shakespeare's *Lear* actually exits in *three* versions: in the First Quarto version, printed in December and January 1607–8; in the First Folio version, printed in 1623; and in a Second Quarto version, printed in 1619, three years after Shakespeare's death. Quarto 2, the Norton editors argue, is "only a slightly improved copy of Q1" (2315). Quarto 1, on the other hand, contains some three hundred lines not printed in folio 1, while folio 1 contains approximately one hundred lines not printed in the quarto.

"There is a growing scholarly consensus," Stephen Greenblatt writes in his introduction to the play in *The Norton Shakespeare,* "that the 1608 text of *Lear* represents the play as Shakespeare first wrote it and that the 1623 text represents a substantial revision" (2308). The question remains: which of the two texts was the one Shakespeare "first wrote"? "The fact that Quarto precedes Folio in print," George Walton Williams argues, "does not necessitate that it should have preceded it in composition." Because folio 1 was printed later than quarto 1 and because it contains far fewer obvious errors, it was long preferred as the most authoritative text. But was the text on which the folio is based also written first—or does it represent Shakespeare's second thoughts? Such questions open onto the issue of *when* the two major versions of *King Lear* were composed and onto whether one prefers an original or an amended text. In the case of *King Lear,* it turns out that we will probably never know with any certainty which is which.

The 1623 folio (folio sheets are folded only once, making two leaves or four pages front and back, while quarto sheets are folded twice, yielding eight pages) was edited by two of Shakespeare's friends. It brought into print eighteen never-before-published plays and grouped the plays into comedies, histories, and tragedies. Only two plays not included in the First Folio, *Pericles* and *The Two Noble Kinsmen*, would later be added to the canon. As the editors of *The Norton Shakespeare* conclude, "The first collection of Shakespeare's plays was not, as far as we know, the product of the playwright's own design" (65).

The two friends who edited the First Folio "claimed to be using 'True Originall Copies' in the author's own hand" (65). None of these copies has been found. Little of what Shakespeare wrote in his own hand has survived, and for the plays, there are "neither foul papers nor fair copies nor promptbooks" (70). And yet the existence of multiple versions of a number of the plays argues that somebody did set about to revise them.

Alexander Pope's 1723–25 edition of Shakespeare's *Complete Works* addressed the problem of multiple versions by inaugurating an editorial tradition that held for some 250 years. The subtitle to his edition—"Collated and Corrected by the Former Editions"—announces what was to become a standard editorial approach: collation, or what came to be called "conflation." Folio and quarto texts were intermingled. But Pope went further, regularizing Shakespeare's meter and consigning lines considered to be bad verses to the bottom of the page. Samuel Johnson was later to remark that Pope "collated the old copies, which none had thought to examine before, and restored many lines to their integrity; but, by a very compendious criticism, he rejected whatever he disliked, and thought more of amputation than of cure."

The practice of offering a conflated text of *King Lear* persisted until 1986. In that year, and in "a startling departure from the editorial tradition," as the editors of *The Norton Shakespeare* write, Stanley Wells and Gary Taylor, the leading editors of the new *Oxford Shakespeare*, "printed two distinct versions of *King Lear*, Quarto and Folio" (73). It was necessary to print both texts, Wells and Taylor argued, because they serve as "independent witnesses to two distinct Shakespearean versions." In a review of the *Oxford Shakespeare*, and despite the claims being made to the contrary, David Bevington pointed out that "the two texts presented here are not in fact the pure Q1 *Lear* and F *Lear*, each is edited to some degree in light of the other." "The difficulty," he concludes, "is in knowing where to stop in what is after all a kind of conflation."

When it came to producing a text for the Oxford World's Classics series some fourteen years later, Wells had to choose what he called a "base text." Noting that "it is the general policy of this series to base an edition on the text that lies closest to performance" and that the folio "brings us closer to performance than the Quarto, it might have seemed logical to present an edited text of that version, too." But Wells nevertheless went with the quarto. The first reason given for that choice: "The Quarto text has rarely been edited in its own right." The New Cambridge Shakespeare had earlier decided otherwise. Jay L. Halio based his 1992 edition of *Lear* on the folio, not the quarto.

Wells proceeded to admit that despite having argued against conflation in his monumental 1986 edition of the plays, he had now decided to engage in it: his new edition of *Lear* "necessarily incorporates a number of the Folio's alternative readings." Why would Wells consent to alter his practice? Because at "points the Folio offers readings which are arguably superior to those of the Quarto." Wells thereby worked his way back to where Pope started, not by producing a text that closely follows Pope but by conceding that the best text of the play he can offer will be, too, a conflated one—and thus another *King Lear* came into being.

Given the ever-shifting text of *King Lear*, a fate also shared by a number of Shakespeare's other plays, it is no wonder that twentieth-century theories of textual editing often had their genesis in a study of the playwright's art. In *The Editorial Problem in Shakespeare*, W. W. Greg attempted to lay out five rules that "should govern the procedure of an editor of Shakespeare," rules that also could be applied broadly to the making of any scholarly edition. Rule 1 states: "The aim of a critical edition should be to present the text, so far as the available evidence permits, in the form in which we may suppose that it would have stood in a fair copy, made by the author himself, of the work as he finally intended it." Greg then immediately issues a warning: "A fair copy is postulated in order that the original may be supposed to have accurately represented the author's intention and that all obvious slips may be ascribed to defective transmission." The use of the word *intention* carries with it the hope that such a thing once existed and might now be determinable. But to speak of intention with regard to an author as fugitive as

Shakespeare calls upon us to become as one of "God's spies." Lear voices this fantasy as he and Cordelia are about to be taken away to prison. "So we'll live," he imagines, "And take upon's the mystery of things / As if we were God's spies" (5.3.11–18). For these lines, Johnson supplies a wonderful note. Where a previous editor of the play had "interpreted this as 'spies' to 'watch' God's 'motions,'" Johnson writes, "I rather take the other meaning. As if we were angels commissioned to survey and report the lives of other men, and were consequently endowed with the power of prying into the original motives of action and the mysteries of conduct." Johnson's sense of a spy of God comes close to describing the imaginative capacities of Shakespeare himself. His editors, however, can scarcely lay claim to such a power, and as much as Shakespeare may have probed the mysteries of conduct, he was, as Keats affirms, also possessed of "*Negative Capability*, that is when man is capable of being in uncertainties, Mysteries, doubts, without any irritable reaching after fact and reason." The acquisition of that capability is the promised end of reading Shakespeare and one that ought to chasten any reaching after such a thing as authorial will or intention.

My text of *King Lear* is derived from the 1997 edition of *The Norton Shakespeare*. The Norton editors chose to follow the *Oxford Shakespeare* by printing both *The History of King Lear*, based on quarto 1, and *The Tragedy of King Lear*, based on folio 1. But confronted with the fact that centuries of audience response and commentary were based on a conflated text of the 1608 and 1623 versions, the Norton editors also chose to include in their edition a *King Lear (Conflated Text)*, prepared by Barbara K. Lewalski. They do so "so that readers will have the opportunity to assess for themselves the effects of the traditional editorial practice" (76). Unless otherwise indicated, all quotations from *King Lear* in this chapter, along with any plot summary, rely on Lewalski.

In the final moments of *King Lear*, Kent asks a question about endings themselves: "Is this the promised end?" (5.3.262). Given the apocalyptic series of closing events, the question is generally understood to refer to Doomsday itself. But Kent's question can also be taken as an invocation of the hope of the reader. Does the scene we are witnessing serve, in Johnson's phrase, as the promised "end of expectation," or is it, to recall Coleridge's pejorative term, only a terrible "surprise"? And more narrowly, and given our readerly hopes, who ought to enjoy the privilege of speaking the play's last lines? Before taking up these questions, a summary of the closing events may be useful.

As act 5, scene 3, opens, Lear and Cordelia are brought on as prisoners. They exit, and Edmund commissions the Captain to kill them both. Albany, Goneril, and Regan enter, and the two sisters argue over Edmund. Albany attempts to arrest Edmund for treason, but the trumpet sounds, Edgar enters, fights with his brother, and mortally wounds him. Albany produces Goneril's love letter to Edmund, and as she leaves the stage, she says, "Ask me not what I know" (5.3.159). Edgar reveals his identity and tells his brief tale. A Gentleman runs on stage with a bloody knife—Goneril and Regan are dead. Kent enters and asks after the king. The bodies of Goneril and Regan are carried onstage. Edmund, meaning to do some good before he dies, sends to the castle to stay the ordered executions. Edgar exits, carrying Edmund's sword. Then comes the stage direction, "*Re-enter* LEAR, *with* CORDELIA *dead in his arms*" (5.3.256). Lear strains after the breath of life—"This feather stirs" (5.3.264)—and manages to recognize Kent. Edmund's death is announced, and Albany grants Lear his "absolute power" (5.3.299). Still looking for signs of life, "Look on her, look, her lips / Look there, look there!" Lear dies (5.3.309–10). And then the last words are spoken:

> The weight of this sad time we must obey;
> Speak what we feel, not what we ought to say.
> The oldest hath borne most; we that are young
> Shall never see so much, nor live so long.
>
> (5.3.322–25)

"Speak what we feel, not what we ought to say": coming as it does in the final speech in the play, the plea has a kind of built-in authority. But the difficulty of doing what is here being recommended is one of the major subjects of *King Lear*. Moreover, it is not even clear who is meant to be the speaker of the closing lines. "It was a convention of Shakespearean tragedy," Jonathan Bate reminds us, "that the new man in power always has the last word." Given this rule, the last speaker in the play ought to be the Duke of Albany. It may therefore be somewhat disturbing to learn that the closing lines of *King Lear* are assigned in the surviving texts of the play to two different characters. In quarto 1, the play's closing lines are given to Albany. In the folio, they are assigned to Edgar.

Shakespeare may have authored both endings, or one may have entered the text by way of an editor or a mistake. Either way, we now have a complementarity. A crux like this need not, however, act as a bar to interpretation but, rather, as an invitation to making more meaning. Given that equal validity has been ascribed by scholars to coexisting versions of quite different *Lears*, a thought experiment centering on Edgar and Albany may therefore be in order.

The case for Edgar. Of the five children in *King Lear*, the best hope lies with Edgar. Can he hold his own against his brother Edmund's stagings? Deploying a forged letter, Edmund convinces Gloucester that Edgar is planning to supplant him. At first, Edgar says very little. Edmund speaks for him, even putting words in his mouth, as in the "'Thou unpossessing bastard!'" speech in act 2.1. Two scenes later, Edgar shares with the audience his plan "to take the basest and most poorest shape" of a beggar (2.3.7), and the counterplot begins. Edgar's performance of madness will exceed Hamlet's as he descends into a language almost indecipherable and yet strangely pregnant. By the middle of the play, he appears to be speaking as if out of the British unconscious, of Flibbertigibbet, old hunting ballads, Jack and the Beanstalk. Lear deems Edgar's poor Tom o' Bedlam a philosopher, in part because his beggar self appears to have taken to heart Lear's advice to himself: "Take physic, pomp" (3.4.34). Engaging in a willed self-humbling, Edgar attempts to purge himself of the self-pity that leads so many other characters in the play to disaster. "How light and portable my pain seems now" he manages to say, after sharing the storm and the heath with Lear (3.6.101).

Edgar is changeable, capable of amendment. The capacity to amend his actions is noticeably lacking in Lear, although of Shakespeare's tragic figures he will, by the end, have been most altered. "Mend your speech a little," Lear says to Cordelia (1.1.93), after she has told him that she loves him "According to my bond; nor more nor less" (1.1.92). "Mend when thou canst," he says to Goneril, when she proves unwelcoming (2.4.224). Lear knows the meaning of the word. But he never applies the imperative to himself—not, at least, until it is too late.

Amendment is the great theme of *A Midsummer Night's Dream*. In act 5 of the play, Shakespeare makes a case for amendment as generous revision. When Hippolyta finds the play staged by the mechanicals to be "the silliest stuff that ever I heard" (5.1.207), Theseus answers: "The best in this kind are but shadows, and the worst are no worse if imagination amend them" (5.1.208–9). *If imagination amend them.* Having earlier accused the imagination of performing tricks, Theseus now finds himself defending the imagination and its amending powers. It comes as little surprise, therefore, that when Robin arrives to deliver the epilogue, he asks the audience, as Ariel does at the end of *The Tempest,* to "give me your hands" (15–16). Applaud—respond—forgive any offense taken, each epilogue enjoins us, and the doing so "shall restore amends."

Amendment requires empathy, a temporary emptying out of the self in order to make room for the imagination of the other. Something like this is going on when Edgar stages the suicide scene with his father in act 4.

He does so reluctantly: "Bad is the trade that must play fool to sorrow" (4.1.39). Edgar is the fool, and Gloucester, now blind, is the sorrow. While Edgar would rather speak and reveal himself, there is still a role to be played. "I cannot daub it further," he admits, "And yet I must" (4.1.53–55). Then he creates the illusion of a hill by the sea.

As he does so, Edgar moves into a different verbal register, and his father notices it: "Methinks thy voice is altered, and thou speakest / In better phrase and matter than thou didst" (4.6.7–8). Edgar is moving out of the role of Tom o' Bedlam, back into blank verse and back into his role as a son. "Give me your hand," he says to Gloucester, as he moves him toward a spot he describes as the "extreme verge" of the imaginary cliff (4.6.25–26). In an aside, Edgar directs an answer at any audience member who may be questioning his methods here: "Why I do trifle thus with his despair / Is done to cure it" (4.6.33–34). Gloucester kneels and then "falls forward and swoons" (4.6.42), thus ensuring that the audience has to confront the sheer manipulation involved on Edgar's part, a tactic he will later confess to be a "fault" (5.3.191).

As T. S. Eliot once wrote to an actor playing Gloucester's older son, Edgar "seems to me a very difficult part."

Borrowing a word from *Hamlet,* Edgar then expresses a fear that his "conceit" (4.6.42)—the imagined scenario he has just put everyone through—may have created a shock sufficient to kill his father. Instead, Gloucester picks himself up, dusts himself off, and resolves to

> bear
> Affliction till it do cry out itself
> "Enough, enough," and die.
>
> (4.6.75–77)

Lear then enters, fantastically dressed with wild flowers. Thinking nothing about himself, Gloucester's interest and concern are all with Lear. "I know that voice," he says, as he abides the deranged King's jokes about his gouged-out eyes (4.6.94). "Your eyes are in a heavy case," Lear bandies with him, "Yet you see how this world goes" (4.6.143–44). Gloucester then makes his supreme response: "I see it feelingly" (4.6.145).

In uttering these words, Gloucester provides a compressed understanding of one promised end of Shakespeare's art. The gentle self-mockery implicit in Gloucester's brief sentence accounts for a good deal of its power; he now must literally move through the world by touch, as a blind man feeling his way. But the four words also speak to the fact that what we take in through the eye or the ear means little unless we can convert sensation into feeling. For Shakespeare's plays to do their work, they must be completed through an overpassing and amending heart.

Gloucester has been brought to this verge of feeling by way of a little play staged by a disguised and loving and manipulative son; it is as if there is something too raw in the lesson the child must impart to the parent for Edgar to appear in the cliff scene as himself. Having been met with such anonymous empathy, Gloucester can then extend acknowledgment to Lear.

At the end of *King Lear*, Goneril and Regan and Edmund and Cordelia are dead. Edgar is the last child standing. It looks as if he has been spared so that someone will be left to run things, and to sum up. Along the way, however, Edgar has had to give up almost too much of himself. And given his continuing decision to assume a role, little of what Edgar says could be called frank speech.

Stephen Orgel observes that the "good" Edgar can in fact appear "singularly obtuse," as when he says "the gods are just" (5.3.169). The outcomes of the play in no way support such a judgment. Summary is one of Edgar's preferred modes. He likes rhyming couplets and the way they snap shut, although, as Stanley Wells reminds us, "the use of rhymed couplets to close a play," as does the last speaker in *Lear*, "is conventional." "Ripeness is all" comes out of Edgar's mouth, and the sentence sounds impressive when quoted as an epigram. Gloucester responds to the utterance, however, as if unimpressed: "And that's true, too" (5.2.11). He might just as well say, "Whatever!"

In choosing to stage the duel with Edmund and then in telling his "brief tale" (5.3.180), Edgar takes up precious time. Edmund almost flatters him into delay: "but speak you on; / You look as you had something more to say" (5.3.199–200).

The case for Albany. "More to say"—how often this becomes a temptation for the characters in *King Lear*. Albany's response to Edmund's invitation is abrupt: "If there be more, more woeful, hold it in" (5.3.201). The folio has Edgar heeding the entreaty—it is clear that Albany has begun to take control of the action. In this version of the end, Edgar stops talking, and then the Gentleman enters with the bloody knife. The quarto, however, gives Edgar fifteen more lines. In them, he describes an emotional meeting with Kent. Lewalski, according to her decision to conflate, includes Edgar's second brief tale. In these lines, as Edgar admits, he might better have put a "period" on his speech (5.3.203). "To amplify too much would make much more / And top extremity" (5.3.205–6). But amplify he does, and in the interval—we by now must be wondering what is happening offstage—Cordelia is killed. Here the folio is to be preferred to the quarto—preferred, that is, if we wish those talking on the stage to "Be brief," as Edmund puts it (5.3.244), rather than to keep prolonging what turns out to be a fatal interval.

The opening lines of *King Lear* make reference to Albany, when Kent says "I thought the king had more affected the Duke of Albany than Cornwall" (1.1.1–2). *Affected* means "favored." Albany is caught up from the start by the question of favor—favor by the King; by his wife, Goneril; and by editors who work to enhance or to diminish his stature. In Albany's early appearances in the play, Leo Kirschbaum maintains, he "is dominated by his wife." Reduced to asking impotent questions of her, he says such things as "whereof comes this?" (1.4.267). Then he is gone from the play until act 4, scene 2, where Goneril says to Oswald, "I marvel our mild husband /

Not met us on the way" (4.2.1–2). Oswald responds that he "never" saw "man so changed" (4.2.3). If Albany has changed, he has done so offstage. As Kirschbaum puts it, "Shakespeare has deliberately made our progressive knowledge of him difficult."

"You are not worth the dust which the rude wind / Blows in your face" (4.2.31–32): Albany's greeting to his wife in act 4, scene 2, often prompts audience applause. He now speaks of Goneril and Regan as "Tigers, not daughters" (4.2.41). Were it appropriate—he often stands on ceremony—Albany says he would use his hands "to dislocate and tear / Thy flesh and bones" (4.2.66–67). Yet even as Albany moves into a more assertive posture, he can be described by Edmund as "full of alteration / And self-reproving" (5.1.3–4). In act 5, scene 1, Edmund is worried that Albany, presumably arrayed on his side against an invasion by France and Cordelia's forces, is thinking "To change the course" (5.1.3). Two scenes later, however, Kirschbaum maintains, Albany "has a markedly increased spiritual stature." He confronts Edmund, deeming him "but a subject of this war / Not as a brother" (5.3.61–62), and again he chooses off Goneril, calling her a "gilded serpent" (5.3.84).

The Albany of the folio is not, however, the Albany of the quarto. As a character given limited stage time, Albany therefore offers a convenient focus when comparing the two versions of the play. In *Shakespeare's Revision of "King Lear,"* Steven Urkovitz has made a case for the need to keep both Albany's in view.

Albany appears in only five scenes in the play. As Urkovitz observes, while the folio gives Albany more lines than the quarto in "the opening movements of the play," lines like "Dear Sir forebear" (1.1.163), Albany "perceives rightly, but he takes no action." Until act 4, scene 2, "the Folio's additional material associates Albany more completely with the ideals and interests of Goneril's party."

Then, in act 4, scene 2, Albany begins to speak out. But the lines about tigers and the tearing of flesh exist only in the quarto. In this version only, "Albany abruptly emerges as a character with a complete moral system, sharply opposed to that of his wife."

Albany's big scene is the play's last scene. Having argued that Albany is stronger in the quarto, Urkovitz is now confronted with a character in the folio who seems to be taking charge. But while Albany does issue orders and challenges Edmund to a trial at arms, on the most important point he defeats the hope of the reader, if that reader shares Johnson's aversion to the loss of Cordelia. Here is Urkovitz: "Each time the audience is led to hope that Albany may act in some way to aid Lear and Cordelia. Each time Albany fails to act on their behalf. He does not try to help them and then fail; he simply does not try." This judgment seems a fair enough summary of the action in the folio. It therefore allows Urkovitz to conclude that "Albany's pattern of delay seems to be a characteristic response to heightened emotional stress." Most fatefully, he also allows Edgar and Edmund to enjoy their time-consuming duel. "Great thing of us forgot!" he suddenly admits. "Speak, Edmund, where's the king? and where's Cordelia?" (5.3.235–36).

In comparing the two versions of *Lear*, the portrait of Albany can be said to waver, although Urkovitz sees him as more assertive in the quarto than in the folio. Giving Albany the play's last words is therefore "perfectly consistent with Albany's character in the Quarto.... He acts as if he is still in complete control of himself and of the action.... He takes upon himself the responsibility of closing the scene." On the other hand, Urkovitz can also argue that "the ending in the Folio, with Albany withdrawing himself after he has expressed his need for mourning, seems highly appropriate to the Folio."

To put it simply, the quarto paints an assertive portrait of Albany, while the folio does something similar for Edgar. But these effects are the result of the cutting or adding of lines. The assignment of a speech is another matter altogether.

Choosing between Edgar or Albany as last speaker in *King Lear* involves a value judgment that no amount of textual evidence can resolve. Any decision made about assigning the play's last four lines to either the one or the other speaker necessarily involves "what we feel" about the force and meaning of the whole. Only "imagination," as always in Shakespeare, can at once acknowledge an undecidable crux even as it accepts the responsibility to choose for either Edgar or Albany and, in choosing, to "make amends."

"Speak what we feel, not what we ought to say." Whoever is assigned the line, it reverberates backward though the play with a descriptive force, capturing as it does the conflict the good characters experience between the demands of obligatory and sincere utterance. "Speak frankly as the wind," Agamemnon says to Aeneas in act 1 of *Troilus and Cressida* (1.3.250). This call to frank speech is surely an ironic summons in a play so filled with guile and self-deceit. No speaker in it can find a position free from the taint of compromised utterance. "Words, words, mere words," Troilus rails upon receiving Cressida's letter, "no matter from the heart" (5.3.109–10). Troilus is one of a number of characters in Shakespeare attached to the notion that there might be some means of access to the heart free from the mediations of language. "What his heart thinks his tongue speaks," Don Pedro says of *Much Ado*'s Benedick, and this is meant as praise (3.2.10). Yet Benedick habitually says the opposite of what he feels and remains so captivated by his verbal facility as to fail to notice that he is falling in love. Finding herself in a more desperate situation, Isabella admits to Angelo in *Measure for Measure* that "To have what we would have, we speak not what we mean" (2.4.119). To save her brother from execution and herself from rape, that is, she can find herself excusing "the thing I hate" (2.4.120). The crooked path from the heart to the tongue remains one of Shakespeare's great subjects, and the way in which each character chooses to travel that path comes to define his or her personal style. No character in *King Lear* is more torn between heart and tongue than is Cordelia.

At the end of his career, Michel Foucault began writing about what he called "frank speech." Frank speech, or *parrhesia,* as the Greeks called it, is exemplified for Foucault in the career of Socrates, a man willing to risk death in the free and fearless expression of himself. "In *parrhesia*," Foucault maintains, "the speaker makes it manifestly clear and obvious that what he says is his *own* opinion. And he does this by avoiding any kind of rhetorical form which would veil what he thinks." The frank speaker "says what he *knows* to be true . . . there is always an exact coincidence between belief and truth." This "practice of telling the truth about oneself" necessarily relies upon and appeals "to the presence of the other person who listens and enjoins one to speak." The proof of the sincerity of the speaker is "his *courage,*" a bravery that will lead Socrates to the drinking of the fatal hemlock.

Cordelia pays the highest price in *King Lear* for her commitment to frank speech. And the fate to which she is subjected involved a profound revision of the "chronicles," to use Johnson's word, that Shakespeare drew upon when writing his play.

The complex afterlife of *King Lear* had its beginnings in what might be called the play's "preexistence." The story of a king and his three daughters is an old one. It started out as an ancient folktale, although Shakespeare probably came across a reworking of it in Holinshed. But he also borrowed heavily, as was his habit, from many others, from Spenser and Higgins and Montaigne and even the diabolist Harsnett. In none of these sources does the king fail to be restored to his throne, and once he dies, Cordelia succeeds him. "It is true that, in some sources, Cordelia ends a suicide," writes Russell Fraser, "but that is an irrelevant epilogue."

The version on the boards by 1594, *The True Chronicle History of King Leir and His Three Daughters,* contains a lovely recognition scene in which Cordella and Leir meet again. The king is hungry, wandering out of doors, and his daughter brings him to a table and invites him to eat. At first he fails to recognize her. Once Cordella kneels before him and calls herself "thy loving daughter," Leir understands and says, "O, stand thou up, it is my part to kneel, / And ask forgiveness for my former faults." It's a long way from this scene to the words Shakespeare gives him in act 1:

> Here I disclaim all my paternal care,
> Propinquity and property of blood,
> And as a stranger to my heart and me
> Hold thee, from this, for ever.
>
> (1.1.113–16)

In *Leir,* all the father wants is to marry his daughter to the man he has chosen so as to ensure the succession. But in *Lear,* there is no such clear reason given for the staging of the love test. As Stephen Greenblatt says, "Shakespeare makes Lear's act seem stranger, at once more arbitrary and more rooted in deep psychological needs" (2310).

Stanley Cavell thinks he knows what that need is: to accomplish the "avoidance of love." Lear loves Cordelia so much that he sets up a scene in which he knows she will not be able to speak and therefore manages to protect himself against the vulnerability to which he will open himself in having to acknowledge the full force of his feelings for her. Maynard Mack Jr.—Sandy Mack—finds this a "preposterous idea." As he writes, "The play appears to have all kinds of other (equally complicated) reasons for Lear's staged show of love."

There is what each meant and what each said:

> what can you say to draw
> A third more opulent than your sisters? Speak.
> Nothing, my lord.
> Nothing?
> Nothing.
> Nothing will come of nothing, speak again.
> Unhappy that I am, I cannot heave
> My heart into my mouth. I love your majesty
> According to my bond; no more nor less.
> How, how, Cordelia! mend your speech a little,
> Lest it may mar your fortunes.
>
> (1.1.84–94)

As Cavell sees it, the father wants the beloved daughter to respond as she responds; it is easier for him to have her do so than to endure the unpacking of her heart. But Lear does not anticipate the rage that Cordelia's "nothing" will provoke in him; it is as if he forgets the purpose of his design in the very act of executing it. Had he simply allowed for the playing out of preordained parts and been content with a merely formal profession of the love that so possesses and appalls him, all might have lived happily ever after.

Lear holds it against Cordelia that she has spoken with plainness. As he says, "Let pride, which she calls plainness, marry her" (1.1.129). But this is not quite right. Unlike Kent, Cordelia never characterizes her speech as "plain"—the word is the king's. It is more accurate to say that she does not speak at all; it is as if she is trying to negotiate some uncrossable gap between what she feels and what she "ought to say." Later the Fool will find himself in something of the same bind, "whipped for speaking true," whipped for "lying," and whipped "for holding my peace" (1.4.160–61). Kent also repeats the word *plainness* (1.1.148); it is apparently the best one he and Lear can come up with. Kent proceeds to modify and complicate this word choice when he adds, "Nor are those empty-hearted whose low sounds / Reverb no hollowness" (1.1.153–54).

Low sounds comes closer to the case. As Lear stages the love test, Cordelia is reduced to sounding out instead of speaking, to talking back in a language within or below language, a register that can only be heard if the listener is willing to attend to tone. That the father proves tone-deaf goes without saying, and when Kent enjoins him to "see better" (1.1.158), he really means "hear better." But the audience need not remain tone-deaf as well, prepared as it has been by its experience of other Shakespeare plays to "see" and to hear "it feelingly."

But what then is being felt? What do we talk about when we talk about love? In Shakespeare, love is an experience often talked into being, and he more than once suggests that the less said, the more felt. *Love's Labour's Lost* is his intense study of the problem of overclaiming. In it, a courtier skilled at protesting too much about his love is sentenced to attempt twelve months of jesting in a hospital. A kind of cracked mirror of Cordelia, he must learn to mend his speech by saying less, not more.

As suspicious as he may be of words, Shakespeare also knows that feelings come into being when we put words on them. Yet his "honest" characters—and the word is a slippery one in Shakespeare—struggle to do just this. Hamlet's "words, words, words," in act 2, scene 2, gets repeated by Troilus's "Words, words, mere words, no matter from the heart." In *All's Well That Ends Well*, Helen's standard four word-sentence, as in "I love your son" (1.3.178), also indicates the ongoing agon with articulation.

If one task of *poesis*—of any act of literary making—is to purify the dialect of the tribe, a writer soon comes up against the limits of his or her own style as well as the limits of language itself. Wordsworth's frequent admission that

> I should need
> Colours and words that are unknown to man
> To paint

the contours of his experience is a central example of the case. Literary language can be distinguished from ordinary language by its open admission of the problem.

Much of *King Lear* turns upon the verb *to say*. In asking "Which of you shall we say doth love us most?" (1.1.49), Lear anticipates the repetition of the word *say* in the play's last four lines. His usage in act 1 is curious: he does not directly ask his daughters to say something but instead anticipates the response (what "shall we say") he will make to the declarations he is soliciting. The implicit demand being made becomes doubly preemptive, revealing Lear to be less concerned with hearing something than with what "we," not his daughters, will eventually be able *to say*.

By not speaking, Cordelia may be speaking up for literature itself. "It is as if speech itself," Harley Granville-Barker observes, "were not a simple or genuine enough thing for the expressing of her deep heart." In admitting all that it cannot say, literature purchases its uncanny authority. It knows that there are thoughts and feelings that lie too deep for tears, or words.

The safe thing to do in a tragedy by Shakespeare is to leave the stage. Just leave. Otherwise, you are likely to be carried off.

In *King Lear*, only the Fool seems to understand this; he in any case simply disappears from the play after act 3, well before the promised end.

Why do people stay? In part because they want to keep performing themselves—to keep talking. Not to be seen, not to keep saying, not to be *in play*—this is the worst fate of all. "Tell my story," Hamlet says to Horatio as he lies dying (5.2.291). The point is to survive in the language of the play, if not as a character still upright on the stage. Shakespeare is trying to show his audience that the best way to deal with danger is to deny access, but this his characters cannot do.

Among Shakespeare's major characters, Cordelia is perhaps the least present. She appears in only four scenes and speaks not many more than one hundred lines. She is there in the opening scene, of course, for the love test. In the conflated text of the play, Cordelia does not reappear onstage until act 4, scene 4. In this brief scene, she converses with a Doctor and urges her men to retrieve her now "mad" father (4.4.2). "Soon may I hear and see him!" (4.4.30).

Three scenes later, in act 4, scene 7, Cordelia and Lear finally meet again.

Then, in her final scene, act 5, scene 3, Cordelia makes two appearances. As the scene opens, she and Lear are brought on as prisoners. The last thing she says is "Shall we not see these daughters and these sisters?" (5.3.7). She and Lear are then carried off under guard.

In a play so concerned with "distribution" (4.1.70), Cordelia is given very little stage time; it is as if there is little room for such a spirit in the world of the play. Once she disappears in the first scene, we hear nothing about her until well into act 4. In the folio version of the play, this does not happen until she sends for her mad father. But as it turns out, Shakespeare wrote her *one more scene*.

The scene appears only in the quarto 1 version of the play. For some reason, it was omitted from the folio edition of *King Lear*. Because the folio edition was generally credited as the more authoritative version of what Shakespeare wrote, the scene might have dropped out of the repertory but for the intervention of Alexander Pope.

Pope brought back into the folio text of *Lear* more than one hundred lines from quarto 1 and also added an entire scene, numbered scene 17 in the quarto and act 4, scene 3, in the Norton conflated text. It therefore directly precedes the scene in which Cordelia speaks with the Doctor. "This scene," Pope wrote, "left out in all the common books, is restored from the old edition, it being manifestly of *Shakespear's* writing, and necessary to continue the story of Cordelia, whose behavior is here most beautifully painted." Eminent Pope scholar Maynard Mack chooses to disagree: in act 4, scene 3, he argues, "Kent and a Gentleman . . . wrap Cordelia in a mantle of emblematic speech that is usually lost on a modern audience's ear and difficult for a modern actor to speak with conviction."

Cordelia does not appear onstage in the scene restored by Pope; in it, Kent and a Gentleman talk about her. The scene opens with Kent inquiring of the Gentleman why France has so suddenly gone back to his country. But Kent's real concern lies elsewhere: "Did your letters pierce the queen to any demonstration of grief?" (4.3.9). These are letters Kent has earlier sent to Cordelia to apprise her of Lear's tortured condition. Kent is not quite sure of where Cordelia's heart lies, but the Gentleman assures him that she took the letters, read them, and that tears trickled down her cheeks. "O, then it moved her," Kent responds (4.3.14).

The Gentleman continues:

> Not to a rage. Patience and sorrow strove
> Who should express her goodliest. You have seen
> Sunshine and rain at once: her smiles and tears
> Were like a better way. Those happy smilets,

> That played on her ripe lip, seemed not to know
> What guests were in her eyes, which parted thence,
> As pearls from diamonds dropped. In brief,
> Sorrow would be a rarity most beloved,
> If all could so become it.
>
> (4.3.15–23)

No other scene in *Lear* places its audience at such a remove. The core event is narrated rather than enacted: attention is directed to Kent as he listens to a character without a name describe the responses of an offstage character as she reads a letter. Why, at this moment, has Shakespeare chosen to create such a distancing effect?

Shakespeare is taking time out to remind us of how empathy works and also about how it is created.

As the opposite of sympathy, empathy is feeling with rather than feeling for. In her wonderfully sympathetic account of Edgar's role in *Lear*, Janet Adelman notes that "*feeling with* is what the play demands of us as spectators." When we empathize, we do not say to ourselves, "I identify with you." Instead, we acknowledge the gap between our situation and the one in which the object of our empathy finds herself. We say to ourselves, "I see that you feel like that," not "I feel that too." Empathy acknowledges the opacity of the other as well as the capacity of persons to have feelings we may never feel.

And how might we develop such a capacity? By watching a play in which people have powerful responses and express complicated feelings. Or by reading something as intimate as a letter, or a novel. In doing so, we learn how to be "moved," to use Kent's word. The work begins early, as we listen to our parents read us fairy tales in which the good and the bad are easily parsed. It continues until we find ourselves drawn into a world like *King Lear*, where such judgments become much more difficult to make.

Shame blocks empathy. It does so by freezing a self in postures it knows to be wrong but which it is too ashamed to acknowledge. William Zak advances this view in his *Sovereign Shame*, where he argues that *Lear* is a play calling us not "to be so ashamed of what is shameful in us that we fail to face ourselves." It is "burning shame" over "his own unkindness" that "detains" Lear from yielding to see his daughter (4.3.45, 41, 46).

The play begins with a father blushing in shame over a bastard son. Gloucester jokes about Edmund's conception as if his son were not even present. Edmund internalizes the judgment in the very act of attempting to fend it off and so wastes time trying to prove himself, to get revenge, to annihilate rather than to face his shame. He is stuck, in part, because his father never asks his forgiveness, as Lear finally does of Cordelia. And yet Edmund will finally confess himself "moved." As Cordelia is moved by Kent's letters, Edmund is moved at the end of act 5 by Edgar's brief tale. Being moved—finally feeling some empathy for his father—he resolves to do "some good" (5.3.245). But it is all too late.

To face our shame is to engage in an act of self-recognition, a judgment that completes itself in an act of forgiveness. Not a seeking of forgiveness from others, or of others, but of ourselves for our own shameful thoughts and deeds. Only then can we love, the play is trying to show us, because only then do we acknowledge the "relatedness" Maynard Mack views as the central revelation of the play.

Cordelia's response to the letters delivered by Kent is complex: why smiles and tears at once? Perhaps Shakespeare means to convey a sense that adult emotions are sometimes profoundly mixed. She does not in any case entirely lose herself in empathetic response. "Made she no verbal question?" Kent asks the Gentleman (4.3.23). No, she cried out some words, shook the holy water from her eyes, and then went off "To deal with grief alone" (4.3.31).

Cordelia is grieving here over the report of her father's sufferings. But when she goes off to grieve alone, she also grieves for herself and for the shame she still feels over being compelled to wound publicly the parent she loves. In the asides in the opening scene, when Cordelia says things like "my love's / More ponderous than my tongue" (1.1.76–77), she is facing up to this shame even while she is beginning to earn it.

And so, when Cordelia and Lear meet again, in act 4, scene 7, she is able to handle her shame. She begins by kissing her father. When he awakens, she asks the doctor to "speak to him" (4.7.42). "Madam, do you, 'tis fittest" (4.7.43). Cordelia then asks her father a few brief questions. Lear answers, "You do me wrong to take me out o' the grave" (4.7.45). Father and daughter continue talking, and Lear, fearing he is not in his right mind, guesses the truth: "I think this lady / To be my child Cordelia." She responds, "And so I am, I am" (4.7.70–71). Lear continues to be disoriented and ashamed, and the Doctor counsels her to "trouble him no more" (4.7.82). When Cordelia invites her father to walk, he answers, "You must bear with me: / Pray you now, forget and forgive. I am old and foolish" (4.7.84–85). The Doctor and Lear and Cordelia then exit the stage.

The reunion scene is most delicately handled. Lear's unsteadiness of mind spares him from the shock of recognition and allows his plea for forgiveness to emerge almost as an afterthought. It is something he feels the need to offer rather than a response to an implicit request. Adelman again: "All the miracles of the play are triumphs of a love that goes beyond cause."

"This speech of yours hath moved me." Given that the capacity to be moved is a supreme test of character in Shakespeare's art, it may be surprising to recall that it is Edmund who speaks these words. But he speaks for anyone who is moved, as I am, by the scene in which the Gentleman describes Cordelia's response—"Oh, then it moved her"—to the letters delivered by Kent. Witnessing this capacity to be moved prepares the audience for the beauty and the power of the reunion between Lear and Cordelia, and the play is all the richer for the inclusion of the earlier scene.

"Of all Shakespeare's heroines," A. C. Bradley says of Cordelia, "she knew the least of joy." Yet the experience of *King Lear* works, Bradley argues, to bring about "the feeling that what happens to such a being does not matter; all that matters is what she is." This seems like a strange claim indeed. Isn't a Shakespeare play all about "what happens," especially, in the case of *King Lear,* what happens between a parent and a child? Yes, usually, given that in Shakespeare, "Family Romance" often provides much of the drama. And does not the hope of the reader cry out that, in the end, Lear's youngest daughter might be spared? Cordelia's behavior is meant, however, to call into question the value of drama itself, where that term is understood to refer to the need of the self to make "large speeches" (1.1.185), to brood upon its hurts, and to act upon its emotions in a big way. Cordelia offers instead a model of a self defined not by what is done to it but, rather, by how it takes things. In doing so, she embodies the play's ideal of "a better way."

The words *a better way,* appearing only in quarto 1, scene 17, might have been lost to the future but for the intervention of Alexander Pope and the tradition of conflation established by him. Many readers and audiences have nevertheless enjoyed versions of *King Lear* from which the scene has been omitted, and it is surely possible to be moved by those versions. While an acquaintance with the textual history of the play can enrich those responses, the play, in whatever form it comes to us, can scarcely fail to evoke both smiles and tears. Each of us finds ourselves alone with our own hopes when reading *King Lear,* and those hopes may lead us to expect any number of different kinds of ends. On the capacity of editing to educate those hopes, perhaps Samuel Johnson deserves the last word:

> Let him, that is yet unacquainted with the powers of Shakespeare, and who desires to feel the highest pleasure that the drama can give, read every play from the first scene to the last, with utter negligence of all his commentators. When his fancy is once on the wing, let it not stoop at correction or explanation. When his attention is strongly engaged, let it disdain alike to turn aside to the name of Theobald and of Pope. Let him read on through brightness and obscurity, through integrity and corruption; let him preserve his comprehension of the dialogue and his interest in the fable. And when the pleasures of novelty have ceased, let him attempt exactness, and read the commentators.

TWO

Wordsworth, the Loved One, and the Making of *The Prelude*

"Who do you love?" My friend the poet Jane Shore likes to ask the question when confronted by "the wavering balance" of some man's mind (*The Prelude* of 1805, 1:650). If, like Wordsworth, you are "not used to make / A present joy the matter" of your song (1805, 1:55–56), the question can take a lifetime to answer. Wordsworth worked on his long autobiographical poem for over forty years, and the "loved one" who may have mattered most only surfaced late in the activity of revision. In *The Prelude*, she remains unnamed.

In book 1, when Wordsworth first writes of "human love," he is not speaking about people at all. Memory itself is the love object, and Wordsworth seems uneasy with the admission.

>   I began
> My story early, feeling (as I fear)
> The weakness of a human love for days
> Disowned by memory.
>
>   (1805, 1:640–43)

The confession being made here is complex. Wordsworth owns up to at least two recognitions: first, that he has begun his story as close as he can get to its beginning, with the earliest memories of childhood. In addition, the love being expressed is for the "days" themselves—for past memories the poet may have forgotten ("disowned") and is now, in writing his poem, attempting to recover.

Memories already re-owned in book 1 of *The Prelude* include three instances of theft. As a boy, Wordsworth stole woodcocks from a trapper's snare, eggs from a raven's nest, a shepherd's boat. Each act of "stealth / And troubled pleasure" resulted in a sense of being followed by "low breathings" or "strange" utterances or "huge and mighty forms" (1805, 1:388–89, 330, 348, 425). These acts of transgression schooled Wordsworth in "the impressive discipline of fear" (1805, 1:631). In having survived and re-owned these fearful experiences, the remembering Wordsworth honors all that he had to overcome to make possible the growth of the poet's mind.

As Wordsworth will discover as he writes his way deeper into his poem, these early memories can be deemed incomplete. They lack a "loved one." It is when he returns with someone he loves to a fateful spot that the full meaning and value of what once happened there can bloom into being. Memory acquires a "radiance more divine" when it is shared (1850, 12:267), with the true secret sharer of *The Prelude* being the reader herself.

Before the reader comes the editor. None of the claims I have been making would have been arguable before the compositional history of *The Prelude* was recovered by Wordsworth scholars. And the process of discovery continues, as new editions of the poem vie with their predecessors for pride of place. Three dates in the emergence of *The Prelude* are of particular importance: 1850, 1926, and 1974. In each of these years, an essential version of the poem came before the world.

Wordsworth made no provision for the publication of *The Prelude* while he was alive. Mary Wordsworth arranged the first publication of the poem in 1850, some three months after her husband's death. Mary gave the poem its title, and for over seventy years, the fourteen books of the 1850 version were all the world knew of *The Prelude*. The version Mary chose to publish was also the one that Wordsworth had continued to revise over the course of his long life, with the major periods of revision occurring in 1819, 1832, and 1838.

In 1926, Ernest de Selincourt brought another *Prelude* into print. This came to be known as the 1805 *Prelude*. Comprised of thirteen books, de Selincourt's edition captured the moment in time when Wordsworth, at the age of thirty-five, felt he had completed his long poem and *before* he set out to revise it.

In 1974, the editors of the third edition of the *Norton Anthology of English Literature* published "The Two-Part Prelude." The composition of some 960 lines dated from 1798 and 1799 and represented Wordsworth's earliest attempt to uncover the hiding places of his power. Remarkably concrete and almost absent of any philosophizing, "The Two-Part Prelude" contained a number of the most beloved episodes found in the two longer versions of *The Prelude*, including the boat stealing, the ice skating, the drowned man, and, most important, the two "spots of time."

Behind these three publishing events lies an even more complex manuscript history. In his Penguin Classics edition (1995) of the various texts of *The Prelude*, Jonathan Wordsworth lists fifteen extant manuscripts containing a portion of this or that version of Wordsworth's long autobiographical poem. Some are written in Wordsworth's almost indecipherable hand; others are fair copies made by Dorothy Wordsworth, Mary Hutchinson, or the poet's daughter, Dora. Given this embarrassment of riches, Jonathan Wordsworth concludes that "there never was a fair copy that represented a single point in time—that is to say, a single version of *The Prelude*" (li).

"The Two-Part Prelude," while having the authority of a beginning, was to have a vexed history. As early as 1931, de Selincourt revealed that he had found "the earliest extant drafts" of passages from book 1 as well as drafts of passages appearing in later books. "I have called the newly discovered manuscript JJ," de Selincourt wrote. That manuscript became the basis for all later editions of "The Two-Part Prelude." In 1959, Helen Darbishire produced a revised edition of de Selincourt's 1926 text and printed a version of JJ as an "appendix" at the back of the book. But her version of JJ did not organize the contents of the manuscript into a readable work. Only in the *Norton Anthology* did the poem first appear as a "compact and rounded whole." A scholarly controversy over the suitability of any version of "The Two-Part Prelude" for a student-centered edition then caused Norton to drop the poem from the fourth edition of its anthology. Despite the debate surrounding the emergence of this ur-text, it has come to be valued by critics such as Jonathan Wordsworth as offering "in a simpler and more concentrated form much of what one thinks of as the best in the thirteen-book poem."

This long-deferred process of recovery, in which the earliest work is the last to be uncovered but in which vying versions of the past continue to pile up, and to frustrate closure, reveals the Wordsworth industry as involved in the same work of recursion that had engaged the poet himself. Moreover, the complex layerings comprising Wordsworth's poem reveal self-revision to be his chosen lifework. A poem on one's own life, like an autobiographical self, these many versions attest, is, as Wordsworth wrote in book 6 of *The Prelude*, "something evermore about to be" (1805, 542).

Wordsworth has anticipated the complexity of retrospection in a memorable image from book 4 in which he finds himself "incumbent o'er the surface of past time" (1805, 247–63). In a long simile, he imagines himself "As one who hangs down-bending from the side / Of a slow-moving boat." As he stares down into the "still water" through reflections of things standing along the shore, and then to "the deeps," the view is also sometimes "crossed by gleam / Of his own image." This work of "remembering back," as Hemingway calls it—or looking down, in the case of Wordsworth's simile—is inevitably marked by quandaries and resistances. Is the project worth the candle if, as it turns out, the seeker concludes that the story of the self has no beginning? Where does the eye choose to stop, Wordsworth seems to be asking, as it seeks to locate in the past some stabilizing *point d'appui*? How much do present reflections intrude upon and color the "then"? Is the "great and cresive self," as Emerson once described it, ever to be trusted not to intrude as one attempts to look back to the days before the reign of the egotistical sublime?

The three extant versions of the first of the two spots of time, when brought into careful alignment, do provide a kind of answer to these questions. From the moment he began to compose *The Prelude*, Wordsworth understood the spots of time to have, for him, a peculiar power and therefore a unique status in his poem:

> There are in our existence spots of time
> Which with a distinct preeminence retain
> A fructifying virtue, whence, depressed

> By trivial occupations and the round
> Of ordinary intercourse, our minds—
> Especially the imaginative power—
> Are nourished and invisibly repaired;
> Such moments chiefly seem to have their date
> In our first childhood.
>
> ("The Two-Part Prelude of 1799," First Part, 288–96)

The spots of time appear in all three versions of *The Prelude*. As they continue to be revised, one figure remains central to Wordsworth's rememberings, the figure of a woman.

Here is the opening of the first spot of time as it figures in "The Two-Part Prelude":

> I remember well
> ('Tis of an early season that I speak,
> The twilight of rememberable life),
> While I was yet an urchin, one who scarce
> Could hold a bridle, with ambitious hopes
> I mounted, and we rode towards the hills.
> We were a pair of horsemen: honest James
> Was with me, my encourager and guide.
> We had not travelled long ere some mischance
> Disjoined me from my comrade, and, through fear
> Dismounting, down the rough and stony moor
> I led my horse, and stumbling on, at length
> Came to a bottom where in former times
> A man, the murderer of his wife, was hung
> In irons. Mouldered was the gibbet-mast;
> The bones were gone, the iron and the wood;
> Only a long green ridge of turf remained
> Whose shape was like a grave. I left the spot,
> And reascending the bare slope I saw
> A naked pool that lay beneath the hills,

> The beacon on the summit, and more near
> A girl who bore a pitcher on her head
> And seemed with difficult steps to force her way
> Against the blowing wind.

(296–319)

The lines detail an event occurring when Wordsworth was five years old. His encounter with the gibbet and the girl took place on the eastern side of Penrith Beacon, near his mother's birthplace. As Mary Moorman points out, "This is the only incident recorded in *The Prelude* of which the setting belongs to Penrith."

The boy rides out with honest James, gets lost, stumbles down into a bottom and finds a gibbet where a murderer was once hung in irons, reascends, and comes upon a naked pool, a stone beacon, and a girl who bears a pitcher on her head and who seems, with difficult steps, to force her way against the blowing wind.

In his book on *The Prelude*, Richard Onorato calls the first spot of time "the truest memory of early childhood." He does so because in it a child attempts to do "a man's things," because it is the only extended memory in *The Prelude* dating from the time before the mother's death—Wordsworth lost her just before his eighth birthday—and because in surviving, if not exactly mastering, this experience of loss and separation, Wordsworth rehearsed for the real losses, of both parents but especially of his mother, that were to come.

In what sense does this memory deserve to be taken as "truest"? It is true, perhaps, because it will happen to anyone who outlives a parent. He or she *will* survive. And this survival can be accompanied by all sorts of feelings, some of them difficult to forgive. In Wordsworth's case, the outcome was that he became the possessor of a power he calls "visionary." As Onorato reads the passage, along with the celebration of the word *visionary* throughout *The Prelude*, "The child did *not* cry out for the mother, but proceeded—to survive, to seek the visible world, to discover his 'visionary' powers." Those powers allowed Wordsworth to see through the visible world so as to discover, as he was to write in book 11 of the 1805 *Prelude,* how

> the mind
> Is lord and master, and that outward sense
> Is but the obedient servant of her will.
>
> (270–72)

Any act of remembering is an act of choosing, especially when it involves writing something like a memoir. Therefore, "it is only in retrospect," as Onorato points out, "that Wordsworth's mind is making this earlier memory into his *first* experience of what was to become the characteristic experience of the Poet, being alone in what could be a too fearful reality."

The issue of beginnings haunts Wordsworth. As he writes in the second part of "The Two-Part Prelude":

> Hard task to analyse a soul, in which
> Not only general habits and desires,
> But each most obvious and particular thought—
> Not in a mystical and idle sense,
> But in the words of reason deeply weighed—
> Has no beginning.
>
> (262–67)

In his roundabout way, Wordsworth is complaining here about the difficulty of tracking the growth of a soul when none of its thoughts and behaviors can be assigned a locatable starting point.

In *Father and Son*, Edmund Gosse notes that Wordsworth "could name no moment, mark no 'here' or 'now,' when the wonder broke upon him." The phrase *no beginning* gestures toward a mise en abyme in which even words like *mother* and *father* begin to lose their authority. As a writer telling the "story of my life" (1805, 1.667), Wordsworth does, however, need to start somewhere, and the first spot of time is the earliest memory given in any detail. In doing so, he commences the work of being an author to himself, where that work is best understood as the continual refiguring of the past so as to free the self from its literal beginnings even as it pays homage to its parents by placing the loss of them at the center of the two core memoires it chooses to own.

Memories, Wordsworth also set out to demonstrate, are subject to revision. When amending the first spot of time for the 1805 version, he added lines that deliver a new emphasis. Wordsworth removed the lines about the rise of turf whose shape is like a grave and then interposed these lines:

> The gibbet-mast was mouldered down, the bones
> And iron case were gone; but on the turf
> Hard by, soon after that fell deed was wrought,
> Some unknown hand had carved the murderer's name.
> The monumental writing was engraven
> In times long past, and still from year to year
> By superstition of the neighborhood
> The grass is cleared away, and to this hour
> The letters are all fresh and visible.

(11:290–98)

In point of fact, the turf at Penrith Beacon was inscribed not with a name but with the letters T P M—Thomas Parker Murdered. Parker was the man who had killed his wife and then been gibbetted in the valley below the beacon.

Jonathan Wordsworth finds all this a "cumbersome" addition. Wordsworth's "revisions are normally—not always, but normally," he writes, "for the worse," and for him, the new lines found in the 1805 text are one such example. But a case for them can be made, as Thomas Weiskel has shown.

However grisly the murderer's story, it is being kept fresh and visible. The added lines deliver a fantasy of a kind of writing that will not decay and that is communally maintained. They also indicate that the order of death is written into the very earth itself. The details surrounding the murderer's name thus carry with them both intimations of immortality and mortality—of writing that lasts, of lives that do not. Even if they therefore call up a kind of paradox, the lines about the "fell deed" can easily be read. But Wordsworth is out to make a more difficult and a more important point. By revising the first spot of time into a Scene of Writing, he is able to express his deep ambivalence about the work of signification itself.

In Weiskel's words, the revision reveals that it is "against the fact that things may come to signify that the boy is forcing his difficult way." Or as Wordsworth goes on to write,

>   I should need
> Colours and words that are unknown to man
> To paint

the experience at the spot, along with what it meant and continues to mean to him. When he pulls away from the concrete situation to brood upon it, he can offer his reader little help. The lines from "The Two-Part Prelude" and the 1805 text are essentially identical:

>   It was, in truth
> An ordinary sight, but I should need
> Colours and words that are unknown to man
> To paint the visionary dreariness
> Which, while I looked all round for my lost guide,
> Did at that time invest the naked pool,
> The beacon on the lonely eminence,
> The woman and her garments vexed and tossed
> By the strong wind.
>
> (1805, 11:307–15)

The wind, an image so often deployed by Wordsworth as a stand-in for his own powers, is moving against the girl and almost into her as it also reveals her bodily shape. The figure with the pitcher on her head can be read as a highly eroticized image; she becomes a "woman" in the space of a few lines. The theme of his own maturation, especially into a man capable of love, emerges even more clearly during two further rounds of revision Wordsworth chose to impose upon the first spot of time. Those changes also involved the poet's evolving perspective on the women central to his adult life.

Dorothy Wordsworth was born some twenty months after her brother, William, on Christmas Day 1771. They were separated when she was six, after the death of their mother, and were reunited nine years later at Penrith, in 1787, when Dorothy was fifteen. She first went to live with William in 1795—first at Racedown, then at Alfoxden, to be near Coleridge, then at Dove Cottage, in Grasmere, and finally at Rydal Mount—and lived with him until he died.

William and Dorothy moved to Dove Cottage after a brief and unhappy sojourn in Germany, where much of "The Two-Part Prelude" was written. In the following May, she began keeping a journal of their life together; the final entry is for January 16, 1803, the day on which they walked out to visit the blind man and his wife and sister sitting by the fire and bought some gingerbread.

In a late poem called "Yarrow Revisited" (1831), Wordsworth writes of "Life as she is—our changeful Life, / With friends and kindred dealing" (*Major Works*, 367). By the time Wordsworth wrote these lines, the ties with friends and family Wordsworth and Dorothy had enjoyed in the early years at Grasmere had suffered considerable alteration.

Soon after Wordsworth and his sister established themselves at Dove Cottage, Coleridge moved to nearby Keswick. He of the godlike forehead had by then become a part of Wordsworth's extended family, one including brother John and the two Hutchinson sisters, Mary and Sara. Despite being married to another Sara, Coleridge had fallen in love with Sara Hutchinson, and his "Dejection: An Ode," published on William's wedding day, records the impossibility of this love. There were many triangles developing within the Wordsworth circle; John, for instance, seemed to be in love for a time with Mary, who married William on October 4, 1802.

There was a public way on which William and Dorothy often walked the thirteen miles to visit Coleridge at Keswick. On the day when Dorothy first copied out the poem she called "the Leech Gatherer"—its formal title is "Resolution and Independence"—she and her brother met Coleridge upon the way, explored a waterfall, ate their dinner, took tea at a farmhouse. "We parted from Coleridge at Sara's Crag," Dorothy writes, "after having looked at the Letters which C carved in the morning. I kissed them all. Wm deepened the T with C's penknife."

On Sara's Crag, or Sara's Rock, as it came to be called, Coleridge carved six sets of initials: "W.W., M.H., D.W., S.T.C., J.W., S.H." How complicated a task it would be to draw the many lines connecting these six hearts. Brother John loved Mary but gave way to William. Later it was assumed that John might marry Sara, but once he left Grasmere, in 1800, John never returned, and in 1805, he was drowned at sea. Friend Coleridge had married one Sara but wanted another. William and S.T.C. had each other, surely, and felt perhaps a bond no other soul was able to violate. Dorothy loved William but gave way to Mary. "Do not make loving us your business," she wrote to Mary, and this only six months before the marriage to her brother. Then, to another friend, Dorothy wrote, "I half dread that concentration of all tender feelings, past, present and future which will come upon me on the wedding morning."

On that morning, when Dorothy slipped William's wedding ring "from my forefinger where I had worn it the whole of the night before," she could not bring herself to attend the ceremony. When Dorothy saw "the two men running up the walk, coming to tell me it was over, I could stand it no longer & threw myself on the bed where I lay in stillness, neither hearing or seeing any thing, till Sara came upstairs to me & said 'They are coming.' This forced me from the bed where I lay & I moved I knew not how straight forward, faster than my strength could carry me till I met my beloved William & fell upon his bosom."

The Hutchinson sisters, like the Wordsworth children, had grown up as orphans. Mary and Sara had met Dorothy when they were girls and were to remain her friends for life. After Wordsworth and Mary were wed, Sara Hutchinson, who never married, continued to live with her sister and brother-in-law until her death in 1835.

The feelings passing between Wordsworth, his sister, and his wife would have been enough for any man to manage. But there was another complicating figure. In the year leading up to Wordsworth's marriage, and at times when Mary was staying with William and Dorothy at Dove Cottage, there arrived letters from France. These were letters from another life. No wonder that William could write

> so wide appears
> The vacancy between me and those days
> Which yet have such self-presence in my mind
> That sometimes when I think of them I seem

> Two consciousnesses—conscious of myself
> And of some other being.
>
> (1805, 2:28–33)

The letters were written by Annette Vallon and by her almost ten-year-old daughter, Caroline.

Soon after he arrived for a second visit to France, in November 1791, Wordsworth made his way to Orléans, where he met twenty-five-year-old Annette Vallon. Annette came from a family of devout Catholics and later became a strong supporter of the royalist resistance. "She and Wordsworth rapidly became lovers," Mary Moorman writes, "and when Annette returned home"—back to her father's house in Blois—"probably in March, she was already with child by him." On December 15, 1792, and within a few days of Wordsworth's return to England, Anne-Caroline Wordsworth was baptized in Orléans Cathedral.

Wordsworth left France for many reasons, an "absolute want / Of funds" being, he claimed, foremost among them (1805, 10:190–91). England's declaration of war on France in February 1793 made any return to Annette difficult to accomplish, although there is some conjecture that Wordsworth did manage to cross the Channel one more time, in September 1793. Even if Wordsworth did reenter France, there is no evidence that he was able to get to Annette.

Wordsworth and Mary Hutchinson had originally planned to marry in the spring of 1802. But the letters from Annette changed all that. Her first letter to William arrived on December 21, 1801. As more letters followed, and were answered, Wordsworth decided he needed to talk to Mary. He rode out to see her on Valentine's Day. He met her, Dorothy wrote, "for a couple of hours between Emont Bridge & Hartshorn Tree." Dorothy's note would seem to indicate that the engaged couple met in the road. "They discoursed, no doubt," Moorman writes, "chiefly about Annette." In the weeks following this encounter, more letters from France arrived, and as Dorothy wrote in her journal, on March 22, 1802, "we resolved to see Annette, & that Wm should go to Mary." William was to *go* to Mary a second time to explain that he had, before marrying her, to *see* Annette.

And so William and Dorothy went to Calais. "We walked by the seashore almost every Evening with Annette & Caroline or Wm & I alone." The remainder of Dorothy's entry about the time spent in France deals with the play of light on walls and water. In *The Ballad of Dorothy Wordsworth*, Frances Wilson notes that when it comes to Dorothy's faithful entry keeping, "there is no more frustrating silence in her journal than the one she keeps about their month in Calais."

Dorothy deploys a more striking ellipsis in the paragraph beginning, "On Sunday the 29th of August we left Calais." Less than a page later and having jumped forward over a month in time, Dorothy's journal records, "On Monday 4th October 1802, my Brother William was married to Mary Hutchinson."

The object of unsanctioned desire is thereby nicely elided in Dorothy's journal by the turn toward the wife, although, as it turns out, Dorothy appears to have experienced ambivalence equal to or even greater than anything Annette may have felt about William and wedlock.

After Caroline's birth, Annette had written to Dorothy: "When we are there, Oh sister, how happy we shall be!" She went on to imagine William "surrounded by your sister, your wife, your daughter, who will only breathe for you." Such an arrangement did eventually occur, although the wife in the picture was Mary Hutchinson, not Annette Vallon.

In 1820, Wordsworth published the freestanding "Vaudracour and Julia," a somewhat coded account of his affair with Annette. An earlier version of the affair had appeared in the 1805 *Prelude*, but, in revising the poem, Wordsworth decided to remove it. His leaving behind his lover and child had to do with his behavior as a man, behavior that he would be the first to remind us had its roots in the losses of early childhood. As G. Kim Blank writes, "He was capable of abandoning because he himself was abandoned." After Wordsworth's death, the "surviving family decided to suppress all reference to the affair and forbade his first biographer, his nephew Christopher, to make any mention of it."

In the act of refiguring his love affair in France, Wordsworth disowned most of the feelings that must have been his as he experienced his fall into sexual love. In the 1805 version of the story, Julia and Vaudracour yield to each other "through effect / Of some delirious hour" (9:596–97). In the 1820 version, the tone is censorious:

> So passed the time, till, whether through effect
> Of some unguarded moment that dissolved
> Virtuous restraint—ah, speak it, think it, not!

The power Wordsworth names "the sexual appetite," in his "Preface to Lyrical Ballads," no sooner asserts itself here than it is banished from the lines themselves (*Major Works,* 610). Vaudracour is not allowed to be *in* his story, however much Wordsworth may have been in his.

Yet "think it, not!" Wordsworth writes, as if such experience were simply to be ruled out of bounds. Apart from the story of Vaudracour and Julia, no version of *The Prelude* makes reference to sexual experience as it plays its part in the drama of personal growth, and even in that tragic tale, the narrator's reticence finally wins the day. When *The Prelude* does recur to the "glad animal movements" recalled in "Tintern Abbey," they are performed by the self and the self alone (*Major Works,* 133). Yet Wordsworth's reticence about the sexual life, in its condensations and displacements, acts as a strange kind of gift to his readers, reminding them as it does of the difficulties growing souls can experience when it comes to acknowledging and being honest about the role desire has played in making them who they are.

Mary and Dorothy did, however, make it into the big poem, although never by name. Their most important appearance in *The Prelude* has to do with the first spot of time. In "The Two-Part Prelude," the Penrith Beacon episode contains no mention of either woman at all—but there is the presence of the "girl" who becomes a "woman." When he came to write the 1805 version, Wordsworth decided to add lines to the poem, lines intervening directly after the poet recalls the figure with her garments vexed and tossed by the strong wind:

> When, in a blessèd season
> With those two dear ones—to my heart so dear—
> When in the blessèd time of early love,
> Long afterwards I roamed about
> In daily presence of this very scene,
> Upon the naked pool and dreary crags,
> And on the melancholy beacon, fell

> The spirit of pleasure and youth's golden gleam—
> And think ye not with radiance more divine
> From these remembrances, and from the power
> They left behind? So feeling comes in aid
> Of feeling, and diversity of strength
> Attends us if but once we have been strong.
>
> (11:315–27)

The pool, the crags, and the beacon were all elements present in Wordsworth's original experience at *this very scene,* an event occurring when he was only five years of age. That melancholy event somehow acquired divine radiance when Wordsworth returned to the spot with "two dear ones," by which he means Dorothy and Mary.

The blessèd time of early love refers to the summer of 1787, when Wordsworth was first reunited with Dorothy at Penrith after a separation of many years. Mary Hutchinson, one of Dorothy's oldest friends, also happened to be living at Penrith, and the poet and his sister and her friend were often together. On one of their walks, they happened upon the very scene where the five-year old Wordsworth had once been lost. Whatever the poet may have felt for Mary at the age of seventeen, it is doubtful that he made any declaration of his feelings.

What can be the reason for this lovely flash-forward in the 1805 spot of time to the blessèd time of early love? And why then the elision of Dorothy, in *The Prelude* of 1850, when William amended the memory, dropping the plural *those two dear ones* and replacing it with the phrase *the loved one.* The altered lines begin:

> When, in the blessèd hours
> Of early love, the loved one at my side,
> I roamed, in daily presence of this scene.
>
> (1850, 12:261–63)

In his initial rendition of the blessèd time of early love, the sister and the wife-to-be are fused—or confused. Perhaps it is true, as Frances Wilson argues, that "the closer Wordsworth became to someone the less he was able to give them form." But by not naming Dorothy and Mary, Wordsworth achieves the important effect of converting his actual intimate partners into characters in a generic developmental romance. The revisions to the first spot of time show this intention at work.

In the 1799 version of the Penrith Beacon episode, the boy is alone, or alone only with a female figure whose clothing is being vexed by a strong wind, "wind" or "breeze" being Wordsworth's recurring image of a violence from within pressing back against a violence from without. In 1805, Wordsworth adds the memory of a later wandering over that very scene, in the time of early love, with the unnamed Dorothy and Mary. Finally, in the 1850 version, Dorothy drops out, and Wordsworth writes only of "the loved one at my side"—by which he means Mary. The movement of Wordsworth's imagination through these three stages of revision suggests his having survived his early losses and his having developed the capacity for mature sexuality and love.

We see here a man trying to make his way against and within a world of lost and found women. Behind all these unnamed yet present female figures, as Richard Onorato has shown, stands the lost mother: the first spot of time is the only one of two memories in any version of *The Prelude* that dates from a time *before* the death of Ann Wordsworth in March 1778. The five-year-old boy who rode out with such proud hopes into the first spot of time and who then became lost came to remember the experience as his "truest memory" because he had survived it. In surviving, he discovered his power to support himself when "The props of my affections were removed." There was something chastening and yet reassuring in the discovery: "And yet the building stood as if sustained / By its own spirit!" (1805, 2:294–96).

The second spot of time does similar work. Its focus is not the mother but the father.

In his thirteenth year, Wordsworth and his brothers were away at Hawkshead Grammar School. Christmas coming on, he repaired to a height where he could see by which road the "expected steeds" might arrive. He "sat half sheltered by a naked wall" and was accompanied by "a single sheep" and a "whistling hawthorn." But he did not simply wait; he worried—he was beset by an "anxiety of hope." The palfreys did eventually show up, but

> Ere I to school returned
> That dreary time, ere I had been ten days
> A dweller in my father's house, he died.

Wordsworth goes on to experience the loss as "A chastisement." And so he bends low "To God who thus corrected my desires" ("The Two-Part Prelude," 330–60).

But desire for what, exactly? Wordsworth's desire, surely, was to be taken home in a timely fashion. His anxiety that this might not happen seems an emotion common enough to any child whose parent has at one time or another failed to pick him up after school. It is a simple enough adolescent sort of doubt—the anxiousness that a father might not come. But for the fact that the father died within ten days after the boy was brought home, the anxiety might have passed notice. But Wordsworth's adolescent mind found it necessary to connect the two events of the anxious waiting and the sudden dying as if the one thing had somehow precipitated the other.

The second spot of time shares the word *naked* with the first. Images of solitary things suffuse them both: a pool, a beacon, a gibbet, a wall, a sheep, a blasted tree. Within this apparent poverty, there lurks an immense richness; each of these lonely things persists, like the girl with the pitcher, against time, the weather, the elements. And each is "single," like the sheep, and destined to survive, as will the boy. Wordsworth lost his parents when he was young and lived to become a great poet and to find friendship and love; it is not as if he was unable to form enduring attachments. Yet the essential solitariness of the soul remained a deep conviction. When pondering Wordsworth's fascination with single figures standing up against the sky, A. C. Bradley came up with the lovely and profound sentence: "What is lonely is a spirit." The lonely figures in Wordsworth's work are his image for spirit itself, where that word is understood as referring to the part of each human being that remains proof against the unimaginable touch of time.

If Wordsworth truly believed himself, at least during his poetic prime, to be "unfathered" (1805, 6:527), and no doubt unmothered as well, why are there, then, the unlooked-for turns toward a loved one in his work? At the end of "Tintern Abbey," for instance, he suddenly brings Dorothy onstage and reveals that she has been standing next to him all the time. In dealing with such cases, it is not enough to say that Wordsworth had a difficult time accepting the reality of other people. It is, rather, that his experience of human bonds was so tangled up with loss that he became practiced at being lonely and so seems sometimes to forget, in his poems at least, that the auditors he has invited to listen in on his musings are, actually, present. Wordsworth was drawn to all those freestanding shepherds outlined against the sky precisely because they figured forth what he understood to be a terminal truth about the human condition, a truth that began for him as a wound and was slowly converted into a bow.

Having made the terrifying discovery of his self-sufficiency in the two spots of time, William still needed Dorothy. He needed her because she shared that "violence of Affection" she detected in him when they were reunited after years of separation. William needed Dorothy because she allowed him to maintain, as he wrote in book 10 of *The Prelude*, "a saving intercourse / With my true self" (1805, 914–15). And he loved her "because in you . . . I fondly view / All, all that Heav'n has claimed, in you." What had been claimed by Heaven were their two parents.

Dorothy was, for William, the desired and initial refinding. The three versions of *The Prelude* trace the mature resolution of this search when the sister is, in the 1850 version, replaced by the chosen wife. Mother Ann, sister Dorothy, wife Mary—each figure played its part in an ongoing drama of replacement. Annette Vallon played her part as well, only to be elided from the final record. Viewed from this perspective, none of the revisions made to the first spot of time, as Jonathan Wordsworth argues, can be judged as "for the worse." It is even possible to argue the opposite—that Wordsworth's additions and revisions testify to the *growth* of the poet's mind and heart. But given that every surviving text contributes to Wordsworth's evolving sense of who he was and what he once felt, the choice is not between but of. Instead of elevating one of *The Preludes* above any of the others, it seems more prudent, as Jack Stillinger argues, to "drop the concept of an ideal single text fulfilling an author's intentions and put our money instead on some theory of versions."

There is no *Ballad of Mary Wordsworth*. Dorothy, long given pride of place as the "woman" in her brother's life, has proven a difficult figure to dislodge. She remains the major documentary source for the months leading up to

Wordsworth's marriage. From all the reports of Mary's behavior during this period, she appears to have acted with extraordinary dignity and generosity. She was confronted with the existence of Annette Vallon: William had had a prior and a secret love. Not only was Mary required to absorb the fact of this liaison, but she saw her wedding day postponed so that William and Dorothy could travel to France.

In her chapter titled "Marriage, 1802–3," Mary Moorman maintains that Wordsworth's "love for Mary was as different from his love for Annette as love can be, and yet remain love. It was, for one thing, the result of long familiarity, whereas his passion for Annette had swept him off his feet in a few weeks." William's pursuit of Mary Hutchinson, Moorman begins, was an "unobtrusive wooing." However obtrusive the wooing may not have been, it did require the female partner to the match to do something extraordinary. Not only was she obliged to acknowledge the fact of William's prior sexual history, but she had to accept the consequences of that attachment as they intruded upon her present life.

But there did come a moment when Mary, so fugitive a character in *The Prelude* and yet one so crucial to the energies sending up the poem, emerged a little from the shadows. It had to do with the belated discovery of *another* set of Wordsworth manuscripts. These were love letters.

In 1977, Cornell University purchased at auction a trove of Wordsworth family papers found in a pile of scrap held by a stamp dealer in northern England. Thirty-one letters were discovered in the holdings, fifteen written by William and sixteen by Mary. The correspondence dated from the years 1810–12, when Wordsworth was away on visits to Coleorton, Hindwell, and London.

Now held in the Wordsworth Library at Grasmere, the letters were edited in 1981 by Beth Darlington. In her introduction to *The Love Letters of William and Mary Wordsworth*, she writes, "These new letters show us, without distortion, who William and Mary were and what sort of love bound them so compellingly together as man and wife."

The letters put paid to any notion that William found Mary "peaceful rather than stimulating." "Every hour of absence now is a grievous loss," he tells his wife, "because we have been parted sufficiently to feel how profoundly in soul & body we love each other." He urges her to be intimate, asking for "a letter for myself and of which I need only read parts to the rest of the family. . . . My soul demands such letters." He bids farewell with "a thousand kisses."

At times, Wordsworth becomes downright sexy. He imagines "thy limbs as they are stretched upon the soft earth; in thy own involuntary sighs & ejaculations, in the trembling of thy hands, in the tottering of thy knees, in the blessings which thy lips pronounce."

Even as Mary is experiencing this second courtship, she remains well aware of the living consequences of her husband's first affair. After being apprised of the difficult circumstance of "William's French family," she can write about Annette: "God bless her I should love her dearly & divide my last with her were it needful." It would not prove needful; Wordsworth's fortunes became sufficiently stable for him to make an annual settlement upon his daughter, Caroline, after her marriage in 1816. Mary was required to share her resources but not to divide her last.

In the emotional sequence Wordsworth lived out between the years 1787 and 1802, there came first the "early love" for Mary Hutchinson, then the affair with Annette in 1792, and finally the marriage to Mary in 1802. One of the letters of 1810–12 adds a significant interval to this sequence. In it, Wordsworth reveals a fantasy dating back to 1797. Mary had been staying with Dorothy and William at Racedown in that year. She spent much of her two-month visit helping to copy out poems, including *The Ruined Cottage*. Mary "slipped easily and naturally into her place beside brother and sister," Moorman notes, "a place which after a few more years she would occupy as William's wife."

Writing to that wife fifteen years after her spring visit to Racedown, Wordsworth projects backward a fantasy of having called upon her in 1797 to be more than an amanuensis: "I fancied that we should have seen so deeply into each others hearts, and been so fondly locked in each others arms, that we should have braved the worst and parted no more." While the circumstances needing braving remain undescribed, this letter shows Wordsworth's revisionary imagination once more at work, this time in the service of remembering his love for Mary as involving deep feelings and painful deferrals.

"Few people much mind what Wordsworth had to say after he married." Frances Wilson makes this somewhat offhand comment in her book on the sinking of the *Titanic*. The conviction that Wordsworth ran out of things "to say" in his early thirties has enjoyed a stubborn survival despite the fact that he wrote much of *The Prelude* after marrying Mary Hutchinson and continued to work on the poem well into his old age. Marriage energized Wordsworth instead of shutting him up, and it did so because he had formalized an attachment that was deeply passionate. Mary Wordsworth also worked at her husband's right hand; the first manuscript of *The Prelude* in fourteen books was made by her early in 1832. If she had not originally inspired his long poem, she can be said to have helped to *keep it going*. In the previous year, he had written that life, like *The Prelude*, was ever changeful. But by that year, some things were settled and done: Wordsworth had long since come to know who it was that he loved.

THREE

Ending *Great Expectations*

Great Expectations encourages a reader to take it personally. It simply cannot work unless one consents to sympathize and even to identify with Pip's deeply compromised attempt to look back upon his life and to arrive at something like a last judgment on it. Dickens means to remind us that we always inhabit two orders of time: the living forward into existential uncertainty and the remembering back on all that we have felt and done. Remembering, as Wordsworth had taught Dickens, has an aesthetic as well as an ethical function: the act of shaping a life story can also be a way of justifying it. But Pip is careful not to confuse his present understandings with the behavior and feelings belonging to his past self. So he can write, "I did not know then, though I think I know now" (78). How we go about coordinating the "now" and the "then" will differ for each person, but Pip's courageous and somewhat masochistic willingness to expose this process at work in his own life can feel uncannily familiar. In bringing this process to light, Pip earns the right to suddenly cry out to his audience, after admitting the hopelessness of some hope, "Why did you who read this, commit that not dissimilar inconsistency of your own, last year, last month, last week?" (285).

Orphaned Pip lives with his stern older sister and her kindhearted husband, the blacksmith Joe Gargery. Pip's first strong memory of "the identity of things" comes one day on the marshes, when he is confronted by an escaped convict who scares seven-year-old Pip into supplying him with food and a file (9). In the next phase of his story, Pip is invited to Satis House to meet Miss Havisham, an embittered and jilted bride still all dressed in white. Pip is commanded to play with Miss Havisham's ward, Estella, and soon falls in love with her. When, in a surprise announcement, Pip is informed by a lawyer named Jaggers that he has "come into a handsome property" and must be "removed from his present sphere of life . . . and be brought up as a gentleman," Pip assumes Miss Havisham to be his benefactor (109). Pip renounces a career as a blacksmith, moves to London, and becomes the gentleman he has been instructed to become. In scorning the forge and in pursuing the equally scornful Estella, Pip comes close to selling his soul, a fate he only escapes when his true benefactor turns up. It is Magwitch, Pip's convict, who, having escaped the law and amassed a fortune, has decided to "make" himself a gentleman. The complete upending of Pip's great expectations culminates in a series of ordeals and recognitions delivering him to a closing scene with Estella in which both characters discover that "suffering has been stronger than all other teaching" and so find themselves, depending on which of the two endings written for the novel a reader chooses to prefer, resolved to live together, or apart (358).

 I can still remember my face firing up as I finished the last pages of Pip's narrative. Lying in the single bed next to the radiator in my bedroom at Davenport College, I was visited by a shock of self-recognition from which I am still trying to recover. By my senior year in college, I had become Pip, the scholarship boy who left home in the pride of his hope and who had remade himself in ways prohibitive of any simple return to the sunbaked streets of Southern California. And if I was Pip, or in many ways like him, was I not also then in need of saying, as Pip does to Biddy and Joe near the end of his story, "forgive me!" (355)?

 But forgive me for what, exactly? For believing in the dream of success? Rising, as Pip does in nineteenth-century England, cannot have meant for him what it did for me in twentieth-century America; the class lines being violated in the 1960s were, for one thing, less marked and distinct. But my initiation into new ways of thinking and talking and dressing did surely make me guilty of distancing myself at times, if only in my mind, from the devoted unworldly parents who brought me up. While I never suffered "mortification" on their account, as Pip does during Joe's visit to London (168), and while I continued to make visits home and to enter into its routines, and this especially after my mother was killed in an automobile accident in 1971 and the family was reconfigured, there were also moments of awkward disagreement and even violent argument over the kind of person I had become.

As with Pip, money was at the heart of the change. My parents had none to spare. I never consulted them about the schools to which I applied, and when the letters from Harvard and Yale and UCLA arrived, I took the offer from Yale—not because I was given more support there, although I was, but because Yale had been the object of my boyhood fancies. With a full scholarship, free room and board, and a work-study job, I graduated without a penny of debt and went on to become the English professor I had dreamed of becoming.

The generous pots of money deposited almost daily into Yale's endowment were, in the mid-1960s, parceled out to scholarship boys in somewhat arbitrary ways. In my case, it was a surprise to learn that my Magwitch was the Alfred P. Sloan Foundation, a representative of which passed through New Haven once a year to check up on my progress during a lunch at Mory's. I cannot say that I was, any more than Pip, sufficiently grateful. While General Motors can be said to have put me through school, I have bought Fords and Plymouths but never a Chevrolet.

Was it all, as Humphry House writes of Pip, a "snob's progress" (644)? There was some of this, surely, and I must confess to moving through the world with a considerable dose of disdain. But I also understood literature to be the best antidote to any deformation of self the professional study of it might have induced. I knew that in *Great Expectations*, Dickens had told a story of "soul error"—of Pip's failure to give sufficient value to his experience—and I also knew that the reader of the novel is given far more assistance in avoiding this error than is its central character. Pip tells his story, but Dickens arranges it, a fact of which we are reminded, for instance, when a framing voice that cannot be Pip's enters the text and announces, "THIS IS THE END OF THE FIRST STAGE OF PIP'S EXPECTATIONS" (125).

As the reader watches Pip commit soul error almost up to the very end, with the last best instance being his absurd notion that he might return to the forge and propose marriage to Biddy, it becomes difficult to resist the thought that Pip may have missed the point of his own narrative. Whether or not Pip has really changed and has therefore earned the forgiveness he seeks from Biddy and Joe when he experiences the shock of his own stupid hope on their wedding day is perhaps the central question left open at the end, and any answer given will depend upon whether or not one believes that Pip has earned the right to a happy ending. In supplying his novel with two quite different endings, Dickens left it for the reader to decide.

Charles Dickens died of a cerebral hemorrhage on June 9, 1870. Four years later, John Forster published the third and final volume of his biography of the author. In it, he made the disclosure that the *Great Expectations* everyone had been reading since 1861 had once had another ending. In "The Original Ending," as it has come to be called, Pip and Estella do not again meet in the ruined garden at Satis House. The novel did not close with the beautiful sentence "I took her hand in mine, and we went out of the ruined place; and, as the morning mists had risen long ago when I first left the forge, so, the evening mists were rising now, and in all the broad expanse of tranquil light they showed to me, I saw no shadow of another parting from her" (501).

Instead of meeting in a garden, in the original ending Pip and Estella come together by chance on a London street. Pip is walking there with little Pip when Estella hails him from her carriage. Pip has already learned that she has survived her marriage to the abusive Bentley Drummle and is now married to a Shropshire doctor. Estella offers to shake hands and then asks to kiss the pretty child. "I was very glad afterwards to have had the interview," Dickens wrote in the concluding sentence, "for, in her face and in her voice, and in her touch, she gave me the assurance, that suffering had been stronger than Miss Havisham's teaching, and had given her a heart to understand what my heart used to be" (492).

Dickens once wrote his friend the novelist Bulwer-Lytton about "an insuperable aversion I have to trying back" (430). He preferred to revise "as I write." But "trying back" was just what Bulwer urged upon Dickens once he had received the proofs of the final chapters of *Great Expectations*. The original ending, he argued, simply did not work. There is no written record of the nature of Bulwer's objections to the meeting in Piccadilly, although a letter sent by Dickens to Wilkie Collins on June 23, 1861, sheds some light on the matter: "As yet, I have hardly got into the enjoyment of thorough laziness. Bulwer was so very anxious that I should alter the end of Great Expectations—the extreme end, I mean, after Biddy and Joe are done with—and stated his reasons so well, that I have resumed the wheel and taken another turn at it. Upon the whole I think it is for the better. You shall see the change when we meet." A day later, Dickens sent Bulwer "the whole of the concluding weekly No. of Great Expectations, in order that you may the more readily understand where I have made the change.... I have done it in as few words as possible; and I hope you will like the alteration that is entirely due to you." "I have put in as pretty a little piece of writing as I could," Dickens wrote to his friend and eventual biographer John Forster on July 1, 1861, "and I have no doubt the story will be more acceptable through the alteration" (536).

The question of how one might best end a novel was one Bulwer and Dickens had confronted only a month earlier. As the editor of the weekly journal *All the Year Round*, Dickens had solicited from Bulwer a new novel, and it was agreed that *A Strange Story* would appear in the magazine once *Great Expectations* had finished its run. Dickens was reading Bulwer's novel even as he was finishing up his own, and at one point, Bulwer solicited his friend's advice about whether or not to kill off his heroine. Dickens supported the idea of killing her "so long as that, beyond question, whatever the meaning of the story tends to, is the proper end" (519).

In his biography of Dickens, Forster printed the original closing lines of *Great Expectations* in a footnote to his commentary on the novel. His transcription of the unhappy ending remained the sole proof of its existence for more than one hundred years, until Edgar Rosenberg, acting on a tip from K. J. Fielding, steamed open some suspiciously bulky manuscripts at the Morgan Library in New York and found therein the "most nearly impeccable text" of the chance meeting in a London street (507). Photographs of the unhappy and happy endings at proof stage can be found on pages 492 and 493 of Rosenberg's superb Norton Critical Edition of the novel.

Editors usually ignored the unhappy ending until George Bernard Shaw restored it to the text of the novel he prepared in 1937 for the Limited Editions Club. "Since the late 1940s," Rosenberg informs us, "it has been customary to print both endings, editors unexceptionally concluding the text with the revised ending and running the original as a trailer" (506).

Shaw was happy that Dickens "got rid of Piccadilly and substituted a perfectly congruous and beautifully touching scene and hour and atmosphere for the meeting" (638). He objected, however, to "Pip and Estella as reunited lovers who were going to marry and live happily ever after"; noting that in qualification, "Dickens, though he could not bring himself to be quite so explicit in sentimental falsehood, did, at the end of the very last line, allow himself to say that there was 'no shadow of parting' between them." After misquoting the final sentence of the happy ending—it should read *no shadow of another parting from her*—Shaw proceeds to argue that Pip could never have made a life with Estella. The novel's "beginning is unhappy; its middle is unhappy; and the conventional happy ending is an outrage on it." Some twenty-five years later, Julian Moynahan was to agree with Shaw: "the cruelly beautiful original ending of the novel remains the only possible 'true' ending. Estella and Pip face each other across the insurmountable barrier of lost innocence. The novel dramatises the loss of innocence, and does not glibly present the hope of a redemptory second birth for either its guilty hero or the guilty society which shaped him" (663).

Despite the objections raised against the happy ending by Shaw, Gissing, Chesterton, Howells, and any number of others, it is a great boon to the history of literature in English that Dickens had "second thoughts" about the original ending of his novel (502). The happy ending is fully earned, earned both by prefiguring words and scenes in the novel itself and by doing "double duty," as Jerome Meckier demonstrates, "as a reviser of texts beyond itself." In choosing in his second ending to refigure the last lines of *Paradise Lost*, Dickens accepted that the story he had been telling sought for its conclusion, as did Milton's, the image of a human couple facing the prospect of marriage in a fallen world. Whether this can be judged to be the novel's "proper end" depends upon a reading of the whole.

Falling in love, we say, as if the event involved being dropped from a height. When we fall in love, we are usually struck quite suddenly by the way someone looks; we are attracted to appearances. The phrase proves strangely apt to the lived experience of looking across a room and saying to ourselves, "I want that." If things go well, we "get to know" the object of our gaze, and thereafter, we may come to love the inner as well as the outer being.

"The theme" of *Great Expectations,* as E. M. Daleski writes, "is the need for love." "At this stage in his development," however, Dickens is able to "express reciprocally powerful emotion . . . only within the framework of the parent-child relationship." "Every finding is a re-finding," Freud has been rumored to say, and whether or not we agree with him that achieving a mature sexual love somehow enacts a repetition of our earliest attachments, his gnomic little saying does usefully define the human task as the finding of a replacement for the love once felt for, and by, the originating parent.

Is Pip more defined by the Magwitch or by the Estella plot? Anyone who reads *Great Expectations* as a love story may be unsettled to learn that when Dickens worked up an outline for a dramatic performance of the novel, he omitted from it much of the narrative about Estella. And yet—she is the one standing with Pip at the end. If there is any real hope for an abiding love between Pip and Estella, it is only made possible, as Daleski maintains, once Pip engages in the work of forgiveness with his "fairy godmother" and his "second father" (122, 241).

Pip falls for Estella hard and fast; by the time he leaves Satis House for the first time, we can sense that he is a goner. He falls for her despite and perhaps even because of her coldness, as if her very inaccessibility made for the attraction. In doing so, he acts out the part of "the young Knight of romance," in which romance is fueled by and kept alive by the frustration rather than the fulfillment of the lover's desire (179).

By making Estella one of the least deserving or responsive love objects in English fiction, Dickens means to draw our attention toward how mystifying our choice of such objects can be. In offering us no access to Estella's inner life, Dickens also chooses to render her as opaque. She moves and speaks and distributes her charms, but what she may feel, or whether she can feel at all, remains an open question. What we are then being asked to witness is a one-sided love affair, one in which Pip continues to refine feelings that remain unreciprocated.

Because Estella is a figure so mediated by these feelings, it is therefore difficult to think or to write about her without adverting to Pip. Over the course of the reading experience, Estella becomes, as a result, a study in the power of self-nourished fantasy. As another novelist has written, "No amount of fire or freshness can challenge what a man will store up in his ghostly heart." This is Fitzgerald, commenting on Gatsby's equally fantastic love for the undeserving Daisy.

Perhaps Pip, like Gatsby, is not so much in love with Estella as in "some idea of himself that had gone into" loving her. There is certainly little enough about Estella that is lovable. When she and Pip first meet, she calls him "boy" and, while seeming to be about his age, "was as scornful of me as if she had been one-and-twenty, and a queen" (49). She mocks his card playing and finds his hands "coarse" (52). Her contempt for him, he notes, is so strong that it becomes "infectious," and Pip catches it. "I had never thought of being ashamed of my hands before; but I began to consider them a very indifferent pair." When Estella brings him bread and meat and a little mug of beer, she gives him the food "as insolently as if I were a dog in disgrace" (53). Pip later complains to Joe "that there had been a beautiful young lady at Miss Havisham's who was dreadfully proud, and that she had said I was common, and that I knew I was common, and that I wished I was not common" (59). Joe responds: "If you can't get to be oncommon through going straight, you'll never get to do it through going crooked." But Joe's lesson is lost on Pip, who retires to bed on the night of that "memorable day" now bound by a "chain of iron" to the thought of "how common Estella would consider Joe" (60). J. Hillis Miller argues that "Pip's first visit to Miss Havisham's determines everything which follows in his life, because it determines the way he reacts to everything which happens to him thereafter." The keyword here is *reacts*. Pip's is a story about how we take things, where taking is defined as the reaction to a surprise or to an affront or to a gift. Pip reacts to being humiliated by falling in love with the humiliator. As Miller writes, "On this day he makes the original choice of a desired self, and binds his destiny inextricably to Estella." Estella—the distant star—then becomes emblematic of Pip's desire to rise above a home he has suddenly agreed to view as common. Hence the need for Pip to kick the brewery wall and twist his hair, a way of getting rid of his injured feelings by displacing them away from the cruel love object that his engendered them.

Pip founds his great expectations on the belief that Miss Havisham is his "patroness" and that Estella has been "designed for me" (179, 243). It has been reserved for him, Pip assumes, to "do all the shining deeds of the young Knight of romance, and marry the Princess" (179). Then he learns not only that Magwitch is his true benefactor but Estella's father as well. So both Pip's money and his love originate from a tainted source. Moreover, his Family Romance proves an amateurish affair indeed compared with the strength and efficacy of the fantasy being orchestrated by Magwitch. In a somewhat desperate attempt to keep his romance alive—he "cannot say," he tells us, why he does so (303)—Pip becomes hot to track down Estella's mother. At the same time, once Pip learns of Estella's engagement to Bentley Drummle, he begs Herbert Pocket never to speak of her, as if this will somehow prevent the event. "Why I hoarded up this last wretched little rag of the robe of hope that was rent and given to the winds, how do I know! Why did you who read this, commit that not dissimilar inconsistency of your own, last year, last month, last week?" (285).

In so openly aligning himself with his readers, Dickens, through Pip, calls out those among us who have also indulged in great expectations, expectations less about money than about love. Part of the deep appeal of the novel lies in its power to allow a reader to travel again along such a path. Insofar as we may want our hero to get what he wants, the happy ending Dickens was eventually convinced to provide allowed him to gratify "the hope of the reader," as Samuel Johnson calls it, a hope any writer frustrates at his peril.

An early reviewer of *Great Expectations* spoke of hopes having little to do with the novel's ending. In the review, appearing in the *Spectator* on July 20, 1861, the reviewer contends that Dickens's reader

> is placed in much the same position as the hero. He has great and well-founded hopes at the beginning which are bitterly disappointed before the novel is half completed. The disappointment, however, is of an opposite kind. The reader is led to hope, when he begins the tale, that its course is to run continuously through that low life which Mr. Dickens describes with such marvelous accuracy and such delightful humour . . . but the circumstances which raise Mr. Pip's hopes gradually depress ours; when his Ideal fairly enters the tale, we are discomforted, and when Mr. Dickens bursts into lyrics, melodrama, and recitative, we almost make up our mind finally to abandon the story.

By "his Ideal," the reviewer means to refer, it seems, to Estella.

By calling attention to the problem of expectation in his novel's title, Dickens means to alert us to the fact that in expectation begins responsibility. As Kate Flint writes of the experience of reading *David Copperfield,* when we "wish for something awful"—or happy—"to happen, because we have been set up to expect it, and it hence forms the subject of our anticipation," that wish becomes "a device which implicates the reader." The something in which we have been encouraged to invest is Pip's Family Romance, although of course he gets it wrong. If our "*readerly* expectations," as Nicola Bradbury calls them, parallel Pip's, then they, too, are frustrated when Magwitch shows up and reconfigures Pip's story as one about a son rather than a lover.

As Jerome Meckier argues, "The expectation process—one's ability to formulate what one wants from the future—is a major reason the human situation remains ironic and unsatisfactory: not only are one's hopes regularly frustrated, but their attainment can be demanding, if not disastrous.... One must continually expect before one is qualified to evaluate the worth and consequence of one's expectations—i.e., before one knows what to expect. In other words, Pip has had to look forward in hopeful but ignorant expectation and backward with comprehension and regret."

The comprehension and regret only arrive for Pip sometime after his story is over. Once Pip loses Estella to Bentley Drummle, he invests in her Family Romance with the same avidity he has shown in constructing his own. Even as Miss Havisham solicits Pip's "understanding," he finds himself drawn back into his preoccupation with parentage (298). In answer to her question "Is there nothing I can do for you?" he asks one of his own: "Whose child was Estella?" (296, 298).

Because Herbert Pocket has already filled him in on the Molly-Magwitch story, Pip knows the answer to his question. But he is so wedded to the fancy built up around Estella that even in his soul-bearing exchange with Miss Havisham, he recurs to his essential fascination. "What purpose I had in view when I was hot on tracing out and proving Estella's parentage," Pip later admits, "I cannot say. It will presently be seen that the question was not before me in any distinct shape, but was put before me by a wiser head than my own" (303).

The identity of Estella's mother is revealed to him not by Miss Havisham but by way of an impressive feat of induction performed in the scene in which Pip dines in Jaggers's rooms. As the woman called Molly serves at table, "a certain action of her fingers as she spoke arrested my attention" (291). Jaggers dismisses Molly, and she glides out of the room.

"But she remained before me," Pip continues. "I looked at those hands, I looked at those eyes, I looked at that flowing hair; and I compared them with other hands, other eyes, other hair, that I knew of, and with what those might be after twenty years of a brutal husband and a stormy life." Pip's sentences continue to unfold through a series of "I looked's" and "I thought's" until they come to rest on a deeply felt and earned conviction: "And I felt absolutely certain that this woman was Estella's mother" (292).

Pip's attempt to trace out Estella's parentage culminates in the interview with Jaggers in which the lawyer argues, without in any way admitting that Pip has uncovered Estella's origin story, that Pip is better off not knowing it. "For whose sake would you reveal the secret?" Jaggers asks, and Pip has no answer (308).

Is the reader, his curiosity having been so fully aroused, also better off not knowing the story as well? For Dickens has revealed to us that an investment in Pip and Estella, if Pip is Magwitch's "boy" and Estella is Magwitch's child (241), is also an investment, according to Carolyn Brown, with a "wisp of incest." That this is all treated as a secret to be teased out only further calls attention to the most open secret of all, one usually at work in a Dickens novel—that families are built on secrets and that the keeping of them is not only a way of maintaining power over children but of keeping their love in the family. Pip does not know that his love for Estella is an inward-turning love, but the discovery of his second father having been her first one reveals it, at least on a symbolic level, to have been the case.

Biddy is the girl Pip talks to about the other girl. She is the kind of confidant one falls in love with without knowing it until it is all too late. "If I could only get myself to fall in love with you," Pip says to Biddy in chapter 17, as they are out on one of their walks together (103). If the invidious comparison is not thereby drawn, it is because Pip has already told the reader that Biddy "was not beautiful—she was common, and could not be like Estella" (100).

The scene in which Pip shares these observations turns upon the question of learning. Pip is "writing some passages from a book, to improve myself" (100). Biddy sits nearby, working her needle. Pip notes that although he never sees her "turn to at it," Biddy somehow manages "to learn everything that I learn." A few lines later, he says, "how improved you are!" When Pip then notices a tear in her eye, he is amazed.

Like so many of the things Pip says to Biddy, his comments are condescending. Biddy brings out Pip's admonishing self, yet even as he continues to run her down, he senses in her something "immeasurably better" that he will one day be required to take into account (105).

But that day is indeed far off. In the meantime, Dickens places Pip and Biddy in a series of awkward scenes of instruction. As Pip seeks to impose what he calls "my knowledge" on Biddy, he is being subtly instructed not only in what is worth knowing but in when and how to impart it (100).

"You were my first teacher," Pip notes to Biddy, and the "lesson" she would set him has to do with expressed emotion. Throughout his narrative, Pip keeps his most self-critical comments to himself, sharing them only with the reader, while in his spoken exchanges with other characters, he attempts for the most part to save face. "What put that in your head?" Biddy says to Pip, after he points out that she is crying (101). Here Biddy is trying to spare Pip the knowledge that his comment about her having improved has moved her to tears. Once she asks the question, Pip turns inward, away from dialogue and into narration.

Narration is about keeping one's words in one's head. "What could have put it in my head, but the glistening of a tear as it dropped on her work?" Pip asks himself, after Biddy delicately denies that his words may have hurt her. Then he is off into the interior, off into a memory of Biddy's "hopeless" and "miserable" early circumstances, of how he had nevertheless "turned to her for help," and of something "latent in Biddy that was now developing." This is all accurate enough, if still not a little condescending—Pip assumes it is Biddy who needs to develop, not himself—and it is rounded out by Pip's thinking that "perhaps I had not been sufficiently grateful to Biddy" (101). None of this, however, gets said.

Instead, Pip makes his remark about Biddy being his first teacher "and that at a time when we little thought of ever being together like this, in this kitchen." Biddy makes her reply, "Ah, poor thing." Pip takes this as referring to Joe and to his grief over the recent attack on his wife: "It was like her self-forgetfulness, to transfer the remark to my sister" (101). But it is precisely Biddy's pity for Pip, as a poor thing, here and elsewhere, that characterizes her interactions with him. She often expresses this pity in her discreet refusals to correct him.

The Pip-Biddy relation opens a window onto Dickens's theory of how people do actually "improve." Dickens certainly has little faith in formal education as it is imparted in school. And in *Great Expectations*, the words *instructions*, *lessons*, and *schooling* are too firmly associated with Miss Havisham's upbringing of Estella to escape a sense of opprobrium. That form of schooling has, however, worked well enough, although more through example than any coherent pedagogy. The Pip-Biddy relation works to question the efficacy of outright instruction itself—of being given direct lessons in a subject or corrected in one's errors in behavior. Change may occur, and personal growth may be possible, but it cannot be coerced out of people by telling them what to do. In Pip's case, improvement takes place slowly, and painfully, in private scenes of self-recognition and only after he has learned to listen to people and to respond to them more generously, in the way a reader might come to "read" the characters in a Dickens novel.

It might seem that Pip has finally learned the necessary lessons when, with most of the novel's action said and done, he makes a last trip home. At the end of chapter 57, after Pip recovers from his illness, he realizes that Joe has paid his debts and resolves to go to him and to engage in a "penitent remonstrance." After making this decision, Pip adds that he also hopes to relieve his mind and heart of "a vague something lingering in" his thoughts now "formed into a settled purpose" (350). That purpose is the proposal of marriage to Biddy. But Dickens meets this desire with a painful irony. Resolved at last to speak his feelings, Pip will be met with a blocking surprise. His feelings must remain, once again, unspoken, although not this time from any inhibition in himself.

"I went down to the old place, to put it in execution," Pip says about his plan, in the closing sentence of chapter 57, "and how I sped in it, is all I have left to tell." But the execution of Pip's purpose has already occurred in the preceding paragraph. In it, Pip rehearses his proposal to Biddy: "I would show her how humbled and repentant I came back . . . I would tell her . . . I would remind her . . . I would say to her." Without once using the word *love* or *marriage*, Pip carefully outlines for the reader what he intends to say. He plans to ask Biddy, and in a way perhaps not likely to recommend him to a future wife, to "receive me like a forgiven child" (350).

When Pip arrives at the forge, it is to discover Joe and Biddy dressed for their wedding day. After collapsing from the shock—"They had taken me into the kitchen, and I had laid my head down on the old deal table"— Pip congratulates the couple and announces his intention to be "soon going abroad" (354).

But Pip is not quite done: "I must say more." He then engages in one of the "Tell Me" scenes a reader of the novel may by now have come to expect.

These are scenes in which a character attempts to put words into another character's mouth. While these are scenes of great seriousness, Dickens anticipates them in a comical way in chapter 4, in which during Christmas dinner, Wopsle and Pumblechook "point the conversation" at Pip and afflict him with a series of "moral goads" (26).

While the Tell Me scenes involve characters attempting to mend their ways, they do not suggest that those seeking forgiveness have completed their journey toward it. The scenes have a complex purpose and effect. On the one hand, they allow something awkward or painful to be said; on the other, they place the burden of utterance not on the person who ought to be saying the thing but on the person who deserves to be hearing it. In the resulting encounters, intense feelings are aroused without seeming to *belong* to anyone.

"Don't tell him, Joe, that I was thankless," Pip says about "some little fellow" who may someday be born. "Don't tell him Biddy, that I was ungenerous and unjust; only tell him that I honoured you both." This curious way of apologizing for sins of ingratitude and pride deflects attention away from the acts themselves and toward some future in which they will *not* be spoken about. Once again, something is being denied even as it is being admitted. Pip completes his displaced atonement by saying, "Pray tell me, both, that you forgive me!" (355).

Joe responds as Pip requires by saying, "God knows as I forgive you, if I have anythink to forgive!" Biddy cannot go quite so far and simply says: "Amen! And God knows I do!" (355). More discerning than Joe, Biddy senses that Pip has preempted the very forgiveness he wishes to receive. She will not use the word *forgive* because she knows that in doing so she will only be quoting Pip. Somehow he has managed to reduce what could have been an authentic emotional exchange to "a form of words" (270).

This last phrase comes from Estella. She utters it in chapter 44, in response to Pip's "you know I love you" (270). Estella is described as "unmoved" by Pip's claim; Dickens repeats the word three times. The inability to be moved by such a declaration points to something more than the success of Miss Havisham's schooling. Estella's hearing what is being said to her as only a form of words reminds us once again of the challenge Pip faces throughout his narrative—the challenge to be in, *really in,* what he is saying. For Estella, the word *love* has been so hedged about by her schoolmistress's hysterical repetition of it as to have become the ultimate empty signifier. "I know what you mean, as a form of words," the complete sentence reads, "but nothing more." Given the many difficulties Pip faces when he attempts to put his thoughts and feelings into spoken words, Estella's response to his declaration of love calls up all the missed opportunities, those behind and those yet to come. Whether love is more than a word Pip wants to be *in* remains a poignant and, for many readers of the novel, an ever-looming question.

The Tell Me scene with Biddy and Joe is anticipated in one with Miss Havisham closing out chapter 49. The scene can be said to begin five chapters earlier, when Pip speaks as directly as he ever will, and Miss Havisham is listening: "'Estella,' said I, turning to her now, and trying to control my trembling voice, 'you know I love you.'" She looks at him with an unmoved countenance. Pip continues: "It would have been cruel in Miss Havisham, horribly cruel, to practise on the susceptibility of a poor boy, and to torture me through all these years with a vain hope." Estella makes her response. "There are sentiments, fancies—I don't know how to call them—which I am not able to comprehend. When you say you love me, I know what you mean, as a form of words; but nothing more" (270). After Estella announces her intention to marry Bentley Drummle and tells Pip to "get me out of your thoughts," his feelings overflow, and he is for once able to meet the moment:

> Out of my thoughts! You are part of my existence, part of myself. You have been in every line I have ever read since I first came here, the rough common boy whose poor heart you wounded even then. You have been in every prospect I have ever seen since—on the river, on the sails of the ships, on the marshes, in the clouds, in the light, in the darkness, in the wind, in the woods, in the sea, in the streets. You have been the embodiment of every graceful fancy that my mind has ever become acquainted with. The stones of which the strongest London buildings are made, are not more real, or more impossible to be displaced by your hands, than your presence and influence have been to me, there and everywhere, and will be. (272)

Pip has come a long way from the novel's opening scene. Then he was lost in a landscape where he could not read—it was all indecipherable "lines" (12). Now he celebrates not only his ability to read a "line" of print but to put words onto his feelings. As with Mary and Dorothy Wordsworth in the first spot of time, the emotional experience of loving a woman has been superimposed upon Pip's initial melancholy encounter with landscape in such a way as to irradiate it. She has become the beloved spot. Having fully acknowledged what he feels, Pip can therefore end by saying, "Oh, God bless you, God forgive you!" (272).

The effect of Pip's candor becomes clear five chapters later, although hints as to its efficacy have been given during the confession scene itself as we watch Miss Havisham "put her hand to her heart" and perceive, through Pip's eyes, her "ghastly look" (270, 271). In chapter 49, when the climax comes, she begins seeking Pip's forgiveness by adverting to one of the metaphors he used with Estella. "'I want,' she said, 'to pursue that subject you mentioned to me when you were last here, and to show you that I am not all stone'" (295).

Miss Havisham's Tell Me scene unfolds on two levels: on the level of agonized feeling as registered through the repeated cry "What have I done!" (297); and on a discursive level in which the prose repeatedly calls attention to the acts of speaking and writing and reading that bring those emotions into an interpersonal space. After Pip says some reassuring words, Miss Havisham addresses him in "an unwonted tone of sympathy" (296). Later there will be mention of the "order" of her "sentences" (300). Once Pip has assured Miss Havisham that there is nothing more she can do for him, she looks "about the blighted room for the means of writing. There were none there, and she took from her pocket a yellow set of ivory tablets, mounted in tarnished gold, and wrote upon them with a pencil in a case of tarnished gold that hung from her neck" (296). After authorizing the payment to Herbert, Pip tells us, "She read me what she had written" (297). Then she hands Pip her pencil.

"My name is on the first leaf," she continues. "If you can ever write under my name, 'I forgive her,' though ever so long after my broken heart is dust—pray do it!" (297). She will utter the words *I forgive her* again in her verbal wanderings after she has been burned in the fire and a third time just after Pip kisses her on the lips, in the last sentence of the chapter.

Chapter 49 did not always end in this way. Edgar Rosenberg notes that "originally Dickens had taken his leave" of Miss Havisham in a separate paragraph: "It was the first and last time that ever I touched her in that way. And I never saw her more" (453). As for Dickens's reasons for striking the original chapter ending, Rosenberg cites three possibilities: "because he wanted to foreground the act of forgiveness, not the farewell, or perhaps because he wanted to keep the options open—that Pip might see her again—or because he thought it important to stress the liturgical repetition, the identical sentence having appeared some lines before."

Here, as he summons even more affect than in the late scene with Biddy and Joe, Dickens shows a character struggling with forgiveness. Miss Havisham's attempt takes the form of dictation. "Take the pencil and write" is an imperative, a kind of command. But since the seeker after forgiveness casts the possible response to the imperative into the future, the act is necessarily deferred. It is a rehearsal for something that may never be enacted, like Pip's "I would's" at the end of chapter 57. As a rehearsal, it cannot yet be said to have actually happened. Perhaps it is, after all, only a form of words. Where and when, Dickens appears to be asking in his Tell Me scenes, is forgiveness to be found?

"You know with whom forgiveness lies, as the highest attribute conceivable" (83). So speaks Crisparkle, the Minor Canon in *The Mystery of Edwin Drood*. He seems quite sure where forgiveness is to be found—outside the self as a gift from on high. But well before attempting a last novel Dickens had begun to conceive of forgiveness as occurring in an inner space where selves work to forgive themselves. And what they seek to forgive in themselves are not the bad deeds that are usually easy enough to identify and to redress but the pride and guilt and the resulting self-blame and bitterness or deadness of heart that alienates them from those they are attempting to connect with when forgiveness is being either granted or sought. Forgiveness in this sense is being redefined as acknowledgment, and what is usually being acknowledged is a failure of feeling. Only after resolving to come alive again in one's own life by taking the risk of feeling and expressing what is felt can the work of forgiveness really begin.

In *Great Expectations*, Dickens appears to be writing out of a profound disillusionment with the activity of fathering. While "a father's last will is the device that in most novels triggers off the Dickens plot," as Anny Sadrin observes, it is "a matter of the utmost urgency that all the heroes' fathers should be put back where they belong: in heaven, where Dickens placed them." Only secondary characters like Herbert Pocket and Wemmick have living fathers, and they are presented as hair-pulling or cannon-firing oddities.

Pip is about as fatherless as they come, although he will be given another chance at sonship after the sudden appearance of Magwitch, his "second father" (241). Through the Magwitch plot, Dickens affords a character a rare chance to enact a Family Romance in which an elected son moves from repugnance to tenderness.

After receiving his inheritance, Pip's becomes a story of misplaced gratitude. Having come "into great expectations from a mysterious patron," Pip fixes his fancy on Miss Havisham as "the fairy godmother who had changed me" (113, 122). He tells her about his "good fortune" and then adds, as if in thanks, "I am so grateful for it, Miss Havisham!" In the scene where Miss Havisham says to Pip, "Love her!" he feels "a burst of gratitude" that Estella "should be destined for me" (187). All the while, Pip is uncomfortably but only intermittently aware of his "own ingratitude" toward Joe (124).

When Magwitch shows up again in chapter 39, Pip does not recognize him, although the stranger displays "an incomprehensible air of being touched and pleased by the sight of me" (237). All that Pip at first sees is a man with iron-gray hair, a muscular man, a man about sixty browned and hardened by exposure to the weather. "Do you wish to come in?" Pip asks. "'Yes,' he replied; 'I wish to come in, Master.'"

Pip asks his "question inhospitably enough, for I resented the sort of bright and gratified recognition that still shone in his face." Magwitch again holds out his hands to Pip, who then asks, "What do you mean?"

Magwitch hopes for a recognition scene. He has "looked slowly forward" to the reunion (241). "It's disapinting to a man," he says, to have "come so fur; but you're not to blame for that" (238). And then, quickly enough, Pip does see—"for I knew him!" Despite all the intervening years and all the intervening objects, "I could not have known my convict more distinctly than I knew him now." Thus the prodigal father returns, now "looking back at me for recognition."

Pip then shifts the subject from recognition to gratitude: "Keep off! If you are grateful to me for what I did when I was a little child, I hope you have shown your gratitude by mending your way of life. If you have come here to thank me, it was not necessary. Still, however you have found me out, there must be something good in the feeling that has brought you here, and I will not repulse you; but surely you must understand that—I—." And then the words die away on Pip's tongue.

Once he regains his composure, Pip doubles down on his theme: "I am glad that, thinking I deserve to be thanked, you have come to thank me" (239). Pip could not be more mistaken; instead of fending off gratitude, he is the one who will soon be expected to display it. But this he cannot feel; once "the truth of my position came flashing on me"—once Magwitch has told his tale—Pip feels, simply, "wrecked" (240, 243).

The Magwitch plot takes up the question of what it means to *make* somebody in a very literal way. "I've made a gentleman on you," Magwitch declares, even as Pip feels the room surge and turn (240). He goes on to remember his days as a lonely shepherd and the resolve he made while eating his supper. "I'll make that boy a gentleman!" (241). In chapters 39 and 40, the words *make* and *made* are conjoined with the word *gentleman* eight more times.

Magwitch is the proud creator: he feels a "triumph in my story" (255). Pip is repelled by this and likens himself to "the imaginary student pursued by the misshapen creature he had impiously made." The reference to *Frankenstein* is not exact, as Rosenberg points out. "It is Frankenstein himself who eventually embarks on a pursuit of the creature and dies in the chase. Pip is saying that in his case the monster has made the man" (253–54).

While Pip's body language may betray these feelings, he says nothing of them to Magwitch. Pip's creator is thereby spared his creature's "thanklessness" (312). But the entire creator-creature dynamic is given such a sounding in the Pip-Magwitch plot as to render it downright absurd: the wished-for act of making has resulted only in a ruining—in the complete and perfect production of a thankless child.

Magwitch refuses, however, to play the role of the disappointed parent. He may use his own version of the word during the reunion scene, but thereafter, he never rebukes or criticizes Pip for his behavior toward him, sketchy as much of it may be. And in his constancy, he helps to effect a change in Pip's heart.

Pip's sudden loss of his illusions forwards an important series of events. In chapter 44, he makes his declaration of love to Estella. She may remain the unresponsive love object, but that is not the point. As Mike says to Wemmick, "A man can't help his feelings," and Pip's feelings have converted him into a "visionary boy" (309, 272). The making and sustaining of that vision is an act of self-fashioning as determinative as Magwitch's gift of a fortune, and I think we are invited to admire it in the somewhat qualified way in which we may admire Gatsby's stubborn adherence to his dream of Daisy, his "extraordinary gift for hope."

Of course, neither Gatsby's nor Pip's love is reciprocated. But now, as the object of a stranger's constant love, Pip begins to understand what reciprocal love is. He has felt it before, from Joe, but he has failed to honor it. Given a second chance with his second father, Pip slowly rises to the occasion. His project of getting Magwitch "out of England" gradually deepens into a task of loving care.

When, for instance, Pip installs Magwitch upstairs in Old Barley's riverside house, he sees Magwitch holding a light over the stair rail to show him the way downstairs. Pip then notices a pattern and its reversal: "Looking back at him, I thought of that first night of his return when our positions were reversed, and when I little supposed my heart could ever be as heavy and anxious at parting from him as it was now" (283). *Parting* is Joe's word, and having muffed so many partings with Joe, Pip now recognizes that he is being given an opportunity to avoid repeating old mistakes.

Pip engages in another project while preparing Magwitch for his escape: tracking down the parentage of Estella. This quest takes him to Satis House, where he rescues Miss Havisham from the fire, and to Jaggers's rooms, where he discloses to him that he knows Provis—Magwitch—to be Estella's father. The episode with Orlick at the sluice house then intervenes, and Pip, now with burned hands, is almost disabled from being of any use in the planned escape. With Orlick, Pip remains blind to repetitive patterns; he is the aggressive quotient Pip never quite re-assimilates. All the while, Magwitch refuses to "be low" (325).

It is not until the foiling of the escape plan that Pip finally places himself with Magwitch. Compeyson has been drowned, and Magwitch is manacled and carried down to the galley. Herbert and Startop are to go to London by land: "We had a doleful parting, and when I took my place by Magwitch's side, I felt that that was my place henceforth while he lived. . . . For, now, my repugnance to him had all melted away, and in the hunted wounded shackled creature who held my hand in his, I only saw a man who had meant to be my benefactor, and who had felt affectionately, gratefully, and generously, towards me with great constancy through a series of years. I only saw in him a much better man than I had been to Joe" (332).

Once again, Magwitch assists Pip in the recognition of life patterns: his treatment of Pip versus Pip's treatment of Joe. As a result of the comparison, the convict emerges as "a much better man than I had been to Joe." He does so by virtue of his constancy. This, Pip now realizes, is the true gift: being held in love. And Magwitch did so "gratefully." Here the gratitude being felt is for the chance to give love.

Pip now knows that all the money remaining has been lost; Magwitch's possessions will "be forfeited to the Crown." And Magwitch then tells him, "It's best as a gentleman should not be knowed to belong to me now" (332). He renounces his right to any claim over or attachment to Pip whatsoever. Pip gives his answer: "I will never stir from your side." So the orphan and the convict, with nothing at all heritable left between them, make their way. As so often happens in the novel, the pact is sealed by the hand: "I felt his hand tremble as it held mine." The rest is beyond utterance, and all that Pip can hear is Magwitch's click, "that old sound in his throat—softened now, like all the rest of him" (333).

And then we come to the end. Which of the two endings to prefer hinges, in part, on the value a reader places on refiguration—on the pleasure afforded when a work of literature attempts to become, in Meckier's words, "a reviser of texts beyond itself." Dickens's "original" ending does not make such an attempt. But when Dickens tried again and returned to the motif of the hand—"I took her hand in mine, and we went out of the ruined place"—he found himself falling back on an earlier scene of departure and setting out:

> Some natural tears they dropped, but wiped them soon;
> The world was all before them, where to choose
> Their place of rest, and Providence their guide:
> They hand in hand with wand'ring steps and slow,
> Through Eden took their solitary way.
>
> (*Paradise Lost*, 12:645–49)

Given that Dickens has already echoed these lines at the close of the first stage of Pip's expectations—"the world lay spread before me" (125)—the refiguring of Milton's ending as Dickens ends his novel comes as an expectation fulfilled rather than as a surprise. As Rosenberg notes, the parallels between the two endings are so apparent that in discussions of the novel's final scene, "it's a rare writer who forgets to quote Milton at this point" (513). The editors of the Oxford World's Classics edition even characterize the couple in the garden as "a Victorian Adam and Eve."

Paradise Lost, like *Great Expectations*, does not really end—it rebegins. The valedictory tone hovering over the two departures from a garden is mixed with a strong sense of "assurance," to borrow a word from Dickens's unhappy ending, of a future to come. Readers pretty much know what happened to Adam and Eve. And they can project forward and ask, as Shaw does, whether Pip and Estella will "live happily ever after." The question may, however, fade in importance before the awe-inspiring awareness of two human beings once again resolving to go through time together.

Time is the misfortune into which Adam and Eve fall when they fell. As Michael says to Adam at the end of book 12, after completing his preview of the human future, "the hour precise / Exacts our parting hence" (12:589–90). Adam and Eve have never had to be on time before; there have been no exacting hours. The ongoing and open-ended nature of existential time is something they have yet to discover. Adam and Eve will learn, as Pip says to Estella at the end, that "parting is a painful thing" and hence the accuracy of Joe's model of human experience as "ever so many partings welded together" (173).

As Dickens moves through the final paragraphs of his revised ending, he appears to waver on the question of parting versus staying:

> "I little thought," said Estella, "that I should take leave of you in taking leave of this spot. I am very glad to do so."
>
> "Glad to part again, Estella? To me, parting is a painful thing. To me, the remembrance of our last parting has ever been mournful and painful."
>
> "But you said to me," returned Estella, very earnestly, 'God bless you, God forgive you!' And if you could say that to me then, you will not hesitate to say that to me now—now, when suffering has been

stronger than all other teaching, and has taught me to understand what your heart used to be. I have been bent and broken, but—I hope—into a better shape. Be as considerate and good to me as you were, and tell me we are friends."

"We are friends," said I, rising and bending over her, as she rose from the bench.

"And will continue friends apart," said Estella.

"Take leave . . . taking leave . . . part . . . parting . . . parting . . . apart": the momentum of the word choices points in one direction. But then comes the turn, in the final paragraph: "I took her hand in mine, and we went out of the ruined place; and, as the morning mists had risen long ago when I first left the forge, so the evening mists were rising now, and in all the broad expanse of tranquil light they showed to me, I saw no shadow of another parting from her" (358).

Milton's ending also sets up a lovely tension between the desire to stay and the need to go. Eve manages to resolve the tension by making a case for going as a kind of staying:

> In me is no delay; with thee to go,
> Is to stay here; without thee here to stay,
> Is to go hence unwilling; thou to me
> Art all things under Heav'n, all places thou.
>
> (12:615–16)

Eve's lines articulate a paradox at the heart of life in the transient world she and Adam are about to enter. Having helped to bring about the loss of the eternal garden, Eve reaffirms the "Abundant recompense" of loving a living person. Such persons, condemned to mortality by the fall are, even while living, always also dying. Staying with one of them therefore involves a continual experience of going.

Pip and Estella come later and are a little sadder. They have never known anything but life in a fallen world. When they go out of the ruined place, they also go down, like Arthur and Amy at the end of *Little Dorrit,* "down into the . . . usual uproar" (859–60). Neither character has been blessed by the kind of happy childhood that might give rise to the myth of a paradise lost. Still, Dickens shows us, it is possible for them to find a way to follow in the footsteps of their first parents.

The words that see them out of the ruined place remain, however, a matter of debate. It turns out that Dickens provided his novel not only with two endings but with two sets of last words. Its final nine have traditionally been taken to read as follows: "I saw no shadow of another parting from her" (501). Yet in all versions of the novel appearing in print before 1862, there were different words in a different order: "I saw the shadow of no parting from her."

Rosenberg relates that the familiar last words date "from the Library Edition of 1862; it is fair to assume that Dickens introduced it deliberately; it was allowed to stand in the Charles Dickens Edition six years later, and it has been the familiar exit line ever since." In all texts of the novel appearing earlier than 1862—in the serial versions and the first edition, along with early American editions—the novel concludes with "I saw the shadow" rather than with "I saw no shadow." While conceding that the revised clause "beckons to us more rhythmically than the gaunt string of monosyllables it supplanted," Rosenberg rejects the familiar exit line and chooses to end his edition of *Great Expectations* with Dickens's original wording of his happy ending (503). The Oxford World's Classics edition follows him in this choice.

When it comes to last words, however, Dickens's second thought was his best thought. Even Rosenberg, choosing against the "no shadow" construction, admits it to be more rhythmical than the sequence of words Dickens originally wrote. It succeeds, he allows, on the level of style. But the familiar nine words also make a claim upon us as one more instance of Dickens's command of the uses of allusion—this time by echoing a wonderful passage not from book 12 but from book 4 of *Paradise Lost*.

In her first speech in the poem, Eve recounts to Adam her memory of her first day. On waking, she tells him, her initial act was to look into a clear, smooth lake:

> As I bent down to look, just opposite,
> A shape within the wat'ry gleam appeared
> Bending to look on me, I started back,
> It started back, but pleased I soon returned,

> Pleased it returned as soon with answering looks
> Of sympathy and love; there I had fixed
> Mine eyes till now, and pined with vain desire,
> Had not a voice thus warned me, What thou seest,
> What there thou seest fair creature is thyself,
> With thee it came and goes; but follow me,
> And I will bring thee where no shadow stays
> Thy coming.
>
> (4:460–71)

No shadow: that's what God promises Eve. After his voice interrupts Eve's reverie, she gets up, begins to move, and then sees Adam, who looks "less amiably mild / Than that smooth wat'ry image" (4:479–80). So "back I turned." Adam cries out "Return" and explains to Eve that she came out of his side (4:481). His hand gently seizes hers, and finally, as Eve says in conclusion to her story, "I yielded" (4:489).

What Eve first sees in the water is less a shadow than a reflection; she calls it "a shape." The shape returns and answers her. Estella uses the same word: "I have been bent and broken, but—I hope—into a better shape." Suffering has reshaped her—she hopes. Eve is yet to learn how suffering will do this to her as well, and she cannot do so until she is drawn away from a fascination with her own shape.

The word *shape* is quickly replaced by Milton with another and more powerful word: "I will bring thee where no shadow stays / Thy coming." In figuring Eve's image of herself as a "shadow," when the voice of God calls to her, Milton is making a metaphor. The word *shadow* freights Eve's act of self-regard with a long history of dark associations.

We know that Pip is often haunted by the word: "What *was* the nameless shadow which again in that one instant had passed?" (202). In Pip's case, the metaphor of the shadow refers to some part of himself he has chosen to disavow. With Eve, and by extension with Estella, her counterpart, the figure of the shadow takes on a different meaning.

What seems to save the situation between Adam and Eve in book 4 is a spoken word: "Return." As the first word ever uttered by one human being to another, *return* argues for the origin of the self in something outside the self to which it can turn again. Perhaps every finding *is* a refinding. But words alone are not quite enough to accomplish the reunion. What is finally needed, to convince and conjoin, is touch. Only by way of Adam's hand is Eve persuaded to return to him and to abandon her shadow. And it is "hand in hand" that they will walk together out of paradise.

When Robert Douglas-Fairhurst describes *Great Expectations* as "a novel of returns," he is surely thinking of this great scene of return at the end. One small but telling detail indicates Dickens's awareness that he is writing just such a novel. It involves the choice of a verb. "'But you said to me,' returned Estella." Why not write, simply, "answered Estella"? It is as if the longing to return has invaded the very lexicon of the novel itself.

Why does Dickens find himself echoing Milton at the very end? Because, as with Eve, the big problem for Estella has been self-love. Milton's fable of human beginnings argues for a primal narcissism at the heart of things that it takes the love of both God and man to overcome. And what interrupts the sterile circularity of self-return—we may notice that when he cries out, "Return," Adam is trying to break the spell of the shape that "soon returned" every time Eve bends over the water—are the sound of words and the touch of a hand.

As Anny Sadrin observes, when Pip enters Satis House for the first time, "the first object he notices and points out to the reader is a looking-glass." While Miss Havisham is given to "looking at the reflexion of herself" (51), Estella, even more, has become "transfixed" by her own shadow (52), a beauty for which she seems to care nothing and yet which traps her in a series of sterile poses. In keeping with this structure of imagery, in chapter 49, Miss Havisham refigures Pip himself as her true mirror. "Until you spoke to her the other day, and until I saw in you a looking-glass that showed me what I once felt myself, I did not know what I had done" (298). Pip's courageous declaration of love reminds Miss Havisham of what "I once felt myself." He is not a mirror but a suffering subject whose words move Miss Havisham and therefore allow her to escape from her frozen state of self-reflection and to return to her lost history of feeling.

Eve's story in book 4 offers up a compressed fable of human growth. Estella's growth—and it is Estella who is most vividly prefigured by Eve—occurs mostly off the page. As she tells Pip, the years intervening since their last meeting have left her "greatly changed," and we must take the change on faith (357). When she returns to the ruined garden, she is also returning to Pip, and their meeting there is no more coincidental than is meeting on a London street. When Dickens writes of an imagined future in which no shadow will stay their coming together, he is not only echoing Milton but forwarding his promise of a love in which two people, by way of well-timed words and timely touch, are given, like Adam and Eve, a second chance.

At the end, Dickens offers only a qualified affirmation, however, one signaled by the decision to convert this last re-turning into another Tell Me scene. Estella and Pip are not yet quite *in their words* and so must settle for one more displaced attempt at forgiveness.

Estella speaks to Pip in much the same way in which Pip has spoken earlier that morning to Biddy and Joe. After she remembers the day of their last parting, Pip recalls it as having been mournful and painful: "'But you said to me,' returned Estella, very earnestly, '"God bless you, God forgive you!" And if you could say that to me then, you will not hesitate to say that to me now—now, when suffering has been stronger than all other teaching, and has taught me to understand what your heart used to be.'" *Say that to me now:* the most Estella asks or seems to hope for is the repetition of an earlier saying.

She ends by saying "Tell me we are friends." Pip complies, answering, "We are friends."

For the 1868 edition of *Great Expectations,* Dickens supplied descriptive headlines for each chapter, with chapter 59 bearing the headline "The Figure in the Ruin" (490). When Pip first sees Estella along the desolate garden walk, he does not at first recognize her. He sees only "a solitary figure in it." A few more sentences are required before he can make her out:

> The figure showed itself aware of me, as I advanced. It had been moving towards me, but it stood still. As I drew nearer, I saw it to be the figure of a woman. As I drew nearer yet, it was about to turn away, when it stopped, and let me come up with it. Then, it faltered as if much surprised, and uttered my name, and I cried out:
> "Estella!" (357).

In book 4 of *Paradise Lost,* it is Eve who fails to recognize Adam. Here the dynamic is reversed, with the man unable to bring the woman into focus.

Even though, like Eve, Estella does begin to turn away, she stops and allows Pip to come nearer. She speaks first, saying his name. And then, again like Adam, she offers him "the friendly touch of the once insensible hand."

Rosenberg points to the striking use here "of the impersonal pronoun—Estella is as yet an *it*" (446). He sees the two characters as "sleepwalkers, people who are not moving by an act of volition but are drawn along by invisible strings." Perhaps so. But the question of volition, so often a vexed question in Dickens, counts for less here than does the simple fact of one of the great love scenes in English poetry having been reimagined in English prose even as, in important ways, it is being reversed. Making the woman the moving party—there is a definite "moving towards" and only an "about to turn away"—is a good thing not only for Pip and Estella but for the tradition of which they form such a central part.

Dickens had, of course, imagined another kind of ending. Then he conceded to the urgings of a friend and to the hopes of man although not all of his readers. Whether or not his two characters have actually changed enough to have earned a happy ending will remain open to controversy. It was not a debate Dickens survived to adjudicate. But the ending Dickens did choose to publish succeeds in refreshing the language in so many ways that it would be a hard thing to have to do without it. There were words that came back to him, words spoken earlier by Joe or by Pip or by Eve or by God, words that wanted to be repeated, newly, again.

FOUR

Harriet Jacobs and the Ordeal of Reception

In 1861, there appeared in Boston a book with the title *Incidents in the Life of a Slave Girl*. Under the title came the words "Written by Herself." Two quotations followed, and below them, readers were informed that the book had been "edited by L. Maria Child." No publisher was anywhere listed. Bound in dark green, the volume carried one word on its spine, in letters of gold: "Linda."

Inside, a preface by the author opened with an exhortation: "Reader, be assured this narrative is no fiction" (1). The stated goal was "to convince the people of the Free States what Slavery really is" (2). Signed by "Linda Brent," the preface was accompanied by an introduction by the editor. "The author of the following autobiography is personally known to me," Child began. "At her request, I have revised her manuscript" (3). In none of the front matter, any more than on the cover of the book or on its title page, is the author of *Incidents in the Life of a Slave Girl* actually named.

Her name was Harriet Ann Jacobs. "I have concealed the names of places, and given persons fictious names," she admitted in her preface. "I had no motive for secrecy on my own account, but I deemed it kind and considerate towards others to pursue this course" (1). *Secrecy* is too small a word for the complex acts of self-fashioning, confession, and strategic concealment that mark Jacobs's narrative. She had any number of reasons to be oblique: first among them perhaps was the fact that when Jacobs began writing her story, in 1853, the Fugitive Slave Law was still in effect, and a number of persons appearing in her narrative were still living under its sway.

The lived experience of the subject Jacobs had chosen to expose also encouraged her to tell it slant. It was an experience governed by suppressions: "The secrets of slavery," she writes in chapter 6, "are concealed like those of the Inquisition." She then follows this claim with an even more startling one: "My master was, to my knowledge, the father of eleven slaves" (35). The sentence may seem to mark a leap—why this revelation, at this moment? Her narrative will not turn on a "scene of violence," as does the *Narrative of the Life of Frederick Douglass*. There will be no striking back at Mr. Covey. Physical resistance to the white master is a male subject. No, the secret Jacobs has just chosen to reveal is a sexual one.

White rape of female slaves was an open secret, one written in the faces of all too many enslaved children. But "did the mothers dare to tell," Jacobs asks, "who was the father of their children? Did the other slaves dare to allude to it, except in whispers among themselves? No, indeed!" (35). While Jacobs does dare to tell such secrets, her narrative also proceeds by way of the "undertell," as P. Gabrielle Foreman calls it, a strategy adopted to avoid offending her chosen audience, "the women of the North." So it is that "my descriptions fall far short of the facts" (1).

By giving herself and her human actors fictitious names, by re-creating rich passages of dialogue, and by supplying her readers with highly dramatic scenes, Jacobs risked having her narrative being mistaken for a novel. Its very power to move the reader through the use of fictional techniques was to threaten its claim to veracity: in *The Slave Community* (1972), for instance, John W. Blassingame was to find *Incidents* "too orderly" and "too melodramatic." The book's narrative satisfactions somehow marked it as "not credible." Such resistant readings of *Incidents*—and there were many more like it—led to the conclusion, as Jacqueline Goldsby writes, "that, because of the literary stylings of the story, Jacobs's life experiences were not true and that she did not even exist."

But Jacobs was known and named as the author of her book in the decade of its publication. *Incidents* was printed by the Boston Stereotype Foundry early in 1861, and with a volume finally in hand, Jacobs went to work for her book. In Philadelphia, she dropped by the offices of the *Christian Recorder*. In its notice about the appearance of *Incidents*, the newspaper suggested that readers contact "Mrs. Jacobs," now "in this city for a few days." She called upon the city's antislavery circles and by mid-January had sold fifty copies of her book. The *Liberator* published a laudatory letter by activist William C. Nell, the *Anti-Slavery Bugle* praised the style of the book as "simple and attractive," and Child wrote a letter about "Linda" to John Greenleaf Whittier.

Then came the Civil War. Jacobs soon became caught up in the relief of freed slaves migrating north. Her work with refugee populations in Alexandria, where she founded the Jacobs School, was especially taxing. Reporting on his visit to the school in 1864, Samuel J. May Jr. identified Jacobs as the Linda of *Incidents* and praised her as an "invaluable friend" to the newly emancipated slaves. William Lloyd Garrison's son "made a call on Washington St. at the house where 'Linda' lives." The conflation of Linda and Harriet would persist well into the twentieth century. There was no confusion, however, about the identity of Jacobs's editor. "In the mid-1800s," Deborah Pickman Clifford writes, "Lydia Maria Child's name was a household word."

Born north of Boston in 1802, Lydia Maria Child was a best-selling novelist, author of domestic advice books, and the object of lingering fame for having created the song "Thanksgiving Day." She was also a fierce social reformer who published "the first full-length argument against slavery" in 1833. She corresponded with John Brown after his arrest in 1859 and offered to come south to nurse him. Her friends among the abolitionists included Garrison, Wendell Phillips, Angelina Grimké, and Frederick Douglass.

Child had been made aware of Jacobs long before they actually met. In a letter dated June 25, 1842, one Joshua Coffin wrote to Child about an escapee recently arrived in Philadelphia who had been "hidden for 7 years! In a small upper room of a house" (227). The two women were not to meet face to face, however, until 1860.

Jacobs first approached Child to seek assistance with her manuscript after a disappointing exchange with Harriet Beecher Stowe. Once Jacobs's friend Amy Post (1802–89) had encouraged her to write her story, Jacobs considered asking the author of *Uncle Tom's Cabin* to help with the project. "I could give her some fine sketches for her pen on slavery," Jacobs wrote to Post (233). Stowe, however, was about to depart for England. After conceiving the idea that she and her daughter, Louisa, might accompany Stowe on her trip, Jacobs persuaded her employer Cornelia Willis to propose the plan to Stowe. Stowe's rejection, and especially her predictions about Louisa, inflamed Jacobs. As she wrote to Post, Stowe "was afraid that if her situation as a Slave should be known it would subject her to much petting and patronizing." Jacobs was also angered that in her reply, Stowe had returned Post's letter to Willis with a proviso. "Your letter," Jacobs informed Post, "she sent to Mrs. Willis asking might she trouble her so far as to ask if this most extraordinary event was true in all its bearings" (235). Were Jacobs's story verified as credible, Stowe had indicated, "she might use it in her key." This was *The Key to Uncle Tom's Cabin*, which Stowe was rushing to complete before sailing to England. "True in all its bearings": even before Jacobs was able to bring her narrative before the world, it was being met with doubt about its veracity.

Jacobs's first publication occurred in the year she began writing *Incidents*. Aroused by the publication of a defense of chattel slavery written by former first lady Julia Tyler, Jacobs fired off a rebuttal and signed it "A Fugitive Slave." The letter appeared in the *New York Daily Tribune* on June 21, 1853. In October, she informed Post that "I must write just what I have lived and witnessed myself" (236). She then began composing her narrative in the Willis household, working mostly at night. "With the care of the little baby the big Babies and at household calls," Jacobs wrote to Post in the spring of 1854, "I have but a little time to think or write" (238).

Three years later, a draft of *Incidents* had been completed, and in June 1857, Jacobs asked a favor of Post: "I have thought that I wanted some female Friend of mine to write a Preface or some introductory remarks for my Book—and there is no one whose name I would prefer to Yours." A few weeks later, Jacobs alerted Post that hers was above all a woman's story: "There are some things that I might have made plainer I know—Woman can whisper—her cruel wrongs into the ear of a very dear friend—much easier than she can record them for the world to read" (242). The image of the ear was also to appear on the title page of *Incidents*, in a quotation from Isaiah—"Rise up, ye women that are at ease! Hear my voice, ye careless daughters! Give ear unto my speech"—and the receptivity and vulnerability of the ear was to play a central part in the story Jacobs proceeded to tell. In beginning with a demand to be heard, Jacobs also anticipated the difficulties she would face in being credited as having given voice to her own story.

Not feeling heard in the United States, Jacobs decided to sail to England. There she might establish copyright and secure a publisher. This effort, too, was to end in disappointment, but once home, Jacobs took her book to Thayer & Eldridge. The firm agreed to publish *Incidents* if Jacobs could secure a preface from Child, a writer known to Jacobs as the former editor of the *National Anti-Slavery Standard*. A meeting with Child was arranged in Boston. There, Child agreed to write a preface and also offered to assist in editing Jacobs's manuscript. "I have been busy with your M.S. ever since I saw you," Child wrote to Jacobs on August 13, 1860, "and have only done one third of it. I have very little occasion to alter the language, which is wonderfully good" (244).

Because no manuscript of *Incidents in the Life of a Slave Girl* exists, readers curious about the nature of Child's alterings must rely largely on her descriptions of the editorial work in which she then proceeded to engage. Writing to a friend, Child maintained that she had "abridged, and struck out superfluous words sometimes, but I don't think I altered fifty words in the whole volume." "Such changes as I have made," Child wrote in the preface itself, "have been mainly for purposes of condensation and orderly arrangement. I have not added anything to the incidents, or changed the import of her very pertinent remarks. With trifling exceptions, both the ideas and the language are her own" (3). Child did make one major structural suggestion. Jacobs had provided her narrative with an addendum, a chapter on John Brown. Child convinced her to cut the chapter and to conclude her story with her freedom being purchased by Cornelia Willis and the ironic cry, "So I was *sold* at last!" (200).

The style and structure of Jacobs's letters to Amy Post indicate that during the years in which she was composing *Incidents,* she was given to the liberal capitalization of nouns, to unusual word combinations, and to setting off her thoughts with dashes rather than periods—practices also favored by Emily Dickinson. Child may well have faced a good deal of work in bringing the manuscript into publishable shape, but the effort can have been no greater, and was probably far less demanding, than the labors exerted by Max Perkins on behalf of the novels of Thomas Wolfe.

Unlike the other authors under consideration in *Afterlife,* Jacobs did succeed in overseeing and publishing her major work while she was alive. That work, however, eventually became alienated from her. While Child's contributions as an editor in no way compromised Jacobs's literary achievement, the problem for Jacobs lay, rather, in the sheer fact of Child's involvement and in the enduring strength of her reputation. "Even before her death," Jean Fagan Yellin writes, "Harriet Jacobs had been largely forgotten.... The records of her Alexandria school were lost. Her book came to be thought the work of her editor L. Maria Child." Just how and when her authorship was reestablished—how *Incidents* was resurrected as Jacobs's own—is a moving and complex story. And fittingly enough, what might be called "the ordeal of reception" had been anticipated in the reading experience on offer in *Incidents* itself.

That experience begins with a direct address: "Reader, be assured this narrative is no fiction" (1). Such assurances and appeals, made frequently throughout, create a sense of the text as something *overheard*. When Jacobs opens her narrative with a call to the ear, she sets up an expectation that will be generously fulfilled. The exhortations to the reader (Jacobs is imagining a white female audience) are meant to alert her to the imminence of a sexual threat. But Jacobs is also aware that such a reader, in Robert B. Stepto's phrase, may be "an unreliable story listener," conditioned in all too many ways to be unable or unwilling to hear the truth about the life of women under slavery. "Naturally," William L. Andrews writes, "Jacobs would like to break the silence that surrounds these 'wrongs,' 'sufferings, and mortifications,' and her story shows her search in the South as well as the North for someone in whom she could confide. *Incidents* attests, however, to a more excruciating irony that besets the slave woman in Jacobs's situation: the more enormous the crimes committed against her, the less receptive people are to hearing about them, especially from the victim herself."

Child addresses potential readerly resistance in her introduction to *Incidents*. After acknowledging that "the experiences of this intelligent and much-injured woman" deal with "indelicate" subjects, Child delivers a challenge: "This peculiar phase of Slavery has generally been kept veiled; but the public ought to be made acquainted with its monstrous features, and I willingly take the responsibility of presenting them with the veil withdrawn.

I do this for the sake of my sisters in bondage, who are suffering wrongs so foul, that our ears are too delicate to listen to them" (3–4).

"I was born a slave," Jacobs begins (5). Nevertheless, her first six years are "happy" ones. It is only at the age of six, after her mother dies, that Jacobs first learns she is owned. Taken into the home of Margaret Horniblow, Jacobs is taught to read, write, and sew. At twelve, she loses this "kind" mistress and is willed to Horniblow's three-year-old niece, Mary Norcom (7). At this point, Jacobs and her brother, John, are moved into the house of Dr. James Norcom, known as Dr. Flint in Jacobs's narrative.

Only a few years later, the trouble begins. Flint, now Jacobs's de facto owner, begins a relentless seduction campaign. "I cannot tell how much I suffered in the presence of these wrongs, nor how I am still pained by the retrospect. My master met me at every turn, reminding me that I belonged to him, and swearing by heaven and earth that he would compel me to submit to him" (28). Submit to what, the reader may ask? *I cannot tell,* Jacobs answers, and throughout her narrative she makes a highly tactical assault on "the secrets of slavery." They may be concealed like those of the Inquisition, but the core secret is also an open one, a secret announced in the faces of the slaves themselves. Jacobs adverts to the secret on the first page of "Childhood": "In complexion my parents were a light shade of brownish yellow, and were termed mulattoes" (5). Where might such an admixture come from, a reader is thereby invited to ask, except from the mingling of Black and white bodies across the color line?

And yet this is a secret about which it is forbidden to speak. The one enslaved couple who does "dare to tell" is handed over by Flint to a slave trader. The husband has "accused his master of being the father" of his wife's child. As Jacobs reports, "They were both black, and the child was very fair." When the mother is delivered into the trader's hands, she turns on Flint. "'You *promised* to treat me well.' To which he replied: 'You have let your tongue run too far; damn you!' She had forgotten that it was a crime for a slave to tell who was the father of her child" (13).

In a narrative conditioned by a loud conspiracy of silence, extreme pressure is brought to bear on the verb *to tell.* Truths in this world can best be whispered, if they are spoken at all. Jacobs herself adopts a strategic reticence when it comes to "impure things," as she writes in "The Trials of Girlhood" (29): "But I now entered on my fifteenth year—a sad epoch in the life of a slave girl. My master began to whisper foul words in my ear. Young as I was, I could not remain ignorant of their import" (27). The actual content of Flint's speech is never articulated. "He peopled my mind with unclean images," Jacobs recalls, "such as only a vile monster could think of."

Jacobs's refusal to spell things out has the effect of leaving it to the reader to fill in the blanks. As a result, we can actually feel more than were she to give a direct report of her exchanges with Flint. The words *feel* and *more* belong to a passage in A Moveable Feast in which Hemingway describes his early strategy of leaving things out: "This was omitted on my new theory that you could omit anything if you knew that you omitted and the omitted part would strengthen the story and make people feel something more than they understood" (75). For Jacobs, as for Hemingway, the art of Leaving Things Out requires the reader to engage in the work of Putting Them In.

Given the prevailing sanction against frank speech in *Incidents,* a number of its most intense verbal exchanges take place in whispers. The most dramatic example of choked voice occurs in a chapter called "The Jealous Mistress."

Well aware of Dr. Flint's intentions toward Harriet, Mrs. Flint has taken to watching "her husband with unceasing vigilance" (31). Husband and wife often exchange "angry words," and "no terms were too vile for her to bestow upon me" (32). When Flint arranges for his four-year-old daughter, along with Jacobs, to sleep in his apartment, Mrs. Flint intervenes. She orders Jacobs to "tell me all that has passed between your master and you." Jacobs does as she is told. "As I went on with my account"—an account, again, in which words that have been spoken are never quoted—"her color changed frequently, she wept, and sometimes groaned" (33). As a result, the sleeping assignments are rearranged:

> She now took me to sleep in a room adjoining her own. There I was an object of her especial care, though not of her especial comfort, for she spent many a sleepless night to watch over me. Sometimes I woke up, and found her bending over me. At other times she whispered in my ear, as though it were her husband who was speaking to

me, and listened to hear what I would answer. If she startled me, on such occasions, she would glide stealthily away; and the next morning she would tell me I had been talking in my sleep, and ask who I was talking to. At last, I began to be fearful for my life. It had been often threatened; and you can imagine, better than I can describe, what an unpleasant sensation it must produce to wake up in the dead of night and find a jealous woman bending over you. (34)

You can imagine, better than I can describe: Jacobs here makes explicit reference to the method by which she seeks to make her reader—the "you" invoked in the passage—feel something more.

It is difficult to imagine a more abject identification with the oppressor than this scene of a jealous white woman ventriloquizing the voice of her betraying husband. "She whispered in my ear," Jacobs writes, and in that act of appropriation by Mrs. Flint, "the sexual abuse of Linda," as Deborah M. Garfield argues, "is displaced into language." By way of "the trope of the ear and a despoiling speech," Jacobs thereby converts these nighttime encounters with her mistress into a scene of instruction for her audience. As Jacobs creates scenes like these, which "bind fragile reader and slave-author in an appalled female consciousness," they manage "to invade the ear she would ostensibly shield."

Jacobs repeatedly calls attention to the "you" who is reading her book. Not only does she open her preface with the word *Reader*, but the apostrophe to this figure appears as well on the final page of *Incidents*: "Reader, my story ends with freedom; not in the usual way, with marriage" (201). These appeals express a faith that the reader can be relied upon to feel more.

In an essay entitled "Distrust of the Reader in Afro-American Narratives" (1986), Robert B. Stepto takes up the question of "unreliability" in literary texts. Theories of creative reading, he argues, imagine an "ingenious reader" who grapples with "a devious or elusive text" and even manages to subdue it. "In Afro-American storytelling texts especially," however, "rhetoric and narrative strategy combine time and again to declare that the principal unreliable factor in the storytelling paradigm is the reader (white American readers, obviously, but blacks as well) and that acts of creative communication are fully initiated not when the text is assaulted but when the reader gets 'told'—or 'told off'—in such a way that he or she finally begins to *hear*."

Jacobs hails her reader by way of direct address seven times in her narrative. But when, to use Stepto's phrase, does the reader get "told off"? The answer comes by way of Jacobs's complex handling of the gains and losses involved in the act of escape.

From Slavery to Freedom: this is the classic plot of the slave narrative, one so deeply ingrained in the American imagination as to have encouraged John Hope Franklin to choose these words as the title of his 1947 history of African Americans. (The early editions of Franklin's history make no reference to Jacobs, but by the eighth edition, in 2000, he does include a long quotation from *Incidents*—the sentences describing Flint's whispering campaign.) Jacobs, however, cannot fit her narrative into the triumphant pattern invoked by Franklin's title. She will, finally, escape the South. But the complicated nature of that escape, one so hedged about with resistances in the narrator herself, prohibits any wholehearted celebration of a slave's liberation. Instead, "there hangs over the book a kind of sadness, as if freedom and love were incompatible."

This last phrase comes from W. H. Auden and describes his experience of rereading *Adventures of Huckleberry Finn*. Auden could have cited any number of scenes from Twain's novel in support of his claim. One that poignantly echoes the predicament faced by Jacobs occurs in chapter 40, when Jim, finally set free by Huck and Tom during their absurd plot to liberate him from the smokehouse, refuses to abandon Tom after he is shot. "*Now,* old Jim, you're a free man, *again,*" Huck says to Jim, just before they see the bullet in Tom's leg. Jim chooses to stick around and is, in consequence, "chained ... again." Jim has insisted on staying: "Ef it wuz *him* dat 'uz bein' set free, en one er de boys wuz to git shot, would he say, 'Go on en save me, nemmine 'bout a doctor f'r to save dis one?'" The doctor who has been summoned by the boys to treat Tom's wound weighs in on Jim's behalf: "When I got to where I found the boy I see I couldn't cut the bullet out without some help ... and the minute I says it, out crawls this n-- from somewheres, and says he'll help.... I never see a n-- that was a better nuss or faithfuller, and yet he was resking his freedom to do it."

Twain ends his novel with a prolonged satire on the difficulty of escaping—really escaping—from slavery. As he finished work on the book in the mid-1880s and witnessed the failures of Reconstruction, he saw that no one had truly been emancipated. After Jim is chained again, Tom informs Huck that the entire escape plan has been unnecessary given that he has known from the start that Old Miss Watson has already set Jim free in her will. Huck proceeds to wonder why they had gone to "all that trouble and bother to set a free n–– free." But Huck's question makes the central point being enacted in Twain's controversial ending: the (crazy) work in which the boys have been engaged with Jim is going to have to continue, given all the laws and customs still in place, or yet to be enacted, that were to keep African Americans profoundly unfree.

Why does Jim stay? His doing so surely violates the hope of any reader who has become invested in the project of seeing Jim delivered to one of the Free States. And yet, offered a chance to save himself, Jim does not take it. He comes out of hiding to help the doctor, "resking his freedom to do it." Jim does what he does out of love. Love is what makes us stay.

Harriet Jacobs finds herself caught as well between the demands of love and freedom. The form her escape takes testifies to the incompatibility of the two terms. She, too, frustrates the hope of a reader who, in picking up a slave narrative, believes she has signed on for a quite different outcome. In 1838, Angelina Grimké had already recognized that "what was most intriguing about black slave narratives, what made then seem 'real' to white audiences, were the details of the fugitives' escape." It was the climactic moment of gaining freedom that made for the pleasure of such texts.

"I went forth into the darkness and rain" (97). With this beautiful sentence, the story of Harriet Jacobs's escape begins. She flees from Flint about halfway through her narrative, and she is finally prompted to leave after he threatens to send her and her children to the plantation run by his son. There she overhears her new master say that his father "ought to have broke her in long ago" (86). In response, Jacobs begins "meditating upon some means of escape for myself and my children. . . . I could have made my escape alone; but it was more for my helpless children than for myself that I longed for freedom" (89). And yet this is not a move she will make "at the expense of leaving them in slavery."

The solution, for Jacobs, is to escape by staying in the neighborhood. She ends up not in the North but in her "Loophole of Retreat."

First there are the preliminary shelters. Hidden in the house of a friend, Jacobs is forced to flee to a nearby swamp. After suffering a snakebite, she returns to her friend's house and is then offered sanctuary by a "kind" white woman (99). Pursued by Flint, who has arranged to have her aunt and her two children thrown into jail, Jacobs is reduced to hiding under the planks of a floor, where she has "but just room enough to bring my hands to my face to keep the dust out of my eyes" (103).

In the following months spent in hiding, Jacobs even manages to get aboard a ship anchored in Albemarle Sound, but she becomes so sick there that the man assisting her insists that she go to "a place of concealment" provided for her at her grandmother's house in Edenton (113).

For the next six years and eleven months, Jacobs will live in "a very small garret," nine feet long, seven feet wide, and three feet high. "The air was stifling; the darkness total." Rats and mice run over her bed, "but I was not comfortless. I heard the voices of my children" (114). It is voices like these that hold Jacobs in place.

Throughout her narrative, eloquent voices speak up for both love and for freedom, but they are never willing, or able, to speak up for both at once. The situation of an enslaved mother in 1840s North Carolina has truly rendered the two terms incompatible. But then it is not so simple, in any life, to reconcile the two imperatives.

"Why does the slave ever love?" Jacobs asks, at the beginning of the chapter called "The Lover" (37). Despite her anguished question, Jacobs does insist on her right to love in terms she can in some way define. As William Andrews notes, "Between Jacobs and Flint the word 'love' is constantly at issue." Flint flies into a rage when she claims to be in love with a free Black carpenter: "How dare you tell me so!" (39). Jacobs realizes that any children she might have with such a lover will "follow the condition of the mother" and so pass into slavery. She therefore entreats her man to go to the Free States and "not to link his fate to my own unhappy destiny" (42). "He left me," she writes, "still hoping the day would come when I could be bought." She urges him to choose freedom over love.

There comes an interval, however, when Jacobs chooses for love—or something akin to it—on her own terms. After the carpenter leaves, "it chanced that a white unmarried gentleman had obtained some knowledge of the circumstances in which I was placed." Jacobs calls him Mr. Sands. He "constantly sought opportunities, to see me, and wrote to me frequently. I was a poor slave girl, only fifteen years old" (54).

"By degrees," Jacobs writes, "a more tender feeling crept into my heart."

She begins to reason that "it seems less degrading to give oneself, than to submit to compulsion. There is something akin to freedom in having a lover who has no control over you, except that which he gains by kindness and attachment" (55). Knowing that Flint often sells off the children of his Black "victims," Jacobs resolves to make "a headlong plunge." At this point in her narrative, she shifts, as if to recruit the reader in support of her choice, into the second person: "Pity me, and pardon me, O virtuous reader! You never knew what it is to be a slave; to be entirely unprotected by law or custom; to have the laws reduce you to the condition of a chattel, entirely subject to the will of another. You never exhausted your ingenuity in avoiding the snares, and eluding the power of a hated tyrant." Jacobs will have two children, Joseph and Louisa, with Sands. They are called Benny and Ellen in the narrative. It is these children she will overhear from her loophole of retreat.

As she looks back at this "painful and humiliating memory," Jacobs attempts to preempt a reader's response. "I know I did wrong," she writes, but "I feel that the slave woman ought not to be judged by the same standard as others" (55–56).

In her biography of Jacobs, Yellin worries the question of the Jacobs-Sands relation. "Is it possible that they shared some version of love? Can that word be used in connection with a relationship that is so utterly unequal?" These are serious and perhaps unanswerable questions. When confronted herself by an enraged Flint with the question "Do you love him?" Jacobs gives her answer: "I am thankful that I do not despise him" (59). The more important point is that in choosing for Sands, Jacobs has taken control of the matter of sexual access. Her liaison with Sands allows her to defy Flint and to shock him by declaring, "In a few months I shall be a mother" (56).

No, the persons Jacobs loves are her grandmother, her aunt and her uncles, her brother, and her two children. It is her love for these people that holds her in place. She also knows, in the words of William Andrews, that there is a "competition between the master and slave for the right to define and apply the word love" and that the power of her love will be tested by the equally if not more powerful demand made of the enslaved self by the lure and promise of freedom.

The most persuasive case made for going rather than staying is made by a neighbor named Aggie. Some years into her imprisonment in the garret, Jacobs learns that her brother, John, has escaped to the North. His "poor old grandmother"—the woman who is hiding Jacobs—"feels that she should never see her darling boy again. And I was selfish. I thought more of what I had lost, than of what my brother had gained" (134). Against this force field of love, Aggie, who has "witnessed the sale of her children, and seen them carried off to parts unknown," confronts the weeping grandmother (135). That grandmother, called Aunt Marthy in the text, has earlier made the case for motherhood as the barrier to escape: "Nobody respects a mother who forsakes her children; and if you leave them, you will never have a happy moment" (91). Now, with one grandchild in hiding and another lost to freedom, Aunt Marthy is met by the impassioned cry of Aggie, who knows that Jacobs has escaped from Flint but is unaware that she is hiding in town: "'Is *dat* what you's crying fur?' she exclaimed. 'Git down on your knees and bress de Lord! I don't know whar my poor chillern is, and I nebber 'spect to know. You don't know whar poor Linda's gone to; but you *do* know whar her brudder is. He's in free parts; and dat's de right place. Don't murmur at de Lord's doings, but git down on your knees and tank him for his goodness'" (135). In this scene, what is being "told off" is mother love.

As she lives out her captivity, Jacobs begins to experience bouts of paralysis. "I had tried various applications to bring warmth and feeling into my limbs, but without avail. They were so numb that it was a painful effort to move" (132). Serious as her physical condition may be, Jacobs's sense of being arrested between two moral and emotional imperatives is even more painful. Her grandmother's "excessive fear" of what can happen to runaways proves "contagious," and when faced with the prospect of escape by sea, Jacobs finds herself having "to relinquish my project" (151).

In the end, Jacobs is never really required to choose between love and freedom. Instead, a "mischievous housemaid" forces the issue (152). Still in fear of the latest plot to send her granddaughter north, Aunt Marthy realizes that the nosy Jennie may have seen Jacobs on a day when she happened to crawl downstairs from the garret. "Go," she says to her granddaughter. "I ain't got another word to say against it now" (153).

Aunt Marthy can be read as a character suffering from "an excess of maternal feeling, a total surrender to that commitment." The words belong to Toni Morrison and her sense of the character of Sethe in *Beloved*. Morrison's novel acknowledges the generosity and the selfishness of mother love, an emotion exacerbated by the cruel separations enforced by slavery, even as it invites Sethe to see herself, rather than her lost daughter, as her "best thing." Morrison also follows Jacobs by framing Sethe's story as one about "the freedom to love."

The freedom to love is a phrase out of *The Souls of Black Folk*. As he nears the end of the first chapter of his singing book, Du Bois finds himself listing the various kinds of freedom being sought after by a postwar African American population. "The training of the schools we need to-day more than ever," he writes. "The power of the ballot we need in sheer self-defence." There is the "freedom of life and limb," and there is "the freedom to work and think." As a final addition to his list, and as the one freedom that depends upon the accomplishing of all the others, Du Bois invokes "the freedom to love."

Du Bois understands that any number of American bodies have already been comingled across the color line. But this history is not one of love but coercion. It involves "two figures": "the one, a gray-haired gentleman," a white man like Dr. Flint; and "the other, a form hovering dark and mother-like, her awful face black with the mists of centuries," a Black woman like Harriet Jacobs, had she been forced to give way to Flint's whispering campaign. These two linked figures "typify" American history. Their nonconsensual sexual unions have not only "borne a tawny man-child to the world," a body bearing a new mixture of gene pools and skin colors, but their very existence serves as a mockery of any attempt by law or custom to segregate Black and white bodies. Toni Morrison pays homage to Du Bois's claim about the freedom to love near the end of part 1 of *Beloved*. As Sethe circles Paul D in her kitchen, eventually taking them both back to the scene in the woodshed, Paul D thinks to himself: "To get to a place where you could love anything you chose—not to need permission for desire—well now, that was freedom."

Jacobs can be said to inaugurate an African American literary tradition in which the conflicting demands placed upon an enslaved Black female body offer up the most excruciating accounting of the cost that had to be paid by anyone caught up in the terrible romance of emancipation. She does not resolve these claims—she dramatizes their presence and their force. White readers are not asked by Jacobs to do anything so easy and so trivial as to "identify" with the conflict experienced by the character called Linda Brent. As Jacobs writes in her preface, "Neither do I care to excite sympathy for my own sufferings" (1). No, the entire burden of Jacobs's narrative is to bring the reader to the point where she "gets 'told'—or 'told off'—in such a way that she finally begins to *hear*." And what all kinds of readers may be able to hear, if they consent to listen, is a story of a suffering unique to enslaved African American women but one that also invites persons of other traditions and inheritances to recognize the ways in which their own lives may have been shaped by the incompatibility of love and freedom.

In a eulogy delivered after the death of Harriet Jacobs in 1897, Reverend Francis J. Grimké of the Fifteenth Street Presbyterian Church in Washington, DC, spoke of her "kind, benevolent face" and "the warm grasp of her friendly hand." Grimké remembered Jacobs as "a woman of marked individuality. There was never any danger of overlooking her, or of mistaking her for anybody else."

A mistaking of Jacobs for somebody else was precisely what did occur, however, in the years to come. She went uncredited as the author of her book; even well into the 1970s, Yellin writes, "it was generally held that the work was a fiction by the white abolitionist L. Maria Child."

The mistaking had begun even before Jacobs's death. In 1881, Elizabeth Cady Stanton and Susan B. Anthony oversaw publication of the first volume of *History of Woman Suffrage*. On page 324, the name Linda Brent appears as part of a strange catalog: "The same love of liberty that glowed in eloquent words on the lips of Lucretia Mott, Angelina Grimké, and Mary Grew, was echoed in the brave deeds of Margaret Garner, Linda Brent, and Mrs. Stowe's Eliza." The list of six names manages to conflate three well-known writers with an enslaved mother who became the inspiration for *Beloved*, a fictional character out of *Uncle Tom's Cabin*, and a pseudonymous "Linda Brent," as if she, rather than Harriet Jacobs, had committed the "brave deeds" described in *Incidents in the Life of a Slave Girl*. "And so she vanished," Yellin writes in her biography of Jacobs, overshadowed by such looming figures as Harriet Tubman and Sojourner Truth.

The "curious resurrection" of Jacobs as author of her great book was a work of almost single-handed devotion performed by one woman, Jean Fagan Yellin. Yellin brought *Incidents* back into print in an authoritative Harvard University Press edition in 1987. In 2004, she continued her mission by writing *Harriet Jacobs: A Life*. She also began the work of gathering and editing the Harriet Jacobs Family Papers, now available in two volumes from the University of North Carolina Press. To accomplish this work, Yellin had to overcome her own resistances as well as those of a century of resisting readers.

Benjamin Brawley (1882–1939) was one of the first scholars to attempt a history of African American literature. In 1918, he published *The Negro in Literature and Art in the United States,* itself an expansion of a sixty-page pamphlet issued in 1910. In the 1929 revised edition of Brawley's book, a brief chapter on the antebellum period includes mention of Frederick Douglass as an orator but makes only passing reference to the existence of slave narratives: "It was but natural that in this period there should be much writing about the Negro, and that this writing should have a political cast. It was also but natural that the man who was so much discussed should endeavor in some way to present his own case to the public. Lydia Maria Child and other abolitionists took pride in publishing such things as reflected credit on the race; and there were also the narratives of those persons who had themselves escaped from bondage, outstanding being those of Frederick Douglass, Samuel Ringgold Ward, and Josiah Henson" ("Uncle Tom"). It is impossible to determine from Brawley's careful wording if one of the "things" being alluded to as published by Child was a book by Harriet Jacobs.

Vernon Loggins's pioneering literary history, *The Negro Author,* appeared in 1931. William Andrews notes that Loggins "plucked Jacobs out of invisibility by including *Incidents* among the few slave narratives that were 'readable,' although Loggins attributes the readability of *Incidents* to "the 'editing' of Lydia Maria Child." Loggins provides twenty-two pages of analysis of Douglass's narrative but not one about Jacobs. In his index, Loggins includes an entry for "Brent, Linda," but none for "Jacobs, Harriet."

Child continued to overshadow Jacobs in Arna Bontemps's *Great Slave Narratives* (1969). In his introduction, the poet-novelist groups *Incidents* in a list of titles that "were offered as 'told to' accounts." *Incidents* is judged as "comparable" to *The Narrative of James Williams* (1839), "told to John Greenleaf Whittier" but eventually suppressed by its publisher as a fraud.

The first modern edition of *Incidents in the Life of a Slave Girl* appeared in 1973. Published by Harcourt Brace Jovanovich, the volume was edited by Walter Magnes Teller (1910–93). Teller is perhaps remembered today as the author of two books about Captain Joshua Slocum, the first person to sail single-handedly around the world. As a Jacobs scholar, however, Teller fell far short.

On the cover of Teller's edition, the name Linda Brent is printed under its title. Inside, the original "Preface by the Author" has been altered to read: "PREFACE," with "By Linda Brent" beneath it. Teller proceeds to note that Brent gave "fictitious names to all places and persons, including herself—her name was Harriet Brent Jacobs."

The Slave Community (1972), written by John W. Blassingame, was one of the first scholarly works to rely heavily on slave narratives as a source for understanding antebellum culture. Jacobs, however, presents a problem:

> In spite of Lydia Maria Child's insistence that she had only revised the manuscript of Harriet Jacobs "mainly for the purposes of condensation and arrangement," the work is not credible. In the first place, *Incidents in the Life of a Slave Girl* (1861) is too orderly; too many of the major characters meet providentially after years of separation. Then, too, the story is too melodramatic: miscegenation and cruelty, outraged virtue, unrequited love, and planter licentiousness appear practically on every page. The virtuous Harriet sympathizes with her wretched mistress who has to look on all the mulattoes fathered by her husband, she refuses to bow to the lascivious demands of her master, bears two children by another white man, and then runs away and hides in a garret in her grandmother's house for seven years until she is able to escape to New York. In the meantime, her white lover has acknowledged the paternity of her children, purchased their freedom, and been elected to Congress. In the end, all live happily ever after.

Blassingame appeared to moderate these views in his 1976 *Slave Testimony*. There he leads off with a quotation from Stanley Elkins about enslaved people and their testimony: "Much is gained and not much is lost on the provisional operating principle that they were all telling the truth." Having admitted as much, Blassingame devotes much of his introduction to issues of "accuracy," "reliability," and "the ring of truth."

Blassingame's doubts about veracity were shared by Elizabeth Fox-Genovese. In *Within the Plantation Household: Black and White Women in the Old South* (1988), she devotes her entire afterword to an appreciation of

Jacobs. At the same time, she maintains that Jacobs's "pivotal authentication of self probably rested on a great factual lie, for it stretches the limits of all credulity that Linda Brent actually eluded her master's sexual advances."

The first reference to *Incidents* in the *MLA Bibliography* did not occur until 1981. In the same year, Yellin published her breakthrough article on Jacobs in *American Literature*. It, too, concerned itself with veracity. Yellin's great service to the history of American literature was to establish Harriet Jacobs as the author of *Incidents in the Life of a Slave Girl*. Whether or not everything Jacobs wrote in her book might be true was to prove, however, another matter.

Yellin had to make her way *to* Jacobs by going *through* Child. In 1972, she published her dissertation, "The Intricate Knot: Black Figures in American Literature." Prompted by the rise of "the new feminist criticism," Yellin then resolved to begin "re-reading the female writers I had studied." While moving through the works of Lydia Maria Child, she came to *Incidents*, a book she had read as a graduate student but one she had "carefully omitted" from the "list of books I would discuss." "I first read *Incidents in the Life of a Slave Girl* more than a decade ago," Yellin writes in the opening sentence of her Harvard edition, "and, accepting received opinion, dismissed it as a false slave narrative" (vii). During the period of her graduate study, "accepted academic opinion" had held that "the book's author was Lydia Maria Child." But while trying to "solve the puzzle of authorship," Yellin also "recalled seeing at the Schomburg Collection of the New York Public Library, a Library of Congress card with the words 'Negro author' neatly penciled in a librarian's professional hand."

Yellin's big break came with the discovery of a "clutch of letters involving Harriet Jacobs." Aware that the University of Massachusetts was preparing Child's papers for publication, Yellin phoned the people there and was directed by them to archivists at the University of Rochester. Yellin was then informed that they had discovered letters exchanged between Jacobs and a woman named Amy Post.

Amy Kirby Post signed her first antislavery petition in 1837. Collaborating with her husband, Isaac, from her home in Rochester, Post became a founding member of the New York Western Anti-Slavery Society. She worked with Frederick Douglass and William C. Nell, and Sojourner Truth lived in the Post home for several months in 1851. But before that, Post had befriended and provided a home for Harriet Jacobs. As the letters published at the back of Yellin's 1987 edition of *Incidents* reveal, Post repeatedly encouraged Jacobs "to consent to the publication of her narrative" (203). Post remained Jacobs's primary correspondent in the years during which *Incidents* was written.

"I ordered copies of the letters," Yellin remembers, "and when they arrived read in them the story of the conception, composition, and publication of *Incidents*. These letters convinced me not only that Harriet Jacobs had written a book, but that she had written the book Child had edited."

And so it was that writing came in support of Jacobs's writing: Yellin found herself persuaded that "the style of *Incidents* is completely consistent with [Jacobs's] private letters." At the same time, as Yellin admits in a footnote, in "editing Jacobs's letters" for the essay at hand, "I have regularized paragraphing, capitalization, punctuation, and spelling." When it came time to include a selection of Jacobs's letters in her Harvard edition, some six years later, Yellin abandoned the regularizing.

The Amy Post Family Papers held at the University of Rochester contain thirty letters sent by Jacobs to Post. Selections of the letters can be found in Dorothy Sterling's *We Are Your Sisters: Black Women in the Nineteenth Century* (1984) and in the "Correspondence" appended to Yellin's 1987 edition of *Incidents*. Read in sequence, the letters trace the growth of a writer's mind as it confronts the usual concerns: faithfulness to the material, structuring of the whole, intended audience, pace of work, obstacles to completion, securing a publisher.

Jacobs makes her first reference to a writing project in a letter of uncertain date—the year is probably 1852—sent to Post from Cornwall, New York, where Jacobs is working as caretaker and maid of all work in the household of Nathaniel Willis. Post has apparently been urging Jacobs to tell her story: "Your proposal to me has been thought over and over again but not with out some most painful remembrances dear Amy if it was the life of a Heroine with no degradation associated with it far better to have been one of the starving poor of Ireland whose bones had to bleach on the highways than to have been a slave with the curse of slavery stamped upon yourself and Children" (232). When she first came North, Jacobs confesses, "I avoided the Antislavery people as much as possible because I felt that I could not be honest and tell the whole truth." She admits to having been blocked from setting out by her "stubborn pride." "I have tried for the past two years to conquer it and I feel that God has helped me or I never would consent to give my past life to any one for I would not do it with out giving the whole truth." By the end of her letter, and despite all the misgivings expressed earlier, Jacobs has begun to imagine the shape her narrative might take: "I should want the History of my childhood and the first five years in one volume and the next three and my home in the northern states in the second" (233).

On February 14, 1853, Jacobs is writing about the fantasy of having Stowe take Louisa to England. Then, on April 4, Jacobs details Stowe's response to the proposal and her angry reply. She is especially concerned that Stowe include none of her story in *The Key to Uncle Tom's Cabin* and even takes a swipe at the shape Stowe's novel had imposed on the slave experience: "Mrs. Willis wrote her a very kind letter beging that she would not use any of the facts in her key saying that I wished it to be a history of my life entirely by itself which would do more good and it needed no romance" (235).

In June, Jacobs sends Post a letter describing her published response to Mrs. John Tyler. The letter can be found in Dorothy Sterling's *We Are Your Sisters*: "When I was in New York last week I picked up a paper with a piece alluding to the buying and selling of Slaves, mixed up with some of Mrs. Tyler's views. I felt so indignant I determined to reply to it." Jacobs is quick to admit that her letter did require some editing: "The spelling I believe was every word correct. Punctuation I did not attempt for I never studied Grammar. Therefore I know nothing about it, but I have taken the hint and will commence that one study with all my soul."

"It makes my heart sad to tell you," Jacobs writes to Post in October, "I have lost that Dear old Grandmother that I so dearly loved" (236). In her biography, Yellin speculates that "the death of the grandmother she had last seen eleven years earlier now freed Jacobs—a forty-year-old former slave—to write her life.... She could never tell her whole story—she could never reveal her troubled sexual history—while her proud, judgmental grandmother lived." As for that history, "I must write just what I have lived and witnessed myself."

Household duties, especially the care of the Willis children, interfere with the rate of Jacobs's progress. "If I was not so tied down to the baby house I would make one bold effort to see you," she informs Post on January 11, 1854. "If I could steal away and have two quiet months to myself I would work night and day. To get this time I should have to explain myself, and no one here accept Louisa knows that I have even written anything to be put in print. I have not the courage to meet the criticism and ridicule of educated people." Concerns about working conditions surface again a few months later. Friendly visitors to the house in Cornwall "saw from my daily duties that it was hard for me to find much time to write as yet I have not written a single page by daylight Mrs W dont know from my lips that I am writing for a Book" (237). Jacobs proceeds to venture a bold metaphor: "Just now the poor Book is in its Chrysalis state and though I can never make it a butterfly I am satisfied to have it creep meekly among some of the humbler bugs" (238).

The sequence of letters provided by Yellin in her 1987 edition of *Incidents* now jumps to 1857. With a draft of her narrative almost complete, Jacobs finds herself and the Willis household "in expectation of a little Stranger" (240). Bailey Willis is born on May 30, 1857, two months after the *Dred Scott* decision has declared that slaves are not citizens and cannot bring suit in the courts. Jacobs is bitter of heart: "I see nothing for the Black Man—to look forward to—but to forget his old Motto—and learn a new one his long patient hope—must be might—and Strength—Liberty—or Death" (240–41).

By June 1857, Jacobs sounds as if her book is finished. "I have My dear friend—Striven faithfully to give a true and just account of my own life in Slavery" (242). Then follows the passage about a woman having to whisper her wrongs. She has attempted to come before her audience as "a poor Slave Mother" and to write on behalf "of Slave Mothers that are still in bondage." Imagining that Post might go to work for her book, Jacobs continues: "Say anything of me that you have had from a truthful source that you think best. . . . I think it would be best for you to begin with our acquaintance and the length of time I was in your family. . . . My kind friend I do not restrict you in anything for you know far better than I do what to say." One result of these requests was the "statement" Post supplied as an appendix to *Incidents*, dated October 30, 1859 (203).

By the summer of 1857, Jacobs begins to turn her thoughts to the publishing process. "I have been thinking that I would so like to go away and sell my Book—I could then secure a copywright—to sell it both here and in England" (243). Child soon becomes involved, and letters sent by her to Jacobs in August and September 1860 detail her editing work and her attempts to secure a publisher. By October, Jacobs has survived the debacle with Stowe and the failure of the first publishing firm that had "agreed to take" her book (246). The experience with Stowe "made me tremble," she tells Post, "at the thought of approaching another Sattellite of so great magnitude" as Lydia Maria Child, but she summons her courage anyway and finds Child to be "like yourself a whole souled Woman." "I told her of the feeling that had existed between us," Jacobs continues, "that your advice and word of encouragement—had been my strongest promter in writting the Book" (247).

With the failure of Thayer & Eldridge, the second publisher she has approached, Jacobs decides to buy the stereotyped plates they had produced and to publish her book herself. She locates a willing printer and brings out an edition selling for one dollar a copy. In the following year, her book appears in England under the title *The Deeper Wrong*.

After reading the letters Jacobs sent to Post, Yellin believed that Jacobs's authorship of *Incidents* had been established. In addition, she maintained, "the appearance of Jacobs's letters has made it possible to trace her life." Working closely with local historical societies, Yellin was able to determine that Jacobs had been born in Edenton, North Carolina; that Dr. Flint was Dr. James Norcom; that Mr. Sands was Samuel Tredwell Sawyer; and that Nathaniel Parker Willis had been her employer in New York.

Even after "having solved the puzzle of authorship," Yellin was left with "a second question." "Had Jacobs's 'Linda' written a book about her own life—as she claimed? Or had she written a novel?" As Jacqueline Goldsby writes, "The canonical nature of the Harvard edition of *Incidents* rests upon Yellin's effort to set Jacobs's story before the public as incontrovertibly 'true.'" In her exuberant 2022 biography of Child, Lydia Moland also addresses the problem of truth. Despite all the editing in which Child may have engaged, "What is striking here is that, as regards the book's *content*—Jacobs's sexual history, her long imprisonment, her improbable escape—Child never flinched. She believed Jacobs and wanted others to do the same."

No more than with any autobiography, a genre relying primarily on memory, can Jacobs's "adventures" be verified as "strictly true." Given the "incredible" nature of the adventures it recounts, *Incidents in the Life of a Slave Girl* can be accused not of fabrication but of falling far short of the facts (1).

In admitting as much from the start, Jacobs also anticipated the many ways in which her readers might be unwilling to suspend disbelief. "I hardly expect that the reader will credit me" becomes, for Jacobs, a prophetic refrain (148).

In his writing about Shakespeare, Samuel Johnson found himself much concerned with the problem of audience belief. A work of literature "is credited," he concludes, "as representing to the auditor what he would himself feel, if he were to suffer what is there feigned to be suffered or to be done." The frequent mistaking of *Incidents* for a novel turns out to have been a way of paying tribute to its power to generate a response—to make a reader feel "Yes, this is how I might have felt, even and especially when the feelings being felt involve a conflict between the two incompatible imperatives of love and freedom." By being true to *How it felt to me*—the standard to which Joan Didion holds herself—Jacobs transports us into an excruciating waiting game, one that seems to go on forever as she listens for sounds of life from her loophole of retreat. The reader waits with her, anxious for Jacobs to accomplish her escape but equally aware of all the ties of love and fate that hold her in place. To return to Hemingway's phrase, if *Incidents in the Life of a Slave Girl* has the power to "make people feel something more"—please Harriet, either leave or stay—it does so by way of the same power of imagination by which we are moved in reading *A Moveable Feast* or *Huckleberry Finn* or *Beloved,* and it is with such works, and the kind of truth they tell, that it deserves to be remembered.

FIVE

The Dickinson Wars

Emily Dickinson's poems are surrounded by the sound of axes being ground. When she was alive, her gaze may have been toward Eternity, but her afterlife remains mired in an endless elaboration of worldly intrigues. The question of who Dickinson loved—if it were not God himself—continues to provoke heated debate. Scholars disagree about why Dickinson chose not to see her poems into print. As editions of the poems do appear, they are met by counter-editions. The Dickinson manuscripts rescued from the households where they had been disseminated are now in the possession of two institutions that cannot agree as to who should hold copyright. And while the two variorum editions of Dickinson's poems were produced by men, such projects were only made possible by the exertions of and the competitions between generations of extraordinary women.

"Then Vinnie came to me": the sentence appears in a journal entry dated November 30, 1890, although the moment being remembered occurred some three years earlier. Vinnie is Lavinia, Emily Dickinson's younger sister. The author of the sentence is Mabel Loomis Todd, the mistress of Austin Dickinson, the poet's older brother. Vinnie has come to Mabel to ask her to take up a dropped stitch. After Emily's death in 1886, her sister-in-law Susan Gilbert Dickinson had volunteered to edit poems found by Vinnie in a drawer. But according to Todd, Susan had recently concluded that the poems "would never sell—there was not money enough to get them out—the public would not care for them, & so on—in short, she gave it up."

What Vinnie had found after her sister's death were some 250 unbound poems along with forty fascicles, small booklets of poems tied together with string. When all of the poems left behind by Dickinson were eventually located, the count had risen to 1,789. Only 10 of these poems were published during Dickinson's lifetime. In poem number 788 (Dickinson did not title her poems), Dickinson had openly expressed her ambivalence about bringing her work to market: "Publication – is the Auction / Of the Mind of Man."

Mabel Todd began copying Dickinson's poems in the fall of 1887. As she began transcribing Dickinson's handwriting, a task described by Richard B. Sewall as one of "cryptographic proportions," Mabel found that "the poems were having a wonderful effect on me, mentally and spiritually. They seemed to open the door to a wider universe than the little sphere surrounding me which so often hurt and compressed me." It is "safe to say," Sewall concludes, "that without the spiritual kinship she felt with the poet and with the poems we might have had no poems (or letters) at all."

After some three hundred poems had been typed—Todd was working with two early versions of the typewriter—she decided to hire an assistant, but "some of her mistakes in Emily's mad words were so ludicrous as to be pathetic." Todd turned to copying with a pen, and the work went more quickly. By the summer of 1889, she had transcribed seven hundred poems.

The copies made were not and could not be exact, both because of the oddities in Dickinson's handwriting and because of the alternate wordings she had provided for a number of her poems. Todd sometimes registered these variants. But in transcribing, she also changed Dickinson's spelling, omitted capital letters, and altered spacing and punctuation.

During the winter of 1889–90, Todd submitted her findings to writer and editor Thomas Higginson, Dickinson's longtime friend and supporter. Higginson chose about two hundred poems from the selection offered him and arranged them under topical headings: Life, Love, Nature, Time, and Eternity. He also insisted on making changes of his own, the most famous involving his insistence on altering "I wish I were a Hay" to "I wish I were *the* hay." The proposed edition was then submitted to Roberts Brothers. One of the publisher's clients, a poet named Arlo Bates, acted as a reader for the press. He cut the number of poems in half and insisted on some changes of his own. Todd and Higginson pushed back and restored some twenty poems cut by Bates, including "I died for Beauty – but was scarce" and "Safe in their Alabaster Chambers." Of the 116 poems appearing in the first volume of Emily Dickinson's work, as R. W. Franklin writes, "over fifty had been changed in various ways."

Poems by Emily Dickinson appeared on November 12, 1890. The volume sold so well that six reissues had been published by the following March. And so it began—a series of editions of the poems that appears to be unending.

A second series of poems was published in the following November. Todd then turned her attention to Dickinson's correspondence, and the *Letters of Emily Dickinson* appeared in two volumes in 1894. By the time *Poems, Third Series* was published, in September 1896, Higginson had ceased to function as an assisting editor. According to Franklin, "The 1896 volume has more titles and more textual deviations than the previous selections had had." Now working largely on her own, Todd "extended" the editorial practices she and Higginson had initiated.

Neither the *Letters* nor the third series of poems sold well. But Todd broke off her editorial work for another reason: the revival of the "War between the Houses."

The houses in question were located next door to each other on Main Street in Amherst, Massachusetts. "The Homestead," the first brick house built in Amherst, was painted a warm yellow with white trimmings and green blinds. Behind the house stood a grove of venerable oaks. The front gate was shaded by a great pine whose roots spread out under a hedge and a walkway. This was the home in which Emily Dickinson was born and where she spent much of her life. Emily and her sister, Lavinia—"Vinnie"—lived on in the Homestead after the deaths of their parents, and Emily died there in 1886.

"The Evergreens," of Italianate design, was built next door for Austin Dickinson and his wife, Susan Gilbert, at the time of their marriage in 1856. A gravel walk, bordered in summer by hollyhocks, connected the two houses. Martha Dickinson Bianchi, the poet's niece, recalls the Northwest Passage, a hallway that lay between the kitchen and the middle hall at the Homestead.

"Here the two allies often met—as Aunt Emily from her window, seeing my mother coming across the lawn, hurried down to meet her, hoping for a few words about her latest poem sent over to her."

The phrase *war between the houses* originates from a letter written by Mary Lee Hall in 1933. Hall moved to Amherst a few years before Emily Dickinson died and became a friend of Lavinia. Her letter was written in response to a request from Millicent Todd Bingham, Mabel Todd's daughter. Bingham had taken up her mother's editorial work after Mabel's death in 1932 and, knowing that Hall had been close to Lavinia, wrote to her, saying, "I want to know anything, everything that is true regarding Emily and every member of her family."

In the letters she sent to Bingham, Hall produced a narrative in which, as Sewall writes, the "bias is clear; she hated Sue and was fond of Vinnie." After making this admission, Sewall proceeded nevertheless to produce fifty pages of "Documents" about the War between the Houses and chose to make it the dominant theme of his two-volume biography.

Whoever happens to be promoting or dismissing the story of the War between the Houses, the pivotal figure in the argument is Dickinson's sister-in-law. Born in 1830 and orphaned at the age of eleven, Susan Gilbert moved to Amherst in her teens to live with an older sister. She and Emily became friends in the early 1850s, and the attachment, at least on Emily's side, quickly became intense. Her first letter to Sue imagines stealing "a kiss" from her. Meanwhile, Austin had begun a quiet courtship with Sue that resulted in marriage in 1856. Sue eventually moved into the newly built Evergreens and lived there until her death in 1913.

Even before marriage had diverted Sue's attentions away from Emily and toward her brother, something had happened. The nature of the breach is not clear, but its severity is registered in a letter Emily sent to Sue in September 1854. "Sue – you can go or stay," she wrote near the end of the letter. "There is but one alternative – We differ often lately, and this must be the last." Dickinson accused herself of "idolatry" and Sue of neglect. Martha Nell Smith and Ellen Louise Hart speculate that "the differences expressed in this letter may have been over spiritual matters"; it was widely understood that Emily refused to make an open profession of faith. Susan Dickinson nevertheless remained the poet's primary correspondent and received hundreds of poems from her over the following decades. At the same time, local legend has it that when Emily ventured across to the Evergreens after the death of eight-year-old Thomas Gilbert "Gib" Dickinson in 1883, she had not visited her brother's house in fifteen years.

If there was a War between the Houses, it only intensified in the 1880s, after Mabel Loomis Todd moved to Amherst, began an open affair with Austin Dickinson, and then found herself involved in "a family quarrel of endless involutions." Peter Gay was so taken by Mabel's frank account of her sexual experiences with Austin as to give it pride of place in the opening chapter of his *Education of the Senses: Victoria to Freud*.

Professor and Mrs. David Peck Todd arrived in Amherst on August 31, 1881. Hired as the director of the Amherst College Observatory, David Todd quickly became taken up by Austin Dickinson, who was then treasurer of the college. Austin was fifty-two, Mabel twenty-four. The Todds were often entertained at the Evergreens, although on Mabel's first visit to the Homestead, Emily Dickinson remained out of sight. After hearing Mabel play the piano, she sent down a complimentary glass of sherry. Meanwhile, Mabel was endearing herself to Susan Dickinson, who began to preface her letters with "Dear Toddy." In a journal entry dated March 2, 1882, Mabel wrote about Sue, "She appreciates me completely, and I love and admire her equally." In the same entry, she also confesses that Sue's twenty-year-old son, Ned, "worships the very ground I walk on."

By the following September, the father had replaced the son. On a walk with Mabel, Austin admitted to his feelings for her. Once they had consummated their union, Austin began noting incidents of intercourse with "====." The affair, apparently conducted with David Todd's full compliance, lasted until Austin's death.

About this high romance, "sides are still taken, passionately," as Sewall writes in volume 1 of *The Life of Emily Dickinson*. But Sewall himself was encouraged to take sides by the nature of a motivating bequest. "It was in 1946, or shortly thereafter, that Mrs. Bingham [Mabel's daughter] first breathed to me the possibility of this work." Sewall taught at Yale, and Bingham's papers were eventually deposited there and became "indispensable to the project." "She tied no strings," Sewall continues, "and asked for no prior commitments." But the influence of the Todd side of things can be felt throughout Sewall's pioneering biography and nowhere more than in the pages on Susan Gilbert, pages that, for a writer so given to qualified assertions, give Mabel the last word on the Dickinson-Gilbert marriage: "Sue, the alien element, had brought on the war and wrecked their lives."

It turns out that there are actually *three* houses central to the Emily Dickinson story. In 1885, Austin Dickinson agreed to give David and Mabel Todd a piece of property located a block north of the Evergreens. On it, the Todds built "the Dell." Austin cosigned the Todd's building loan, and it was understood that he would have free access to the Queen Anne cottage, located only a five-minute walk from his back door.

In the December after Austin's death in August 1895, Mabel Todd confided to her diary: "I went to see Vinnie just before tea—and had a talk with her. She is going to do one lovely thing." According to Mabel's daughter, the lovely thing was to sign a deed to a narrow strip of land adjoining the Dell. In a letter addressed to "Mrs Todd," although one with "no legal validity," Austin had promised to give the land to Mabel.

Some four weeks after making her diary entry, Mabel went to see Vinnie at the Homestead. She was accompanied by a young man named Timothy Spaulding. When she left the house, Mabel carried with her a signed deed, although Mabel informed Spaulding she did not wish to register the transaction. "If Mrs. Austin Dickinson discovered it were deeded to me," she told him, "she would make trouble, there would be a row."

Two years later, Vinnie sued Mabel Todd, complaining of "misrepresentation and fraud." At trial, Vinnie claimed not to have understood that the paper she had signed was actually a deed, having construed the agreement as merely a promise not to build "on the meadow adjacent to the Todds' house." The court found in Vinnie's favor, and the Todds were ordered to pay all costs and to return the property to Vinnie.

Writing to Mary Lee Hall in 1934, Millicent Todd Bingham asked: "Did Miss Vinnie ever talk to you about her suit against my mother? *Why* did she sue mamma for that piece of land—after all that mamma had done for her?" Hall's answer: "It must have been Sue who held a sword over Vinnie's head, ready to drop it if she did *not* get that land back."

This petty fracas is worth recording for only one reason: "At this point publication stopped." This is Millicent writing in the preface to her *Ancestors' Brocades: The Literary Debut of Emily Dickinson*. "It was not until 1932 that I asked my mother to tell me what happened. She agreed to do so. But it would take a long time, she said, to explain it all." What needed to be explained was why, after the trial, Mabel Todd ended her editorial labors on behalf of Dickinson's work. According to Sewall, she "put all the manuscript materials, including some 665 of Emily's poems, in the famous camphorwood chest and shut the lid, as she thought, forever."

Lavinia died in 1899, and the poems in her possession went to Susan Dickinson. Sue's daughter, Martha Dickinson Bianchi, began adding to the published canon in 1914 with the 146 poems in *The Single Hound* and continued, in the words of Franklin, to issue "a bewildering series of editions." Six volumes quarried from the Gilbert-Bianchi holdings appeared between 1914 and 1935. "Martha was determined to wipe Mrs. Todd out of the record," Alfred Habegger writes, "reclaim Aunt Emily for the family, take the royalties, and vindicate Sue, the spurned wife and tragic mother who had lost both her sons."

Meanwhile, the Todd faction was about to reenter the fray. In 1924, Mabel and Millicent traveled to Amherst and opened the camphorwood chest. The chest contained diaries, letters, and poems. The daughter was struck by Dickinson's preference for one mark of punctuation: "In some poems dashes are sprinkled about so lavishly that they give to the page the appearance of a thread on which the phrases are strung. At times the dashes seem so integral a part of the text that an editor is tempted to perpetuate them, lest without them the words should fall apart."

Working slowly with the recovered material, Bingham brought out *Bolts of Melody* in 1945. The volume contained some six hundred previously unpublished Dickinson poems. All but a very few of the 1789 poems written by Dickinson during her lifetime were now in print.

Dickinson's manuscripts continued to be held by two estranged families. In 1950, the Bianchi holdings, passed down from Susan Dickinson, were acquired by Harvard University. Harvard now claimed ownership of *all* Dickinson manuscripts, even those held by Bingham. Despite this claim, Bingham, with holdings derived from Mabel Todd, eventually donated her papers to Amherst College. The War between the Houses, now reinstated as a tension between two institutions, was eventually to have serious consequences for the attempt to broadcast Dickinson's work in digital form.

By the middle of the twentieth century, it had become clear that the many vying volumes of Dickinson poems needed to be gathered into a single authoritative format. The first variorum edition of Dickinson's poems, edited by Thomas H. Johnson, appeared in 1955. Working under contract with Harvard University Press, Johnson was only able to produce such a volume because of Millicent Todd Bingham's decision to allow him access to the holdings at Amherst. But now another problem arose, one that vexes Dickinson scholarship to this day. As Franklin wrote in 1967: "The variorum tried to make Emily Dickinson's poetry available as she wrote it. The representation, however, is not exact because printing is itself a misrepresentation of the texts as they exist in manuscript." Which to prefer: an "authoritative" printed version of a poem that could be studied and widely circulated or a facsimile of a manuscript page expensive to produce and difficult to distribute? Franklin gave a kind of answer to the question when he published his own variorum edition in 1998, one in which each poem is printed along with any and all of its variants. Yet even Franklin's attempt to capture the many vagaries of Dickinson's compositional habits and self-editings could not, as he had argued in 1967, fully capture the look and feel and even the meaning, some would argue, of the poems as they exist in manuscript. So another "war" sprang up, between the materialists and the believers in print.

Reviewing a volume called *The Riddle of Emily Dickinson* in 1952, Elizabeth Bishop noted that "Emily Dickinson is supposed to have cherished a hopeless passion." Who Did Dickinson Love has remained an open and unresolved question ever since Bianchi, in her 1924 *Life and Letters,* wrote of a trip to Washington, DC, taken by her aunt in the mid-1850s: "Certainly in that first witchery of an undreamed Southern springtime Emily was overtaken—doomed once and forever by her own heart." Bianchi does not name her nominee, but others have been more definite. Genevieve Taggard elects George Gould, a classmate of Austin at Amherst, as Dickinson's love object. Based upon the three "Master" letters Dickinson wrote between 1858 and 1862, Albert J. Gelpi posits minister Charles Wadsworth as "the unquestionable choice" for an unrequited passion. Near the end of Dickinson's life, many critics have concluded, she fell in love with Judge Otis Phillips Lord. "The legend of a broken heart" remains "for most people the only plausible explanation for a life like hers," Millicent Todd Bingham writes in *Ancestors' Brocades*. "So they try to find the man."

Given the power of poems like "I cannot live with You," it seems to have been useful to Dickinson to fail at love. And as Timothy Morris argues, the question of Emily Dickinson's "lover" takes on "explanatory value" because, if settled, it might help to establish the force and meaning of any number of the poems. The object of address clearly matters, and no one has been more diligent in making a case for the identity of that person than Martha Nell Smith.

"Almost no one would dispute," Smith writes in *Rowing in Eden,* "that one of the powerful facts of Emily Dickinson's life is that she was in love with Sue." This is the opening claim in a chapter that ends with the qualification: "I do attempt to cast a skeptical eye about drawing hard and fast conclusions." In Smith's book, as in Sewall's biography, strong assertions consort with a rhetoric of friendly indeterminacy. So, Sue and Emily shared a "powerfully sensual relationship," and yet "the sisters-in-law's desire for one another may have remained unconsummated." Along with these disclaimers, Smith freely applies the word *lesbian* to the relationship, and she would seem to agree with Catherine Stimpson that lesbianism "represents a commitment of skin, blood, breast, and bone."

Vivian Pollack views Emily's desire for Sue as an act of the mind. In the 1850s, Dickinson was "attempting to create a female counterculture with Sue," Pollack writes, in *Dickinson: The Anxiety of Gender.* In the process, Emily "fabulated a romantic tale with herself and Sue as the principal actors." That tale did contain "overt professions of homosexual love," but the first Master letter, clearly addressed to a man, was written in 1858 and "conceived as the alternative to her disappointed love for Susan Gilbert." Pollack's conclusion: "Lesbianism, for Dickinson, was one of the roads not taken."

Not in dispute is the fact that Dickinson sent more poems, mostly in letters, to Sue than to any other correspondent—some three hundred, as the editors of *The Gorgeous Nothings* calculate. In this way, Smith argues, "Dickinson 'published' herself." Sue and Emily even engaged in a "Poetry Workshop," Smith proceeds to argue, with the most salient example involving an exchange of letters over "Safe in their Alabaster Chambers." Pushing back against this hypothesis, Habegger points out that there is no evidence of the two women workshopping another poem and that "induction requires more than one example."

Then there is the problem of the "you can go or stay" letter of 1854 as well as the widely shared belief that, but for one visit to the Evergreens after the death of Susan's son Gib in 1883, Dickinson did not set foot in the house next door for the last fifteen years of her life. Despite the evidence of a "rift," as Sewall calls it, Smith maintains that "Sue and Emily's regular and intimate exchanges did not cease but were continuous."

Because the experience of love does occupy a central place in Emily Dickinson's poetry, readers naturally can wonder: yes, but a love of what kind? If Dickinson did feel same-sex desire, she never encoded it as openly as did Elizabeth Bishop in a poem like "Crusoe in England," in which Crusoe and Friday become plausible stand-ins for Elizabeth and Lota. To miss the matter of loving someone of the same gender in such a poem would be to miss too much indeed.

In *Open Me Carefully: Emily Dickinson's Intimate Letters to Susan Huntington Dickinson,* Ellen Louise Hart and Martha Nell Smith set out "to make a cohesive book that would most effectively relate the human story behind this most generative of literary and emotional unions." Given that the resulting volume includes "manuscripts that editor Thomas W. Johnson did not link to Susan," along with "twenty poems and one letter not previously associated with Susan," *Open Me Carefully* can be considered a new edition of Dickinson's writings. "The letter-poem," Hart and Smith continue, "a category that includes signed poems and letters with poems or with lines of poetry, will be seen here as a distinct and important Dickinson genre. Johnson arranged lines in letters to separate poems and make them look like we might expect poems to look. We do not do this here." Domhnall Mitchell speculates that "enclosing poems in letters can be seen as a strategy for controlling and limiting the social environment in which one published and of guaranteeing *posthumous* literary survival within the cultural terms and conditions privileged by the same social circle."

Open Me Carefully appeared in 1998. In the same year, R. W. Franklin published his three-volume edition of *The Poems of Emily Dickinson*. Franklin's variorum was meant to supersede Johnson's 1955 volume of the same title. Describing Johnson as "the first literary scholar to edit Dickinson," Franklin describes Johnson's purpose as "to publish all of the poems in a literal text, chronologically arranged, with the variant readings, which infested the published texts, critically compared with all known manuscripts." His new edition, Franklin writes, "seeks to intrude minimally and therefore turns again to the manuscripts, accepting them as their own standard, almost the only record we have of her intentions." But, Franklin added, "this edition is based on the assumption that a literary work is separable from its artifact, as Dickinson herself demonstrated as she moved her poems from one piece of paper to another."

And there's the rub. Can the poems be experienced separately from the manuscripts in which they originally appeared? This question has come to dominate Dickinson studies to the extent that debating about how to present the poems threatens to displace the work of how to read them.

What was one to do, for instance, with Dickinson's favorite mark of punctuation—the dash? When handwritten, Dickinson's dashes come in all sorts of shapes and sizes; in *Inflections of the Pen: Dash and Voice in Emily Dickinson,* Paul Crumbley, attempting to capture the primary visual features of Dickinson's handwritten productions, resorts to "the creation of sixteen dash types." Hart and Smith choose, "for simplicity," to "show all these 'pointings' as short, standard en-dashes" except for a mark that angles up, which they "translate as an apostrophe." Yet in *Rowing in Eden,* Smith had protested that in editing "Wild Nights," Todd and Higginson had chosen "to even the long and short dashes by translating them into conventional, equally demarcated signs." Franklin makes no mention of the dash issue in the introduction to his variorum edition and chooses, as do Hart and Smith in *Open Me Carefully,* to indicate all dashes as standard ens.

"While any handwritten text must suffer the inexact representation (the regularizing) of the printed word, the problem is particularly severe for Dickinson's texts, punctuated as they are with dashes of varying lengths and perhaps of varying meanings." So wrote Sharon Cameron in *Lyric Time.* Although Bingham had drawn early attention to Dickinson's dashes in *Ancestors' Brocades,* these "pointings" were first given close critical attention in Charles R. Anderson's 1960 *Emily Dickinson's Poetry: Stairway of Surprise.* Five years later, Brita Lindberg-Seyersted concluded that Dickinson's punctuation did not conform to "a consistent system; it was a conscious, but impressionistic method of stressing . . . it was a creation of the moment, seldom deliberated." Helen Vendler has argued that Dickinson's dashes "served a multitude of purposes." They can become "an enactment of separation" or "can indicate a break in continuity." A dash "becomes especially significant when it concludes a poem," and Dickinson's "concluding punctuation was almost always a dash."

While Dickinson's punctuation may not conform to a consistent system, Jerome McGann argues that the *look* of the poems very much matters: Dickinson's "surviving manuscript texts urge us to take them at face value, to treat all scriptural forms as potentially significant *at the aesthetic or expressive level.*" Susan Howe is more direct about Dickinson's practice: "Her calligraphy influences her meaning." An example of how such an assumption might play out is given by Smith in her reading of "The Sea said." "The sly producer shapes her letters so readers are forced to consider mimesis in the most literal sense. By forming letters that 'look like' waves, Dickinson mocks exclusively mimetic goals for language. Her reminders that words can be cymbals as well as symbols, and of language's self-referentialities, are gleefully comic." In her "experimental edition" of forty late pencil drafts of work done by Dickinson, Marta L. Werner carried this mode of reading to its logical conclusion. Her book contains photographs of all kinds of jottings on all kinds of pieces of paper. The intention seems to be to catch the poet in the moment of the creative act—to get back to the source. Yet, as Werner confesses, "this edition is about undoing." "The drafts and fragments provisionally collected here continue to demonstrate their insusceptibility to collection, their resistance to bibliographic determination."

To print or not to print: that is the question. In *Measures of Possibility: Emily Dickinson's Manuscripts*, Domhnall Mitchell enumerates the characteristics of the poet's handwriting, considers their implications for meaning, and while noting that even "the least intrusive of modern technologies of textual reproduction" can "still involve interpretative alignments," then asks: "Might Dickinson not be equally served by publishing clearly legible and affordable print versions of her poems?" While the implied answer to Mitchell's question is yes, his exhaustive researches have uncovered so many difficult-to-reproduce features of the handwritten text as to yield a somewhat sad "Probably not." Mitchell deals especially with "the problem of blank spaces" in Dickinson's poems. Deploying "an Accu-Spec II transparent metric scale" to measure such spaces, Mitchell has found that no existing print versions of the manuscripts succeed in capturing the number and variety of these spaces.

Printed editions of the poems continue to appear nevertheless, and they have their partisans. "It is my conviction that Dickinson's poems are separable from their handwritten artifacts," Cristanne Miller writes in her introduction to her 2016 *Emily Dickinson's Poems: As She Preserved Them*. In support of her approach, Miller notes that Dickinson often recopied her poems, thereby appearing to accede to the fact that further copies—even print copies—might eventually be made. In printing some eleven hundred Dickinson poems, Miller's edition focuses on a "moment or stage in a work's presentation or genesis." But she also provides generous shoulder notes recording any variants Dickinson herself may have considered. The underlying assumption is that a poem for Dickinson remained a work in progress and that any printing of it captures only an instant in time. This approach forwards Lena Christensen's claim that Dickinson's poems can "be read without any yearning for the lost original." Christensen invites readers "to move away from a heroic narrative of Emily Dickinson's life and the connected assumption of a heroic rescue of her texts."

The first photographic facsimile edition of Dickinson's poems appeared in 1981. R. W. Franklin's *The Manuscript Books of Emily Dickinson* reproduced images of some eight hundred poems contained in Dickinson's fascicles. Now, without having to travel to an archive, readers had direct access to the look of an original text. But Christensen is not convinced. "This is an expensive and exclusive edition, at some level the exquisite epitome of fine art book publishing." In it, "the black and white photography fails to represent various kinds of details with apparent meaning, such as smudges and particular margin widths." As a result, "to someone concerned with the literal 'freedom' of handwritten loose sheets, the edition functions literally as a dead end of representational capacity of the book format: it is only a shadow of the artifact."

Franklin's attempt to offer something like an image of the real thing led, Mitchell argues, to a "dissipation of certainty" about "what constituted a book of Dickinson's poetry or even a Dickinson poem." Franklin's offering appeared at the dawn of the digital age, and what happens, Mitchell asks, "when a writer whose paradigm of literary production and reception was the codex, the (handwritten or printed) book made up of pages made of paper, is published on a screen? Do Dickinson's manuscripts look the way they do because she neglected to publish, or did she refuse to publish to protect and preserve the integrity of her manuscripts?"

There are three major websites dedicated to the digital reproduction of Dickinson's poems as they exist in manuscript. The Dickinson Electronic Archives (DEA) was opened by Martha Nell Smith in 1994 and updated in 2012. The two largest online archives were launched in 2013, the year in which Harvard opened the Emily Dickinson Archive and Amherst debuted the Emily Dickinson Collection. In his 2019 survey of the status and function of these archives, Seth Perlow concludes that they "perpetuate familiar assumptions about the value of seeing her handwriting, encouraging us to invest Dickinson's script with gnomic powers. The manuscript images do not necessarily make her poems easier to read."

The Harvard and Amherst archives are an artifact of The War between the Houses. In 1950, an heir to the Bianchi holdings sold the Dickinson papers to Harvard University. As part of the complicated agreement ensuring transfer of the papers, Harvard "acquired claims to the manuscripts in Bingham's possession," as Franklin writes, as well as "to the Dickinson literary property generally." Meanwhile, Bingham gave her holdings to Amherst.

And there the matter stands. Instead of the Dickinson papers being gathered into one integrated archive, they remain divided between two Massachusetts institutions. When Johnson, and then Franklin, set out to produce their variorums, they were required to negotiate with each institution to gain access to the full range of Dickinson's output. In Johnson's case, for instance, he was allowed to see only photostats of the poems in Bingham's possession.

As Perlow notes, "Harvard's claims of ownership have presented substantial impediments to the new online archives." Although Harvard possesses only a little more than half of the Dickinson manuscripts, its claims to rights over all of Dickinson's writings complicates any attempt to reproduce work by Dickinson in any form. In the acknowledgments to *Emily Dickinson: The Gorgeous Nothings,* there is a chilling sentence: "The President and Fellows of Harvard College assert the sole ownership of and sole right of literary rights and copyrights therein to the texts of Emily Dickinson." Harvard University Press does grant permission and charge fees for any such reproduction, but it "does not offer a schedule of fees." Amherst permits reproduction of manuscript images without fee or restriction. A feud lasting more than three generations has thus led to a situation in which the original Dickinson online archive, the DEA, hoping "to edit and encode all of Dickinson's corpus," was required to limit its initial focus to Emily's letters to Sue.

After all this, it may be a relief to turn to a reading of a poem. Written in late 1861 and found in fascicle 11, the poem is numbered 269 in the Franklin variorum:

> Wild nights – Wild nights!
> Were I with thee
> Wild nights should be
> Our luxury!
>
> Futile – the winds –
> To a Heart in port –
> Done with the Compass –
> Done with the Chart!
>
> Rowing in Eden –
> Ah – the Sea!
> Might I but moor – tonight –
> In thee!

We have counted Dickinson's dashes, but has anyone numbered her exclamation points? The poem contains five of them, a generous number even for so histrionic a poet. These pointings overleap the conditional status (the "should" and the "might") of the wish being expressed here. "Already with thee," they seem to say, "already with thee." Except that *with* gives way to *in*.

But who is the "thee," and just how is the speaker with or in him—or her? An understanding of the kind of arrival or union here being imagined, and of the nature of the desired partner, relies, in particular, on how we choose to interpret the conceit being developed in the final stanza. The image of rowing is perhaps clear enough. It bespeaks a rising and falling effort, a lifting and a straining. But rowing *in Eden* defuses the sense of the effort as one being enacted with another body. Instead, the speaker is rowing across a distance imagined as "the Sea." Robert Hass is helpful here: "Longing, we say, because desire is full / of endless distances." As so often in Dickinson, desire feels haunted by Zeno's paradox: the more proximate the love object, or the closer the speaker draws toward it, the more the gap infinitely extends itself.

This tension is released, however, in the poem's final two lines. While consummation remains only a surmise, the words that follow "Might" create an image concrete enough to allow for a reader to picture, and therefore in some sense to experience, achieved arrival. But there is a complication, and it turns upon the word *moor*.

When John Donne conjures "Two stiff twinned compasses" in "A Valediction: Forbidding Mourning," the logic of the metaphor is clear enough and also gets spelled out; "thy soul," he writes to his wife, is "the fix'd foot," while mine is the other that "far doth roam." He "grows erect" as he "comes home." "Thy firmness makes my circle just," he concludes, "And makes me end, where I begun."

A more accurate imaging of sexual longing, arousal, and consummation could scarcely be accomplished in so few lines. The action of the compasses proves true to the rhythms of happily married love. Donne wants to find metaphors that can stand the test of actual experience, and in doing so, he sets the standard for imagining—while also encoding—heterosexual sex in English.

"One poem only I dread a little to print—that wonderful 'Wild Nights,'" Thomas Higginson wrote to Mabel Todd in 1891, "lest the malignant read into it more than that virgin recluse ever dreamed of putting there." He seemed to deem the poem explicit. And yet as the image of rowing gives way to mooring, how to understand the poem's ending is anything but simple.

A rowboat moors *in* a harbor. While a harbor can be a wide or a narrow expanse, the act of mooring there does not carry a strong sexual valence. "Though some readers take this as an image of penetration," Alfred Habegger writes, "it probably signified enclosure in an embrace, a powerful Victorian image." Helen Vendler also takes up the question of penetration: "The speculation that the speaker of the poem must be a man—a critical interpretation deriving, with a coarseness foreign to Dickinson, from "moor ... / In thee"—seems to me untenable; the poet's diction is that of female romance." Little in Dickinson's closing conceit makes it possible to imagine with any certainty who is doing what or with whom. Left open, once again, is the question of whom Dickinson loved.

Neither Habegger nor Vendler address the fact that the final stanza of the poem, as printed by Franklin, does not reflect Dickinson's original lineation. A photograph of the manuscript of "Wild Nights" printed in *Rowing in Eden* permits the following transcription:

> Rowing in Eden –
> Ah! the Sea!
> Might I but moor –
> Tonight –
> In thee!

According to Martha Nell Smith, this "eye-catching stanza of five lines" invites "readers to passionate pause," while a four-line version works "to mask the breathless sexuality conveyed by the holograph." Moreover, as she proceeds to catalog the various details of the handwritten version, Smith maintains that the typescript reproduction of the poem "levels the effects of letters" and of "Dickinson's extraordinary, somewhat seductive, calligraphy—the wide-mouth *W*, the triangular *T* at the beginning of the sixth line, and the stunning flourish that crosses both *T*'s in 'Tonight.'"

Dickinson's poems present themselves to the eye by way of highly suggestive and yet underdetermined pointings and flourishes. As R. P. Blackmur observed in 1937, "The manner of notation, if it were known, might make a beginning of the establishment of a canon." But how Dickinson meant this notation to be understood is not known and never will be—*and this is a result of the poet's choice*. When general editor Robert S. Levine chose to include Franklin's transcription of "Wild Nights" in the 2022 edition of the *Norton Anthology of American Literature*, he also chose, on the facing page, to print "a reproduction of the manuscript of this poem." Few juxtapositions could be more illustrative of the unresolved debate in Dickinson studies between manuscript and print or more exemplary of choosing not choosing—to use Sharon Cameron's phrase. Perhaps the last word should then go to the much-maligned and much-admired Sue, who, surprised by the publication of Emily's first volume of poems and surely vexed to have Mabel listed as an editor, was moved to comment nevertheless: "'The Poems' will ever be to me marvellous whether in manuscript or type."

SIX

Faulkner Revises
SARTORIS AND FLAGS IN THE DUST

It was time to visit the archive.

At the University of Virginia, where the majority of Faulkner's manuscripts and typescripts are held, you enter the Small Special Collections Library, walk down a winding stair (you are now underground), through an exhibit hall, and into the area where the librarians and computers direct you to the item you are looking for. Inside a further room, one furnished with nicely polished cherry tables, you wait until your request arrives. If you have asked for a Faulkner manuscript, you often see a page divided into four quadrants. The horizontal line leaves a generous two or three inches above it, while the vertical line, meant to define the left-hand margin, moves aggressively into the rectangle on the lower right-hand corner of the page. In this stringently defined space, tiny vertical strokes are bisected by an occasional horizontal: there is a sensation of reading cuneiform. The handwriting sometimes varies the color of its inks. A former director of Special Collections once remarked that the most successful of its decipherers were scholars visiting from Japan.

Any number of the Faulkner manuscripts held in Charlottesville have been heavily revised. Scholars can thereby trace the fits and starts of one writer's imagination as he brought his wares to market. Faulkner oversaw the process of shepherding his works into print with varying degrees of attention, and each of them was given its final, significant form while Faulkner was alive—except one.

I didn't even know what name to give the book I was working on: first published in 1929 as *Sartoris*, a restored text of the novel appeared in 1973 as *Flags in the Dust*—and then another version of *Flags* saw print in 2006. Most scholars seemed to view *Sartoris* as a publisher's artifact that deserved to be replaced, but I had strong reservations about the process. *Sartoris* was, after all, the novel Faulkner scholars had built careers upon for almost fifty years before the new and improved version came along. And I was simply not convinced that *Flags* was the better book. I did take some comfort from comments made by Joseph Blotner in his introduction to the two volumes published as *William Faulkner Manuscripts 5*. The Garland facsimile volumes reproduce the holograph manuscript of *Flags in the Dust* in volume 1 and the Ribbon Typescript in volume 2. Blotner is writing in 1986: "This novel, in both its manuscript and typescript versions, its two published versions, and its missing other versions, presents perhaps the most vexed set of problems to be encountered in all of Faulkner's texts."

Set in the years following World War I, *Sartoris* introduces many of the elements of what could be called the "Faulkner complex":

—the sadness of the *re-*, that things that have happened will happen again;
—storytelling and the listening it enforces;
—the dynamic of the skipped generation;
—women as "cracked" urns or unravished brides (*Light in August*, 538);
—the glamour of the prank versus the efficacy of the act;
—love as incest;
—race as an interaction effect, where, to quote Quentin Compson in *The Sound and the Fury*, "a n-- is not a person so much as a form of behavior; a sort of obverse reflection of the white people he lives among" (943).

In the late 1970s, when I first wrote about *Sartoris*, I argued that in the novel "Faulkner had discovered the shape of his material rather than its significance." As I was about to discover some forty years later, issues of shaping and significance can prove elusive indeed when approaching a novel with such a complex prehistory and such a controversial afterlife.

After consulting the finding aid, I requested two boxes from the Noel Polk Papers. Polk began editing Faulkner for Random House in the early 1980s. Over the next three decades, he managed to bring out readable and reliable editions of most of the major novels and short stories under the Vintage imprint. This editorial work also served as the basis for the five Faulkner volumes published by the Library of America. It was Polk who brought out the second edition of *Flags in the Dust* in 2006, and I was interested in seeing how he did things.

After opening box 1, I pulled out a folder labeled "*Flags in the Dust*—Markup of TS and first edition of *Sartoris* (1 of 5 folders)." The folder contained a photocopy of some one hundred pages from the Ribbon Typescript. The first page was headed by the word *one* and the number 1 typed below it. An opening sentence followed: "Old man Falls roared: 'Cunnel was settin' thar in a cheer, his sock feet propped on the po'ch railin', smokin' this hyer very pipe.'" The page was scribbled over in red, green, blue, black, and purple ink. "Final decision in this color," Polk had written, in purple.

Over the next four hours, I made my way through five folders and 593 pages. At different points, Polk had pasted in photocopies of passages from the 1956 reprint of *Sartoris*. The ink colors—mostly the red—turned up on virtually every page: it was clear Polk felt compelled to make all kinds of insertions and deletions, most of them at the scale of a single letter or word. Each mark, I came to see, indicated a change in the typescript when it had been edited into the novel called *Sartoris*. But who had made those original changes? Who, for that matter, had produced the typescript? My search for an answer to these questions would take me back almost to the beginnings of Faulkner's writing career.

Faulkner's first novel, *Soldier's Pay,* appeared on February 25, 1926. His second, *Mosquitoes,* appeared on April 30, 1927. The one book is located in Georgia, the other, in Louisiana. Faulkner began work on the manuscript he called *Flags in the Dust* in late 1926 or early 1927. With his third novel, Faulkner knew he wanted to shift attention back to the home ground he was calling Yocona County, but he could not have known he was entering a remarkably creative period: "Between 1927 and 1932," Polk reminds us, "Faulkner wrote *Flags in the Dust;* wrote *The Sound and the Fury;* wrote *Sanctuary;* wrote *As I Lay Dying;* revised *Sanctuary;* revised the Quentin section of *The Sound and the Fury;* wrote *Light in August;* and wrote and/or revised about thirty short stories, some of them among the best he would ever write."

Work on *Flags in the Dust* proceeded rapidly; by the early fall of 1927, Blotner estimates, "Faulkner was in the final stages of the manuscript." He began typing it up in sections, and he "apparently did more changing and rearranging than he had done with either of the two preceding novels." "Five lengthy sequences underwent relocation. And there were deletions." By the end, Faulkner had filled almost six hundred pages. At the bottom of the last page, he recorded the finish date: "29 September 1927." He had just turned thirty years old.

In mid-October, Faulkner wrote to his publisher, Horace Liveright: "I have written THE book, of which those other things were but foals." Six weeks later, he sent another letter to Liveright. "It's too bad you don't like Flags in the Dust," he began. On the last day of November, Faulkner had received Liveright's estimate of his achievement: "It is with sorrow in my heart that I write to tell you that three of us have read Flags in the Dust and don't believe that Boni and Liveright should publish it. Furthermore, as a firm deeply interested in your work, we don't believe that you should offer it for publication." The readers of the book had found it "diffuse and non-integral with neither very much plot development nor character development. We think it lacks plot, dimension and projection. The story really doesn't get anywhere and has a thousand loose ends."

This would turn out to be one of the more fortuitous rejections in the history of American literature. By the following March, Faulkner was writing Liveright about having "got going" on a new novel. The project had begun as a short story centered on a Negro laundress named Nancy. Nancy works for a family named Compson, and three of the Compson children—Quentin, Candace, and Jason—find themselves captivated by Nancy's fear of a Black lover who intends to take revenge on her for having become pregnant by a white man. Quentin narrates the story as a young man looking back.

On April 7, 1928, Faulkner began another story. He called it "Twilight" and later described it as about "some children being sent away from the house." The Compson children again appear: Quentin and Caddy and Jason are sent away from the house to protect them from the mechanics of a grandmother's funeral. To the threesome, Faulkner decided to add another perspective. "The idea struck me to see how much more I could have got out of the idea of the blind, self-centeredness of innocence, typified by children, if one of those children had been truly innocent, that is, an idiot." He went on to invent Benjy Compson and decided to begin the story with him. *The Sound and the Fury* was now well underway.

"When Faulkner wrote about the novel's composition five years later," Blotner writes, "he presented it as a reaction, in part, against the rejection of *Flags in the Dust*." With *The Sound and the Fury*, Faulkner found himself turning away from thoughts of publication. In an introduction to the novel written in 1933, Faulkner remembered the turning: "One day I seemed to shut a door between me and all publishers' addresses and book lists. I said to myself, Now I can write. Now I can make myself a vase like that which the old Roman kept at his bedside and wore the rim away with kissing it. So I, who never had a sister and was fated to lose my daughter in infancy, set out to make myself a beautiful and tragic little girl."

Despite his growing reservations about the publishing world, Faulkner refused to abandon the book Liveright had rejected. He began showing *Flags* to friends, but they, too, "told me the same general thing—that the book lacked any form whatever." In the spring of 1928, he wrote to his aunt 'Bama: "I have been trying to get the mss. in some sort of intelligible shape to send you.... Every day or so I burn some of it up and rewrite it, and at present it is almost incoherent."

Faulkner eventually sent a revision of *Flags* to Ben Wasson, a friend now working for the Leland Hayward literary agency. "Will you please try to sell this for me?" he wrote. In September, Wasson invited Faulkner to come to New York. Wasson had sent *Flags* to his friend Harrison Smith, an editor at Harcourt Brace. Smith wrote a favorable report and gave the novel to Alfred Harcourt. Harcourt liked the book but found it overlong. Blotner quotes Harcourt's exchange with Wasson:

> "I don't think he can cut his work," he told Ben. "Will you do it for fifty dollars?"
>
> Ben immediately agreed. Rather diffidently, he inquired about an advance on royalties.

"How about three hundred dollars?" Harcourt asked. Ben accepted.

Wasson sent the money to Faulkner and told him that the typescript had to be cut.

A contract from Harcourt soon arrived. Dated September 20, 1928, it specified a novel of some 110,000 words to be titled *Sartoris*—somehow *Flags in the Dust* had been retitled. Faulkner signed the contract, packed a few things, and headed for New York.

One of the virtues of Joseph Blotner's *Faulkner: A Biography*, and one that makes it unlikely that his achievement will ever be exceeded, is that it does not argue a case. Blotner simply lays out the facts in immense and well-documented detail. In relying heavily on Blotner's vivid account of Faulkner's attempts to secure a publisher for *Flags in the Dust*, I have quoted from passages in the biography containing revealing action words: *changing, relocation, deletions, revision*. By the time Faulkner traveled to New York to work with Wasson on the cuts Harcourt was demanding, he had already subjected his novel to so much reworking as to have moved a considerable distance away from any original impulse. The revisions that were about to occur under Wasson's hand were no doubt considerable, but it is difficult to measure with any certainty whether they were more significant than those the author himself had already imposed on "THE book."

When Faulkner met Wasson in New York, he made it quite clear, however, that he was reluctant to engage in further editing. In his 1931 essay on the composition of *Sartoris*, Faulkner recalled their exchange about the issue of cuts:

> I said, "A cabbage has grown, matured. You look at that cabbage; it is not symmetrical; you say, I will trim this cabbage off and make it art; I will make it resemble a peacock or a pagoda or 3 doughnuts. Very good, I say; you do that, then the cabbage will be dead."
>
> "Then we'll make kraut of it," he said. "The same amount of sour kraut will feed twice as many people as cabbage." A day or so later he came to me and showed me the mss. "The trouble is," he said, "Is that you have about 6 books in here. You were trying to write them all at

once." He showed me what he meant, what he had done, and I realised for the first time that I had done better than I knew.

Wasson's comment about the six books "in here" may be the part of this exchange most widely cited, but the nature of Faulkner's realization deserves to be remembered as well. The value of the thing done comes home to him "for the first time" in response to an act of revision performed by another hand.

Blotner lists some of the cuts made by Wasson: Narcissa Benbow's reflections about old Bayard Sartoris as a boy; long passages about Byron Snopes's torments; any number of scenes involving Horace Benbow. Wasson did most of the work, although, Blotner speculates, Faulkner did take some part in the process of turning his cabbage into kraut. At the same time, Blotner feels compelled to admit in a footnote that "the analysis of BW's deletions is tentative because they were made upon the setting copy of SAR, which is not known to have survived."

About the status of the Ribbon Typescript, Blotner has this to say in his introduction to the Garland volumes: "The typescript which Faulkner retained in his files, and which is reproduced here, is presumably not the one from which Wasson worked, and there is no way to tell how many versions, whole or in a part, were created by Faulkner's revisions before the typescript was produced that Wasson prepared to serve as setting copy for the novel, retitled *Sartoris*." Once the Ribbon Typescript had been generated, more cuts took place: "Wasson would later say that he cut the typescript by a quarter and that Faulkner told him he had done a good job." Blotner ends with something of a dying fall: "Until new evidence comes to light, one will be able only to speculate on these revisions and the extent to which Faulkner was involved in them."

To sum up: beyond Faulkner's holograph manuscript, the Ribbon Typescript is all we have, and we do not know when it was typed or who typed it or who cut it.

Even as Wasson worked to shorten Faulkner's novel, he was seeking to disentangle his friend from his old publisher. Faulkner still owed Boni & Liveright a first look at his next book as well as two hundred dollars from an advance. After a casual exchange with Liveright, the publisher agreed to tear up Faulkner's contract. As Faulkner wrote to his aunt, "Harcourt Brace & Co bought me from Liveright. Much, much nicer there. Book will be out in Feb. Also another one, the damndest book I ever read. I don't believe anyone will publish it for 10 years." The book no one would publish duly appeared on October 7, 1929. But it was not published by Harcourt Brace.

Faulkner may have found Albert Harcourt much nicer to work with, but his firm could not come to terms on *The Sound and the Fury*. Harcourt would prove as resistant to Faulkner's fourth novel as Liveright had been to his third one. But while Liveright had lodged sensible objections to the prolixity and complexity of *Flags in the Dust,* Harcourt ended up rejecting a masterpiece. That outcome was abetted by Smith and Wasson. Each man hoped to join the firm of Jonathan Cape, and, after Harcourt expressed "mingled admiration and doubts" about *The Sound and the Fury,* Smith retrieved the manuscript from Harcourt and told Faulkner he would henceforth be handling the novel himself.

Smith then went to see Harcourt. Blotner sets the scene, in which Smith speaks first:

> "You're never going to publish that manuscript," he told him. "Why don't you let me have it?"
>
> "All right," Harcourt replied. "You're the only damn fool in New York who would publish it."

Smith and Wasson soon joined forces with Jonathan Cape, and on February 18, 1929, a contract for publication of *The Sound and the Fury* was executed by the new firm of Johnathan Cape and Harrison Smith. Faulkner was offered an advance on royalties of two hundred dollars. On the same day the contract was issued, Faulkner wrote Alfred Harcourt: "My copies of SARTORIS came promptly. I like the appearance of the book very much indeed." *Sartoris* had been published a few weeks earlier, on January 31, 1929. *The Sound and the Fury* appeared nine months later.

"*The Sound and the Fury* is an apt title in more ways than one," Eric Sundquist argues, "for as Faulkner's remarks on the writing of *Sartoris* suggest, a creative convulsion of immense magnitude takes place between the two novels, as though Faulkner has entered the dream world, the limbo, that would make available his greatest materials." However great the convulsion taking place *between* the two novels, they were intimately linked by the experience of a deeply disappointing failure inseparable from an even more remarkable success. *Sartoris* can even be said to have produced *The Sound and the Fury* insofar as the frustrations Faulkner experienced in the editing and the selling of it inspired him to turn toward the worlds Sundquist invokes.

In 1973, Douglas Day, a professor of English at the University of Virginia, published with Random House a new edition of *Sartoris* under the original title Faulkner had assigned to it, *Flags in the Dust*. In the following year, Day's corrected edition appeared as a Vintage paperback. The 1973 hardback runs to 370 pages; the 1974 paperback contains 433. In his introduction to the paperback edition, Day describes the original *Flags in the Dust* as having been submitted to an "extensive cutting job ... until almost a fourth of the book had been excised." Day notes that Faulkner had preserved the original holograph manuscript and "a sort of composite typescript of the novel, produced by the combination of three separate but overlapping typescript drafts." Day also records being contacted by Jill Summers, Faulkner's daughter, who "remembered that her late father had spoken often of a restoration of *Flags in the Dust*. Mrs. Summers asked this writer and Albert Erskine, editor at Random House, to undertake the task." The result," Day declares, "is, now, *Flags in the Dust*, which aims at being a faithful reproduction of that composite typescript," although "certain nonsubstantive alterations in spelling and punctuation have been made."

In 2006, there appeared a new edition of *Flags in the Dust*. It, too, was published under the Vintage imprint, and it was edited by Noel Polk. Like Day, Polk had to rely on the Ribbon Typescript. "This typescript," we are informed by the "Note on the Texts" in the Library of America volume containing Polk's edition of *Flags*, "is a composite of several different typings of portions of the novel, done on more than one typewriter and by at least two different typists." At the back of Polk's 2006 Vintage edition can be found another brief editor's note. It pays a kind of strange tribute to Day's earlier efforts:

> In 1973 Random House published an edition of *Flags in the Dust* edited by Douglas Day, who used the typescript dated "29 September 1927" as his text, although he made some editorial alterations and interpo-

lated into his text one passage from *Sartoris* that does not appear in the typescript and which seems clearly to have been written by Faulkner. The result is a conflated text that aims to be as close as possible to the typescript that Faulkner sent to Wasson in 1928.

By preserving Faulkner's spelling, punctuation, and wording, even when inconsistent or irregular, the Polk text strives to be as faithful to Faulkner's usage as surviving evidence permits.

It is difficult to believe that Polk himself wrote this astonishing note. Why, for instance, would he refer to himself in the third person? More important, the sentences quoted here finesse as much as they confront. "The result," Day had written in his introduction, *aims* at something. By repeating this choice of verb, the editor's note of 2006 avoids having to raise the question of whether the aim has hit the target. The phrase *some editorial alterations* leaves a reader wondering just how many changes Day had made. Finally, the one sentence in the editor's note devoted to "the Polk text" remarkably compresses the story of a difficult and also a highly politic labor, given that one Random House editor was redoing work already done by an earlier one.

The critique politely sidestepped by Polk had already been rendered by George Hayhoe in a 1975 *Mississippi Quarterly* review of Day's edition. Day had maintained that he had made "certain nonsubstantive alterations" in the text, but by Hayhoe's count, in Day's edition "there are more than seventeen hundred variants, of which nearly one hundred are substantive." Day had also corrected dialect forms and standardized Faulkner's highly variable usage of dashes and ellipses. He imported material from *Sartoris* that did not appear in the typescript with which he was working, and he "has omitted material which has not been cancelled in the typescript." "Day's apparent misunderstanding of the nature of the text he was editing," Hayhow concludes, "resulted in a confusion of the old problems and the creation of new ones." On top of all this, Hayhoe maintains, Mrs. Summers, in an interview with James Meriwether, "has stated that she did not ask Day to edit the book."

Sartoris centers on the return to Mississippi of two war veterans, Bayard Sartoris and Horace Benbow. Bayard is haunted by the death in France of his brother and fellow pilot, John, while Horace, who served with the YMCA, struggles to reenter the career of a small-town lawyer. Bayard is haunted by namesakes, both by his grandfather, old Bayard, whom he manages to kill in a car accident, and by the Civil War generation of the original John and Bayard, each of whom also met a violent death. The Sartoris and Benbow families are eventually united when young Bayard weds Horace's sister, Narcissa, but marriage fails to quell his restless spirit, and he enacts a kind of suicide by insisting on going up in a plane unfit to fly.

Any plot summary of a novel so bristling with subplots will leave out all too much: Wasson was right about Faulkner having "about 6 books in here." The material Faulkner had begun to amass was to prove rich indeed but virtually unmanageable at this stage in his career, and even a quick glance at Faulkner's holograph manuscript reveals its author's uncertainty about how he ought to begin. In his superb online resource, *Digital Yoknapatawpha*, Stephen Railton locates "three manuscript pages" that "all read like possible first pages."

One set of pages opens in France during World War I and deals with pilots John (here named Evelyn) and Bayard Sartoris. A second set opens in Mississippi in 1918 with old Bayard reflecting on his family history: "Sartoris: Bayard Sartoris: a fatal name." On a manuscript page bearing the number "3," Faulkner wrote another beginning: "It was an afternoon in late spring of 1863 and John Sartoris sat." Taken together, the three attempts forecast a novel in which the author would make ambitious leaps in space and time: the novel's depressed post–World War I present is juxtaposed against a glamorous Civil War past. Faulkner went with "the last of these possibilities," Railton argues, "when he prepared the typescript." In it, the story of Colonel John Sartoris is recast into a first-person narrative being related by old man Falls to old Bayard.

And this is where Day's *Flags in the Dust* begins:

Old man Falls roared: "Cunnel was settin' thar in a cheer, his sock feet propped on the po'ch railin,' smokin' this hyer very pipe. Old Louvinia was settin' on the steps, shellin' a bowl of peas fer supper. And a feller was glad to git even peas sometimes, in them days. And you was settin' back agin' the post. They wa'nt nobody else thar 'cep' yo' aunt, the one 'fo' Miss Jenny come. Cunnel had sont them two gals to Memphis to yo' gran'pappy when he fust went away. You was 'bout half-grown, I reckon. How old was you then, Bayard?"

"Fourteen," old Bayard answered.

"Hey?"

"Fourteen," Bayard shouted. "Do I have to tell you that every time you tell me this damn story?" (3)

In Polk's 2006 *Flags in the Dust*, this exchange appears some eighteen pages in.

Polk begins with a passage appearing on page 4 of the Ribbon Typescript: "As usual old man Falls had brought John Sartoris into the room with him, had walked the three miles in from the county Poor Farm, fetching, like an odor, like the clean dusty smell of his faded overalls, the spirit of the dead man into that room where the dead man's son sat and where the two of them, pauper and banker, would sit for a half an hour in the company of him who had passed beyond death and then returned.... Freed as he was of time and flesh, he was a far more palpable presence than either of the two old men who sat shouting periodically into one another's deafness" (3). Given Faulkner's initial indecision about where and when things might start, it may come as no surprise that Day and Polk do not agree on how *Flags in the Dust* ought to begin.

Day's opening plunges us into a story being told; Polk begins not with the story but with its effect on a listener. And Polk chooses to begin where *Sartoris* begins: his 2006 opening reproduces the novel's 1929 opening. Yet nowhere in Railton's careful survey of possible beginnings does the novel start with "As usual." Polk—and *Sartoris*—have invented a fourth beginning. But it is also a beginning that *works*.

Polk's beginning works because it establishes a dynamic that will recur in Faulkner's fiction with sometimes deadly force. Bringing a dead man "into" a room by way of a story also happens at the beginning of *Absalom, Absalom!*, in which Rosa Coldfield summons Quentin Compson to her father's dusty office and imposes upon him the Sutpen family saga. Like the John Sartoris summoned by old man Falls, the Thomas Sutpen conjured by Rosa becomes "a far more palpable presence than either" the teller or the listener, each of whom, in both novels, has been reduced to the status of a ghost haunted by a more heroic if also self-destructive past. Thus, Faulkner can describe Quentin's body in the same way old Bayard's might be described, "an empty hall echoing with sonorous defeated names; he was not a being, an entity, he was a commonwealth" (9). "I have had to listen to too much,"

Quentin says to himself in chapter 6 of *Absalom!* (172), and in his reluctant acceptance of the role of coerced auditor, Quentin embodies the plight of those readers who may feel kidnapped as well by an author possessed of a never-ending and often repeated repertoire of "damn" stories.

For Faulkner, the test of a good listener is to be able to retell with a difference. In *Absalom!*, with the assistance of Shreve McCannon, Quentin will "overpass to love" as he evolves into an empathetic re-teller in the final chapters of the novel (261). Even as Quentin assists in giving Henry Sutpen and Charles Bon complex and compelling inner lives, the hold of story proves too much for him. In the spring following the winter in which he revises and refines the story imposed upon him, Quentin will take his own life, and he does so, in part, because he sees himself, in his guilty and yet irrepressible love for his sister Caddy, as a failed repetition of Charles, the brother-seducer of his sister Judith, and Henry, the brother-avenger of that incestuous desire.

The hold of story is one of Faulkner's deepest subjects. As Jean-Paul Sartre writes in his 1938 essay on *Sartoris*, Faulkner "dreams of a world in which stories should be believed, where they would truly act upon men; and his novels depict this world of which he dreams." While Faulkner had no trouble coming up with stories, he did need to learn how to arrange and to revise them. In writing his third novel, Carolyn Porter argues, "Faulkner had basically lined up a disparate set of stories, turning now to one, now to another, and linking them loosely around family tales and the failed heroics of war."

Day and Polk may not agree on where the novel is meant to begin, but their opening chapters do each contain the same two stories about the heroics of Civil War, the one about Colonel John Sartoris and his escape from the Yankee cavalry, the other about his brother, Bayard. Each story involves a prank.

As Colonel John is resting up at his home place, some enemy cavalry rides up. The Yankee officer asks John a question: "Whar do the rebel, John Sartoris, live?" (558). He tells the inquiring officer that John Sartoris lives down the road and offers to show them "whar" after fetching his shoes. Once inside the house, Colonel John runs out the back door, Louvinia hands him his coat and boots, and he goes "a-tearin" down to the creek, where his son is waiting with his stallion (559). "And then he tole you to tell yo' aunt," Will Falls says to old Bayard, "he wouldn't be home fer supper."

In the novel's first chapter, the story about the prank performed by Colonel John's brother, Bayard, comes by way of Miss Jenny Du Pre. "It had to do with an April evening, and coffee" (551). Lacking a morning stimulant, General Jeb Stuart and twenty of his men, including Bayard, decide to ride into a nearby enemy camp, "where General Pope and his staff sat at breakfast al fresco." After grabbing a blackened coffeepot, the Confederates offer a Yankee major a taste just before the pot is shot from Bayard's hand. As Stuart and his men ride off through a hail of bullets, the prank would seem to be over.

But Bayard is not yet done. When the raiding party's lone captive says, "At least General Stuart did not capture our anchovies," Bayard whirls his horse, and "with all of Pope's army shooting at him," rides back after the anchovies (554, 555). A cook hidden under a mess tent then kills Bayard with a derringer.

Faulkner seems fond of these two stories and lavishes a good amount of detail on each of them. He may mean to portray John and Bayard as figures of gratuitous gallantry, but the Yankee captive sees it differently: "This is not bravery: it is the rashness of a heedless and headstrong boy" (554).

Faulkner's novel eventually comes to know better than to glorify such pranks. In part 4, after young Bayard has caused another crash, the automobile accident in which his grandfather is killed, he appears to experience a moment of insight. Faulkner even has Bayard quote the Yankee captive: "For an instant he saw the recent months of his life coldly in all their headlong and heedless wastefulness.... *You, who deliberately do things your judgment tells you may not be successful, even possible, are afraid to face the consequences of your own acts*" (816). By way of interior monologue, Faulkner here also renders a judgment on himself: the patterns inaugurated in *Sartoris*, he already appears to intuit, will have to be revised.

Horace Benbow represents the other pole of Faulkner's early vision: he is not the self-destructive hero but the artist manqué. Like young Bayard, he, too, is a returnee from the war dealing with the problem of reentry. Horace brings home to Mississippi an apparatus for glass blowing, and he remains a prisoner of the urn vision, obsessed both with his sister Narcissa's sexuality and devoted to the making of an unravished and inviolate thing. Meanwhile, he conducts an affair with Belle Mitchell and flirts with her daughter. Horace and Belle eventually marry and move to another town.

Polk describes Horace as a man of "lugubrious preoccupations." His chaotic inner life dominates parts 3 and 4 of the Ribbon Transcript. "*Flags in the Dust*," Sundquist argues, "was marred by excessive attention to the character of Horace Benbow and his incestuous attachment to his sister." Many of the most severe cuts imposed on the Ribbon Transcript involved material about Benbow, "revisions," Sundquist believes, "that made *Sartoris* as good as it is."

Day and Polk restore the Benbow cuts. The passages quoted here, each removed in the initial editing of the novel, are taken from Polk's 2006 edition of *Flags in the Dust*.

In part 3, Horace resumes his law practice after returning from the war and finds himself musing on "the unchanging days. They were doomed days; he knew it, yet for the time being his devious and uncontrollable impulses had become one with the rhythm of things as a swimmer's counter muscles become one with a current, and cage and all his life grew suave with motion, oblivious of destination. During this period not only did his immediate days become starkly inevitable, but the dead thwarted ones with all the spent and ludicrous disasters which his nature had incurred upon him, grew lustrous in retrospect and without regret" (176). A few pages later, Horace plays doubles with a young girl:

> Hers was an awkward speed that cost them points, but from the base line Horace retrieved her errors when he could, pleasuring in the skimpy ballooning of her little dress moulded and dragged by her arms and legs, watching the taut revelations of her speeding body in a sort of ecstasy. Girlwhite and all thy little Oh. Not pink, no. For a moment I thought she'd no. Disgraceful, her mamma would call it. Or any other older woman. Belle's are pink O muchly "Oaten reed above the lyre," Horace chanted, catching the ball at his shoe-tops with a full swing, watching it duck viciously beyond the net. Oaten reed above the lyre. (187)

In part 4, Horace talks with Joan, Belle's sister, about love as a chemical attraction: "'But I suppose it's all sort of messy: living and seething corruption glossed over for a while by smoothly colored flesh; all foul, until the clean and naked bone.' He mused again, she quietly beside him. 'But it's something there, something you go after; must; driven. Not always swine. A plan somewhere, I suppose, known to Whoever first set the fermentation going'" (313).

While the complicated negotiations that took place between the author, his various editors, and the publisher of *Sartoris* make it impossible to know who decided upon removing much of the Benbow material from it, the sheer ugliness of the material quoted here makes a strong case for the decisions made. When Faulkner turned to *Sanctuary*, he incorporated "some of the Benbow material that was cut from *Flags*." Then he thought better of it. "The guiding principle behind Faulkner's revision of *Sanctuary*," writes Polk, "seems to have been the felt need to get us outside of Horace Benbow's cloyingly introspective, narcissistic personality." Faulkner eventually chose to replace much of Horace's "modified stream-of-consciousness" with straight narration.

Is it possible for a great novelist to write a "bad" character? Not bad as in the sense of being evil or unlikable but bad as in incoherent, boring, or downright creepy. Faulkner quickly realized that Horace Benbow was such a character, and while offering him a second appearance in *Sanctuary*, the novel he began once *The Sound and the Fury* was published, he dropped Horace from his repertoire thereafter.

Faulkner had only limited success, however, in freeing his imagination from what might be called the "Benbow complex." While Horace never appears again in the Faulkner procession after *Sanctuary*, his sexual obsessions and lofty imaginings pass into Quentin Compson and are dignified there by Quentin's effort to understand the Sutpen family story. Horace is also diffused into lawyer Gavin Stevens, a tedious apologist for the mid-twentieth-century South.

With the Sartoris family, the case is far different.

Faulkner once told an audience that readers of his work should "begin with a book called *Sartoris* that has the germ of my apocrypha in it." Faulkner here seems to imply that his third novel helped to germinate something questionable—apocryphal—or even downright false. And, given the work to come, there is a kind of crazy logic to the claim. While something fundamental had been discovered, it was also a vision of human life that would have to be revised.

The fundamental discovery was of an imaginative world—Yoknapatawpha County—in which a set of fictional families and characters will reappear. These are typically families trapped in stories they feel doomed to repeat. Repetition of names across the generations—names like John and Bayard—underscores the pattern. As John T. Irwin writes in *Doubling and Incest / Repetition and Revenge*, "This feeling that an ancestor's actions can determine the actions of his descendants for generations to come by compelling them to periodically repeat his deeds is the form that the fate or doom of a family takes in Faulkner."

The doom, then, is that things happen again. In *The Sound and the Fury*, Mr. Compson makes the negative case about repetition: "Again. Sadder than was. Again" (950). Mr. Compson finds *againness* sad because in his family, at least, it involves a pattern of inescapable decline.

The prevalence of *re-* words in Faulkner's pages express his fascination with the presence and power of repetition in human life. Of all the *re-* words deployed in the work, the most loaded is the word *revenge*. In *Flags in the Dust*, revenge resolves obligations and relieves guilt. Sartoris women, Miss Jenny admits, "take our revenge wherever and whenever we can get it" (584). Horace Benbow seeks "revenge upon perfection" as it is embodied in his sister, while young Bayard takes revenge against the future, "the long long span of a man's natural life" (683, 669). Old Bayard, otherwise passive before events, "had had his revenge" when he caused his father's tombstone to be re-chiseled with the words "Fell at the hand of —— Redlaw, Sept. 4, 1976" (871). But this revenge of words rather than deeds does not satisfy, as reflected in Miss Jenny's meditation at another grave: "Old Bayard's headstone was simple too, having been born, as he had, too late for one war and too soon for the next, and she thought what a joke They had played on him—forbidding him opportunities for swashbuckling and then denying him the privilege of being buried by men who would have invented vainglory for him" (870). Miss Jenny's reflections suggest that none of the men in her world have yet escaped the vanity of vainglory.

Faulkner will proceed to discover that repetition can be not only a doom but an opportunity. To "re-read," as Faulkner writes in *Absalom!*, is to think and feel again and therefore to give a story a second chance (83). To revise, as when an author chooses to imagine a character newly, can achieve much the same thing. No character in Faulkner is given a more dramatic second chance than the old Bayard of *Flags in the Dust*.

It happens in *The Unvanquished*. In this sequence of Civil War stories, published in 1938, Faulkner invents a childhood and young adulthood for a character who had originally been imagined as an ineffectual old man. Old Bayard's second chance comes in "An Odor of Verbena," the seventh and last in the sequence of stories.

The first six stories in *The Unvanquished* are driven by the desire to get back at an enemy: hence the title of the fifth story, "Vendée." In that story, a sixteen-year-old Bayard and his Black friend Ringo go after Grumby, the man who murdered Rosa Millard, the woman they call Granny. They succeed in killing Grumby and nail his corpse to the old compress door.

"An Odor of Verbena" begins some eight years later. Bayard, now twenty-four, is away at college, boarding with the Wilkins family and reading the law. On an October night, Ringo bursts into the house and says, "They shot Colonel Sartoris this morning" (464). Bayard's father has been shot by a business rival; the Redlaw of *Sartoris* has been renamed Redmond.

Bayard has to decide what he will do. "I dont know how many things I will have to attend to," he tells Mrs. Wilkins, before he begins riding back to Jefferson, but he also thinks to himself, in this deeply interior first-person narration, "of that which I still had no yardstick to measure save that one consisting of what, despite myself, despite my raising and background (or maybe because of them) I had for some time known I was becoming and had feared the test of it" (465–66). Bayard has no yardstick for what he intends to do because his immediate culture has offered him any number of stories about vainglorious pranks but no model for what will prove to be an unprecedented act.

"I did not tell him . . . what I was going to do," Bayard thinks to himself, as he says goodbye to Professor Wilkins. But his narrative has already begun preparing the reader for the event (466–67). It is a narrative haunted by the prefix *pre-*, as when Bayard says, "People talk glibly of presentiment, but I had none" (463). Faulkner here sets one prefix—*pre-*, meaning "before"—against the more habitual *again* of *re-*. The simple substitution of the one prefix for the other alerts the reader to the strenuous work of preparation in which Bayard has already been engaged, a period of reading and thinking during which he has enlarged and changed his mind. Thus he can say, as he rides through the night, "At least this will be my chance to find out if I am what I think I am or if I just hope; if I am going to do what I have taught myself is right or if I am just going to wish I were" (466).

"I should have been prepared," Bayard thinks, when the Professor enters his room without knocking (463). "Or maybe I was prepared," he goes on to admit, prepared by all his reading to live by the words he quotes to himself out of "the Book," words like "Thou shalt not kill" (466, 467). But the real preparation here has been accomplished by Faulkner himself, as if all the reading and writing done by him up until the making of this story has liberated him to create a character who will not repeat.

Everyone expects Bayard to kill his father's killer. Drusilla, the Colonel's wife, even offers him two pistols. "Take, them, Bayard," she says, "take into your bare hands the fire of heaven" (480–81). As she presses the pistols into Bayard's hands, Drusilla begins to laugh, and then to scream, because she has realized what he now intends to do. And the reader now knows as much as well, especially in light of Bayard's meditation on his father's hands, one conducted only a few pages earlier: "The empty hands still now beneath the invisible stain of what had been (once, surely) needless blood, the hands now appearing clumsy in their very inertness, too clumsy to have performed the fatal actions which forever afterward he must have waked and slept with and maybe was glad to lay down at last—those curious appendages clumsily conceived to begin with and yet with which man has taught himself to do so much, so much more than they were intended to do or could be forgiven for doing" (480). The emphasis on the verb *to do* throughout the story enforces a sense that in choosing *not* to do something, Bayard is nevertheless committing an act. An act, as Faulkner understands it, creates something new, although the new thing being created is, as often as not, a work of revision. In Bayard's case, he chooses to go through the motions of revenge while refusing the satisfactions of actually accomplishing it.

After witnessing the scene with Drusilla and the pistols, Aunt Jenny says to Bayard: "You are not going to try to kill him. All right" (482). Then she adds, "I know you are not afraid" (483). On the following morning, Bayard prepares himself for "going to town." "Are you going now?" Aunt Jenny asks him, and he answers: "Yes. . . . You see, I want to be well thought of" (485). However supported he may be by his radical rethinking of the nature of personal honor, Bayard can still fear apprehension about public shame.

Bayard may be in the act of revising his sense of the South's "simple code," but he still cares about how he is seen by others (487). His concern, however, has nothing to do with simple vanity. The kind of shame regulating Bayard's behavior has best been articulated by Bernard Williams in *Shame and Necessity*. It has to do with the experience of caring about an "internalized other" whose existence creates a necessity to act in certain ways. "The source of the necessity," Williams writes, "is in the agent, an internalized other whose view the agent can respect. Indeed he can identify with this figure, and the respect is to that extent self-respect; but at the same time the figure remains a genuine other, the embodiment of a real social expectation. At the extreme, the sense of necessity lies in the thought that one could not live and look others in the eye if one did certain things." Without his abiding sense of an obligation to the real social expectations surrounding him, Bayard's unique expression of courage would be achieved at too little expense.

Bayard and Ringo ride into town and tie up their horses. "I'm going with you," Ringo says. "'No you aint,' I said." Bayard has already seen the outline of a pistol under Ringo's shirt. "So I walked on." Then George Wyatt is beside him fumbling with another pistol. Like Drusilla, he suddenly stands back and whispers in fury. "Who are you? Is your name Sartoris? By God, if you don't kill him, I'm going to" (486, 487).

Much of Bayard's story has to do with living up to a name. "I was now The Sartoris," Bayard thinks to himself, when Professor Wilkins first brings him the news about his father (465). Is it possible to stay in a family, or in a culture, and to save your name when you have decided to act against a cherished shibboleth? The word comes from a passage in *Absalom, Absalom!* in which Faulkner makes one of his most powerful assaults on "the eggshell shibboleth of caste and color" (115)—the ideology, if you will—for which the South fought the Civil War. In the logic of Faulkner's word choice, the South fought for a mere password, a construction as brittle and empty as the simple code of honor dictating the necessity for a son to avenge his father's murder.

As various persons around Bayard approach him with weapons or advice, he continues to walk. "I went on across the square itself now, in the hot sun, they following though not so close so that I never saw them again until afterward" (488). He sees the sign reading B. J. REDMOND, mounts the stairs, knocks on the office door, and opens it. Redmond is sitting behind his desk. "I walked steadily toward him." Bayard thinks of speaking but does not. "I just walked steadily toward him as the pistol rose from the desk." Bayard sees the slant of the barrel, "and I knew it would miss me." He hears no bullet; the gun is fired a second time. Then Redmond rises and crosses to the wall and takes his hat and blunders along the wall and goes through the door and walks downstairs and on to the station, where he takes the southbound train and leaves Jefferson and is never seen there again.

The scene in Redmond's office might at first appear to be shaping up as a repetition of the tracking down and killing of Grumby in "Vendée." But Bayard's solution to the temptation of revenge is a repetition with a difference. Faulkner visually links the two scenes by way of the "orange" flashes from a pistol that appear against Redmond's "white shirt as they had appeared against Grumby's greasy Confederate coat" (489). In both scenes, the antagonist shoots first. In "Vendée," Grumby misses, and Bayard kills him. In "An Odor of Verbena," Redmond misses too; he intentionally shoots to the side. But the big choice, the determining revision, is that in the second scene, Bayard has chosen to be *unarmed*.

Bayard's is an act of facing. He not only faces his father's killer but faces down the shibboleths governing the world in which he lives. By not killing again as his father had killed, and by not killing for his father's sake, Bayard asserts his originality within the southern codes of honor and his indebtedness to a much older code, one expressed by a proverb he quotes to himself as he rides back to Jefferson on the night after being informed of his father's murder and tries to work out what he intends to do: "Who lives by the sword shall die by it" (465).

In giving Bayard the opportunity to revise, Faulkner fully embraces the positive valence of the *re-*. The doing of something again need not always be a sad matter of repeating destructive patterns. Revision is a doing again as well, and when Faulkner affords a character like the old Bayard of *Sartoris* the freedom to change by giving him a life in *The Unvanquished*, in which a much younger version of the same character is allowed to revise revenge itself, he celebrates the artist's freedom to revisit his work and to think, a second time, about the kinds of endings and beginnings his characters have come to deserve.

SEVEN

Plath and the Rabbit Catcher

"It was a place of force," "The Rabbit Catcher" begins. Sylvia Plath dated the poem May 21, 1962. Written ten months before her death, the poem's opening line reverberates backward through Plath's career as a description of it, and especially of the poems published in the 1965 *Ariel*. Plath's last poems invite—even forcefully compel—"the awful daring of a moment's surrender / Which an age of prudence can never retract." But because Plath died before the *Ariel* poems were gathered into a book and was therefore without say in the matters of inclusion and arrangement, the forces acting in and upon these poems remain to this day a matter of considerable debate. How was it, for instance, that "The Rabbit Catcher," written during the period in which Plath was composing *Ariel* and listed by her on a contents page as the third poem in the volume, did not appear there? Given that Ted Hughes became Plath's literary executor, questions about the editing of her posthumous books inevitably shade into questions about the role played by her marriage in her creative life. The complex history surrounding "The Rabbit Catcher" can help us respond to these questions because, as Jacqueline Rose argues, in the Plath canon "it is also the poem in which the weight of biographical reference on poetic interpretation operates with the greatest force."

"The Rabbit Catcher" opens with a woman being gagged, torn, and blinded:

> It was a place of force—
> The wind gagging my mouth with my own blown hair,
> Tearing off my voice, and the sea
> Blinding me with its lights, the lives of the dead
> Unreeling in it, spreading like oil.

She now tastes something:

> I tasted the malignity of the gorse,
> Its black spikes,
> The extreme unction of its yellow candle-flowers.
> They had an efficiency, a great beauty,
> And were extravagant, like torture.

She feels the lure of the trap:

> There was only one place to get to.
> Simmering, perfumed,
> The paths narrowed into the hollow.
> And the snares almost effaced themselves—
> Zeroes, shutting on nothing,
>
> Set close, like birth pangs.
> The absence of shrieks
> Made a hole in the hot day, a vacancy.
> The glassy light was a clear wall,
> The thickets quiet.

As the two enjambed stanzas end, the speaker becomes an "I" again:

> I felt a still busyness, an intent.
> I felt hands round a tea mug, dull, blunt,
> Ringing the white china.

> How they awaited him, those little deaths!
> They waited like sweethearts. They excited him.

At the end, the "I" introduces a "we":

> And we, too, had a relationship—
> Tight wires between us,
> Pegs too deep to uproot, and a mind like a ring
> Sliding shut on some quick thing,
> The constriction killing me also.

Much of the force of a Plath poem rides on the reach of her comparisons, with "The Rabbit Catcher" operating as an object lesson in the tension between simile and metaphor. Some things are openly like other things: the lives of the dead spread *like* "oil"; flowers are *like* "torture"; the snares are set close, *like* "birth pangs"; the rabbits to be trapped wait *like* "sweethearts"; and the mind is *like* "a ring," sliding shut on a thought rather than an animal. Plath's metaphors, on the other hand, enforce likeness without signaling the comparisons being made: the beauty of the gorse is "extreme unction"; the snares are "Zeroes"; the light is a "wall"; "the relationship" is composed of "wires" and "pegs." But whose mind is being compared to a snare snapping shut—the speaker's or the mind belonging to the other half of the "we"? Either way, it is an entrapping mind. Thinking here feels a lot like killing, as if to pounce upon a similitude is to constrict rather than to enrich meaning.

The central comparison being made in Plath's poem is of someone to a rabbit catcher. For many Plath critics, the tenor of Plath's vehicle can take only one name—that of her husband, the poet Ted Hughes.

Marjorie Perloff advanced such a reading in a 1984 essay. "The failure in vision that characterized the poet's marriage," Perloff writes, "is made quite explicit in . . . 'The Rabbit Catcher,' which seems to be the first poem Plath wrote after she found out about Hughes's infidelity." Perloff refers here to the affair between Ted Hughes and Assia Wevill that began sometime in the summer of 1962. "Here the speaker identifies with the rabbits for whom her husband has set traps. . . . In her fevered vision, the poet confuses the rabbit snare with the male hand, squeezing the white china tea mug and, by extension, the throat of the woman who serves him his tea." The poem makes "explicit reference to the broken marriage."

If anyone can be judged an authority on when the Hughes-Wevill connection began, it may be Frieda Hughes, Plath and Hughes's daughter: "In June 1962, my father began an affair with a woman who had incurred my mother's jealousy a month earlier." The editors of *The Letters of Sylvia Plath* maintain that the affair "was discovered" by Plath on July 9, 1962. But "The Rabbit Catcher" was written by Plath in May 1962, by which date, according to Anne Stevenson, "nothing had happened to harm her marriage." It is also not accurate to refer to "her husband who has set traps"; the snares Plath and Hughes came upon were laid by an actual rabbit catcher. The poem originated in a walk taken by Plath and Hughes in the early spring of 1962. Discovering a line of rabbit snares on a clifftop, Plath tore them up. According to Olwyn Hughes, her brother Ted "was sympathetic to the simple economics of village life and saw nothing admirable in Sylvia's harming the rabbit catcher's livelihood."

In *The Silent Woman,* Janet Malcolm reads "The Rabbit Catcher" as a poem "of a mind stirred by something." She has been quoting from letters written by Ted Hughes to Al Alvarez, letters protesting his having written in *The Savage God* a "scenario" of Plath's suicide that claims to have "solved the mystery of *exactly what happened, and how.*" At a certain point in her reading of one of Hughes's long letters, Malcolm is reminded of "perusing the first draft" of "The Rabbit Catcher" in the Smith College Library's Rare Book Room: "On the first page of the draft and on a part of the second page, the poem is unrecognizable—disconnected lines, most of them scratched out. There is the sense of a mind stirred by something, a mind activated but not able to move forward, like a car spinning its wheels in a rut, unable to get a purchase. Suddenly the car surges forward. 'It was a place of force,' Plath writes, and the rest of the poem follows the well-known first line essentially as we know it." Well aware that the poem is often read as about A Marriage Failing, Malcolm sees it also as one of A Woman Thinking.

"It's all drama," a poet friend of mine once remarked about Plath's work. Plath's figurative language is so forceful, and the emotions called up by it are often so extreme, that her critics have often felt compelled to contain the poetry's energies by treating it, to use one of Hughes's words, as "documentary." But it is also possible to read Plath's poems as an inquest into the dangers and pleasures of figuration itself. There is a responsibility involved for the poet in the making of metaphors, just as critics become responsible for the meanings they read into them. As much as any other Plath poem, "The Rabbit Catcher" has managed to ensnare a complex set of critical responses.

One of the most powerful reactions came from Ted Hughes himself in two poems published over thirty years after Plath's death. The poems appeared in the 1998 *Birthday Letters*. In this series of eighty-eight poems addressed to an unnamed "you," Hughes recalls throwing soil clods at Plath's Cambridge window, their first kiss, fishing for flounder off of Cape Cod, "the morning we set out to drive across America." And he also deals with "Life after Death," with the "two babes," Frieda and Nicholas, "who have turned, in their sleep, / Into orphans," and with the impossible fancy that "the pain could be explained."

As he recalls the day of walking with his wife along the cliff top in the spring of 1962, Hughes even borrows the title of her poem. His "The Rabbit Catcher" contrasts two ways of seeing:

> You saw baby-eyed
> Strangled innocents, I saw sacred
> Ancient custom.

But something more serious than a spontaneous attack on local custom is at work here. "In those snares / You'd caught something," Hughes continues.

> Those terrible, hypersensitive
> Fingers of your verse closed round it and
> Felt it alive. The poems, like smoking entrails
> Came soft into your hands.

Knowing that he has long been identified as the rabbit catcher, Hughes here engages in an act of self-defense even as he embraces and amplifies his wife's original conceit. *She* is the rabbit catcher, his metaphor argues—Plath's hands close around her poems with a violence of their own. The logic of this complex metaphor has been worked out earlier in the volume in a poem called "Astringency."

In the poem, Hughes remembers walking with Plath along the banks of the Charles River. They watch "small, ranked waves / Washing over a nipple of rock." Plath then ventures a comparison for the sight of the ripples moving over the stone: "'Like a lariat,' you said."

Not the similitude but the fact that Plath has allowed herself to voice it—this is what Hughes remembers:

> The sole metaphor that ever escaped you
> In easy speech, in my company—
> Past the censor? Past the night hands?
> Past the snare
> Set in your throat by whom? Who caught all
> That teeming population, every one,
> To hang their tortured eyes and tongues up
> In your poems? To what end? The constrictor
> Not to be tugged out, or snapped.

In these lines, Hughes engages in an act of outright refiguration. Borrowing the word *snare* from Plath's "The Rabbit Catcher," Hughes also returns to the theme of a mind "sliding shut on some quick thing, / The constriction killing me also." Here the constriction is not something Plath suffers but, rather, a work originating out of her own throat, out of her own inner "constrictor." Hughes remembers a poet who held her gift for "metaphor" close, not spending it in casual talk. She reserved its expression for the night work during which her teeming population of figurations could escape all in her throat that would censor it. Given the struggle against constriction her poems must have made in order to issue forth, they may well appear as "tortured" as any animal caught in the rabbit catcher's "snare." Plath is both the prey and the snare, since it is out of her own "entrails" that her subject matter emerges, is caught—recognized as worthy—and then transformed into poetry.

I am arguing, then, that the Rabbit Catcher poems, while they may well record a crisis in the Plath-Hughes marriage, can also be read as poems of the act of the mind, poems uniquely attuned to the peculiar violence of imagination two poets felt required to mobilize as they reached for metaphors adequate to contain the pain of experience. In "The Rabbit Catcher," Plath converted her poetic method into her poem's difficult subject.

The constriction the speaker feels at the end of Plath's poem was not, in any case, according to Anne Stevenson, about her husband's affair with Assia Wevill, which, in May 1962, had not yet begun. Wevill and her husband, David, did, however, visit Plath and Hughes that May. Plath had detected a "current of attraction" between her husband and Assia and had written "The Rabbit Catcher" the day after the visiting couple departed. In the poem, which Stevenson reads as "partly a cry for help, partly one of blind terror, and partly an act of emotional blackmail, the poet almost wills the worst to happen." "Yet nothing had happened to harm her marriage other than her upsurge of jealousy," Stevenson concludes. "The shrill pain of 'The Rabbit Catcher' is true only of her own magnified inner terrors and consequent fury."

In "Creative Partnership: Sources for 'The Rabbit Catcher,'" Diane Middlebrook reads the poem as the register of a turning point in, rather than a betrayal of, what had been a fruitful working arrangement. Beneficiaries of "incessant dialogue," both Plath and Hughes were, by 1962, about to experience "developmental growth spurts that go on occurring in adulthood and reveal aspects of character that have long been in formation but haven't yet asserted themselves." Hughes was about to discover that "his life as an artist henceforth would require his wife's acceptance of the 'nocturnal' impulses to which his deepest inspiration was attached," while "Plath had finally outgrown the usefulness of the D. H. Lawrence figure in her education.... The consequence for each of them, as a married couple and as artists, would be a separation."

In these readings of "The Rabbit Catcher," the poem's display of poetic force coexists with the loss—or gain—of personal force. Either way, as Linda Bundtzen puts it in *The Other "Ariel,"* "Plath's textual body is also hopelessly entangled with that of her husband, Ted Hughes."

Jacqueline Rose found herself very much entangled with the Hughes family during her writing of *The Haunting of Sylvia Plath*. While Hughes and his sister, Olwyn, each "saw a late draft of the text and made copious and detailed comments," it was Rose's "interpretation of one poem in particular" that became "the object of heated and unresolved dispute."

Rose was asked to remove her reading of "The Rabbit Catcher." "When I refused, I was told by Ted Hughes that my analysis would be damaging for Plath's (now adult) children and that speculation of the kind I was seen as engaging in about Sylvia Plath's sexual identity would in some countries be 'grounds for homicide.'" In reviewing the nine pages Rose devotes to the poem, it is difficult to locate the possible grounds for objection except, perhaps, when she recurs to the image of "gagging" in the first stanza. "Most crudely," Rose writes, "the wind blowing, that gagging, calls up the image of oral sex and then immediately turns it around, gagging the speaker with her own blown hair, her hair in her mouth, her tasting the gorse (Whose body—male or female—is this? Who—man or woman—is tasting whom?) even while 'black spikes' and 'candles' work to hold the more obvious distribution of gender roles in their place." The objection appears to be less to the mention of oral sex than to the suggestion that here a woman might be tasting another woman. But any such objection misses Rose's central point—"that such fantasies, such points of uncertainty, are the regular unconscious subtexts—for all of us—of the more straightforward reading, the more obvious narratives of stable identity which we write."

Rose attempts to shift her interpretation of "The Rabbit Catcher" away from any literal reference to the Plath-Hughes marriage and toward a meditation on the role of fantasy in life and in the making of poems. Positioned in a chapter called "No Fantasy without Protest," her reading of the poem makes the case for the workings of structures of dominance and desire, of attraction and repulsion, that are products of "a mind," as named in the poem, operating by way of its own unique and yet also archetypal patterns of thought and feeling. Such a reading allows criticism to move beyond questions of blame. "The logic of blame which seems to attach itself so relentlessly to the story of Sylvia Plath needs once and for all to be left behind," Rose argues, and if blame there is, as her reading of "The Rabbit Catcher" attempts to demonstrate, "blame belongs to no one and to everyone because it is something which is passed around."

Few literary careers have been more subject than Sylvia Plath's to the autobiographical reduction and its eager searching for blame. In *Walking in the Shade,* Doris Lessing makes an impassioned plea on behalf of writers like Plath and herself who have experienced the reduction. "Extraordinary, this need for the autobiographical," Lessing writes. "Why do readers always want to make characters in a novel into autobiography? How often have I seen a face fall into disappointment when I say no, such and such a character was imagined, or composed from half a dozen similar people, or transposed from another setting into this one.... Most readers now want to think, as they read: This is *really* what happened to the author." Lessing's sober conclusion: "What we are seeing is a reluctance of the imagination."

At the outset of *The Haunting of Sylvia Plath,* Jacqueline Rose states her position on the attempt to read a writer's life into her art:

> My focus is on writing—its own process, the way it has been edited, presented and read. This is not a biography. I am never claiming to speak about the life, never attempting to establish the facts about the lived existence of Sylvia Plath. First, because what I am interested in is writing, in what—independently of a writer's more concretely lived reality—it can *do;* secondly, because accounts of her life—and nowhere has this been demonstrated more clearly than in relation to Plath—have to base themselves on a spurious claim to knowledge, they have to arbitrate between competing and often incompatible versions of what took place.
>
> Working on Plath, the thing that has seized my interest most strongly is the circulation of fantasy in her texts, how she writes of psychic processes, the way she lets us—with what strikes me as extraordinary generosity—into her mind.

Writing in the early 1990s, Rose could not have anticipated Plath's good fortune when it came to the production of biographies about her: "Like the child caught up in a hideous divorce case between its parents," Rose concludes, "the writing of the life of Sylvia Plath, both by herself and by those who knew her, forces you—and makes it impossible for you—to take sides." Early biographies, like Stevenson's *Bitter Fame* (1989), did take sides, and even a writer as open to ambiguity as Janet Malcolm was to admit, late in *The Silent Woman* (1994), that "in the Plath-Hughes debate my sympathies are with the Hugheses." The side taking had everything to do with the temptation to read Plath's poems as transcripts rather than fantasies. It will be difficult, however, to be led any longer into such temptation after the 2020 publication of Heather Clark's *Red Comet: The Short Life and Blazing Art of Sylvia Plath.*

Clark begins by taking on the Icarus myth: "Previous biographies have focused on the trajectory of Plath's suicide, as if her every act, from childhood on, was predetermined to bring her closer to a fate she deserved for flying too close to the sun." Clark's patient, deliberate approach to her subject results in a book of over a thousand pages. The length of the text is justified by the extent of the research: Clark had access to all of Plath's surviving letters, to her father's FBI investigation, to the Ted Hughes archive at Emory University, to Harriet Rosenstein's interviews of Plath's contemporaries in the early 1970s—and to much more. The result is a story in which "no blame is apportioned": while this is Clark's initial comment on "The Rabbit Catcher," it can stand as a fair description of Clark's treatment of the various traumas that may have shaped Plath and that some have seen as gathering together to force her toward the promised end—her unique brain chemistry, the early loss of a father, the betrayal by the husband, the failure to find an American publisher for *The Bell Jar*, the 1962 Cuban Missile Crisis, even an extraordinarily cold London winter. Each of these is acknowledged by Clark and given the respect it seems to deserve. Her even-handedness is all the more striking in light of the tone taken in her earlier book, *The Grief of Influence: Sylvia Plath and Ted Hughes*. There she reads *Ariel* as directed at Plath's husband. "In 'Daddy' and 'Lady Lazarus,' Plath had attempted to wrest control of her dialogue with Hughes by mocking his adulation of 'positive violence' and 'impersonating' his femme fatales.... As Plath's depression worsened, her resentment towards her husband and poetic rival, which had earlier fueled her rage, became a measure of defeat."

Because Sylvia Plath died intestate, her husband became her literary executor. The control retained over Plath's work by members of the Hughes family was exercised with considerable force. The intensity of their oversight is testified to by Anne Stevenson in the author's note to *Bitter Fame*, in which she describes the "help from Olwyn Hughes" that has made her book "almost a work of dual authorship," and in the preface to Jacqueline Rose's *The Haunting of Sylvia Plath*: "I have faced what I believe to be an attempt to ... impose limits on what may be said about the writings of Sylvia Plath." Even if one wishes to focus, in Rose's words, on Plath's "writing" rather than on its relation to her "lived reality," it is not possible, given the role he played as her posthumous editor, to exclude Ted Hughes from the story.

On February 11, 1963, after Sylvia Plath's body was transported to University College, Ted Hughes entered his wife's apartment on Fitzroy Road and found a volume of poems "neatly arranged in a black binder on her bedroom desk." This was the typescript of the book that came to be called *Ariel*, although Plath had considered other titles for the collection, including "Daddy," "The Rival," and "A Birthday Present." In discussing the cover of her new book with Hughes, Plath had hoped for a red background with large black print. In the fall of 1963, Hughes entered into negotiations with Faber & Faber, and the British edition of *Ariel*, containing forty poems, was published in the spring of 1965. (Appearing in 1966, the American edition, with a foreword by Robert Lowell, added three more poems: "Lesbos," "Mary's Song," and "The Swarm.") Fifteen thousand copies of *Ariel* had been purchased within ten months of its publication, and the volume went on to sell in the hundreds of thousands.

Most of *Ariel* was composed rather quickly. In mid-December 1962, Plath wrote her mother, Aurelia Plath, to say that "the best poetry critic here thinks my second book, which I've just finished, should win the Pulitzer Prize." She had recently shown her manuscript to her friend, the critic Al Alvarez. All but four of the forty-one poems in the volume projected by Plath had been written in 1962. "Morning Song," with which the sequence was to open, was begun as early as February 1961, while the last poem written for the volume, "Death & Co.," was completed on November 14, 1962.

Over half of the *Ariel* poems were composed in a single month. During October 1962, Plath wrote close to a poem a day—twenty-three in all. "These were the poems that would, as she predicted, make her name," and the list included "Lady Lazarus," "Cut," "Ariel," "The Bee Meeting," and "Daddy." On October 22, as Plath wrote in a letter to a friend, "the muse has come to live, now Ted is gone, and my God! What a sweeter companion."

The black binder found by Hughes contained a typed list of the order in which the poems were to appear. The volume was to begin with "Morning Song" and to end with "Wintering," thus ensuring that its first word would be *Love* and its last word would be *spring*. The list Plath left behind did not, however, succeed in determining the order in which the *Ariel* poems were to appear, nor did every poem on her list make it into the 1965 volume. Hughes's edition of *Ariel* does open with "Morning Song," but it ends with two poems not on Plath's list, "Edge" and "Words." Hughes also decided to include nine poems written by Plath in early 1963. Most important, perhaps, he decided to omit twelve of the poems Plath had listed, including "Thalidomide," "Barren Woman," "A Secret," "The Jailor," and "The Rabbit Catcher."

"The Rabbit Catcher" first found a public on September 16, 1962, when the BBC broadcast a reading of the poem in its New Poetry series. Published in the *Observer* on February 7, 1965, four weeks before the publication of *Ariel*, "The Rabbit Catcher" first appeared between book covers in *Winter Trees* (1971), a volume to which Hughes attached a peculiar note: "The poems in this volume are all out of the batch from which the *Ariel* poems were more or less arbitrarily chosen and they were all composed in the last nine months of Sylvia Plath's life."

"The Rabbit Catcher" appeared again in print in *The Collected Poems* (1981), a volume also edited by Hughes and one attempting "to set everything in as true a chronological order as is possible." In his preface to *The Collected Poems*, Hughes looked back at his editing of *Ariel*:

> The *Ariel* eventually published in 1965 was a somewhat different volume from the one she had planned. It incorporated most of the dozen or so poems she had gone on to write in 1963, though she herself, recognizing the different inspiration of these new pieces, regarded them as the beginnings of a third book. It omitted some of the more personally aggressive poems from 1962, and might have omitted one or two more if she had not already published them herself in magazines—so that by 1965 they were widely known. The collection that appeared was my eventual compromise between publishing a large bulk of her work—including much of the post-*Colossus* but pre-*Ariel* verse—and introducing her late work more cautiously, printing perhaps only twenty poems to begin with.

Having admitted as much, Hughes did decide to include in the notes to *The Collected Poems* an entry titled "The 'Ariel' Poems," which came with the following headnote: "Sylvia Plath's own prepared collection of poems, titled *Ariel*, was ordered as follows." He then proceeded to reproduce, it now appearing for the first time in print, Plath's typed list.

"In 1981 my father published my mother's *Collected Poems*," Frieda Hughes was later to write, "and included in the Notes the contents list of her *Ariel* manuscript. This inclusion brought my father's arrangement under public scrutiny and he was much criticized for not publishing *Ariel* as my mother had left it, though the extracted poems were included in the *Collected Poems* for all to see." It is at the beginning and the end of *Ariel* that Hughes's revisions of Plath's list have the most force.

The first five poems in the 1965 *Ariel* are listed here alongside the first five poems on Plath's typed list:

"Morning Song"	"Morning Song"
"The Couriers"	"The Couriers"
"Sheep in Fog"	"The Rabbit Catcher"
"The Applicant"	"Thalidomide"
"Lady Lazarus"	"The Applicant"

Does poem order much matter here? Given that "The Rabbit Catcher" and "Thalidomide" were simply cut from the 1965 version, poem inclusion seems the more vital matter. "Sheep in Fog," on the other hand, was excluded from Plath's list because it had been begun in early December and therefore fell beyond the cutoff date for inclusion she had established. Linda Bundtzen also speculates that for Hughes the positioning of "Sheep in Fog" as poem number 3 in the 1965 *Ariel* "replaces the attack on him in 'The Rabbit Catcher.'" About his choice, Hughes appears to have had second thoughts. In 1988, Hughes gave a lecture on "The Evolution of 'Sheep in Fog'" in which, after surveying the surviving drafts of the poem, he surmised that "realizing perhaps . . . that the mood and 'story' of the body of the poem contradicts the generally masterful programme of *Ariel*," Plath "keeps the poem out of that collection."

Here are the last five poems in the 1965 *Ariel* and the last five poems on Plath's typed list:

| "Poppies in July" | "The Bee Meeting" |
| "Kindness" | "The Arrival of the Bee Box" |

"Contusion"   "Stings"
"Edge"   "(The Swarm)"
"Words"   "Wintering"

Here the ordering of poems seems a more serious matter. The "Bee Poems" that Plath has imagined as an ending suite have been moved by Hughes toward the middle of the volume and are replaced by four poems written in February 1963. "Poppies in July," a poem written in July 1962, appears nowhere on Plath's typed list.

"Edge" is the strongest poem in Hughes's final five, and it is linked to "Wintering" by more than an act of replacement. Plath began writing "Edge" on February 5, 1963, and composed the poem on the reverse side of a copy of "Wintering." From the start, then, "Edge" acted as a kind of alternative ending poem. "The question must remain," Bundtzen writes, "whether Plath's decision to create definite closure in 'Edge,' where there was only an open-ended oracle and unanswered riddle in 'Wintering,' also authorizes Ted Hughes's decision to alter the ending" of *Ariel*. "Wintering" ends with the speaker's questioning whether "the hive" will survive

> To enter another year?
> What will they taste of, the Christmas roses?
> The bees are flying. They taste the spring.

"Edge" begins with

> The woman is perfected.
> Her dead
>
> Body wears the smile of accomplishment,
> The illusion of a Greek necessity
>
> Flows in the scrolls of her toga,
> Her bare
>
> Feet seem to be saying:
> We have come so far, it is over.

A question about surviving for another year in the one poem is answered, in its replacement, with "it is over."

The most incisive response to Hughes's editings came from Marjorie Perloff in her 1984 article "The Two *Ariels:* The (Re)Making of the Sylvia Plath Canon." The two *Ariels* "have a plot," Perloff argued, "but the two plots are so different that we cannot help but wonder what it means to reconstruct a poetic sequence after the fact." Perloff read the newly revealed sequence as one that "begins with the birth of Frieda (hence the inclusion of the earlier poem 'Morning Song') and moves through the despair Plath evidently experienced when she learned, in April 1962, that Hughes was having an affair with another woman, to the period of rage and misogyny that followed upon his actual desertion in mid-September . . . and then to a ritual death and a move toward rebirth, as chronicled in what many critics consider to be Plath's finest poems, the Bee sequence." In the 1965 *Ariel,* "on the other hand, the poems that make it only too clear that Hughes's desertion was the immediate cause of Plath's depression are expunged; instead, the volume now culminates in ten death poems, poems written, as it were, from beyond rage, by someone who no longer blames anyone for her condition and reconciles herself to death."

According to one's predilections, it is possible to discern any number of plots in a book of forty or more poems. While the question of whether a book of poems is a whole greater than the sum of its parts is hardly a settled one, it is the case that the words within a single poem are held together by the strong forces of form and theme and can therefore inspire such terms as *verbal icon* or *autotelic.* But the poems in a volume like *Ariel,* regardless of whether they have been sequenced by an author or by an editor, are more likely to be held together by weak forces and usually find themselves brought together and placed in a book because they have been written during a span of time after which a decision is made to publish them.

Exceptions to the claim just made do exist, and a number of scholars have made a study of what Earl Miner calls "integrated collections." Ben Jonson was one of the first English poets to arrange his poems in volumes with suggestive umbrella titles such as *Epigrammes, The Forrest,* and *Underwood.* In *The Forrest,* it is possible to discern a kind of alternating rhythm between rejection and affirmation. Beginning with a statement of negation ("Why I Write Not of Love"), Jonson moves to praise of the good place ("To

Penshurst"), celebration of the moral hero (Wroth), a second negation, this time addressed "To the World," a swerve toward the subjects negated ("To Celia"), a reason given for the rejection of both women and the world ("That Women Are but Men's Shadows" and "To Sickness"), a series of encomiums, with a final resting on one last turning away in "To Heaven."

The argument for an integrated collection is countered, however, by Jonson himself in his lead poem to *Under-wood*. In "To the Reader," Jonson confesses to having fallen for a unifying conceit: his poems may be mere "Timber-trees, promiscuously growing," but he has taken "leave" to style these "workes of divers nature" as "A *Wood*, or *Forrest*," and "so am bold to entitle / these lesser Poems, of later growth, by / this of *Under-wood*." In so titling his collections, Jonson admits to having imposed upon poems of diverse nature the seductive fiction of growth.

In a 1971 response to an *Observer* review by Alvarez, Hughes looked back on the arranging and cutting of *Ariel*. "In the States," Hughes remembers, even the most vocal of Plath's supporters at his publishers "felt the full collection might provoke some outraged backlash. This introduced new hesitancies because it touched on my own uncertainties." Acting then out of "concern for certain people," Hughes is now left, in 1971, with a mixture of questions but no strong regrets:

> Was the whole book simply unacceptable, did it overdo itself? I was anxious that the collection should not falter in any way, and that the work should be recognized. . . . I had already started rearranging the collection, cutting out some pieces that looked as if they might let in some facile attacker, cutting out one or two of the more openly vicious ones, and a couple of others that I thought might conceivably seem repetitive in tone and form. . . . I would have cut out "Daddy" if I'd been in time (there are quite a few things more important than giving the world great poems). I would have cut out others if I'd thought they would ever be decoded.

This open letter, published in England's oldest Sunday newspaper, is strikingly undefensive in tone. Hughes simply explains his thinking. He even admits to having thought of cutting a poem as admired as "Daddy." Hughes's use of the word *decoded* also foretells the many ways in which Plath's poems would be subjected to a hermeneutics of suspicion.

In her 1984 article, Perloff wrote that "perhaps Sylvia Plath's publishers will eventually give us the original *Ariel*. But it is not likely, given the publication of *The Collected Poems*, which now becomes our definitive text."

Twenty years later, Frieda Hughes, Plath's daughter, did give us the original *Ariel*. In 2004, HarperCollins published *Ariel: The Restored Edition*. In her foreword, Frieda Hughes announced an act of recovery: "This edition of *Ariel* by my mother, Sylvia Plath, exactly follows the arrangement of her last manuscript as she left it." For the first time, the common reader, rather than a handful of literary scholars, was given access to Plath's typed list of poems as well as to a facsimile of Plath's typescript. The *Ariel* sequence now contained forty poems.

Even the "restored" *Ariel* sequence remains, however, open to question. In an article titled "Unstable Manuscripts: The Indeterminacy of the Plath Canon," Tracy Brain points out that in the facsimile of Plath's typed list provided in the Frieda Hughes edition, there is a handwritten notation where "Death & Co." is inserted between "Ariel" and "Magi." Other "last-minute changes of mind are visible" in the manuscripts of *Ariel*, Brain argues, and therefore any published version of the book "should only be regarded as Plath's latest draft." Brain's article addresses the scholarly tendency "to narrativize the circumstances surrounding a given text so that it legitimates what we want to do with it or say about it." In the case of *Ariel*, Brain concludes, "the more we try to establish the 'right' Plath text, the more we find that it eludes us."

One of the best things ever written about *Ariel*, "Sylvia Plath and Her Journals," appeared in *Grand Street* in 1982. (A shorter version of the piece appeared earlier in the year as the foreword to *The Journals of Sylvia Plath*.) "Few poets have disclosed in any way the birth circumstances of their poetic gift," the author writes, but "Sylvia Plath's poetry, like a species on its own, exists in little else but the revelation of that birth and purpose. . . . Her poetry is the biology of Ariel, the ontology of Ariel—the story of Ariel's imprisonment in the pine, before Prospero opened it." And it is "in the last entries of this surviving bulk of her journal," pages written as Plath was finishing up *Colossus*, "where the opening of the pine took place and was recorded."

"Her writing here (as in her poems)," the essay continues, "simplifies itself in baring itself to what hurts her." Because what Plath "did have, clearly, was character—and passionate character at that. One sees where the language of *Ariel* got its temper—that unique blend of courage and vulnerability." In each poem, "the terror is encountered head on, and the angel is mastered and brought to terms. . . . And indeed it was blazingly clear that she had come through, in Lawrence's sense, and that she was triumphant. The impression of growth and new large strength in her personality was striking. The book lay completed, the poems carefully ordered."

Who among us would not enjoy being written about with such insight and such force? The reader may approach such eloquent claims with skepticism, however, given the confessions made by the author of them in an opening paragraph: "Sylvia Plath's journals exist as an assortment of notebooks and bunches of loose sheets, and the selection just published here contains about a third of the whole bulk. Two other notebooks survived for a while after her death. They continued from where the surviving record breaks off in late 1959 and covered the last three years of her life. The second of these two books her husband destroyed, because he did not want her children to have to read it (in those days he regarded forgetfulness as an essential part of survival). The earlier one disappeared more recently (and may, presumably, still turn up)."

"Her husband," the author writes, and throughout the essay the voice remains in the third person. But the author of the piece is none other than that husband himself, as announced in the two words appearing below the essay's title: *Ted Hughes*. In the foreword to Plath's journals, a severely abridged version of his essay, Hughes did write in the first person, ending its few pages with "I destroyed."

Only a year after the publication of *The Collected Poems*, Hughes has once again chosen to admit that in an attempt to save Plath's work, he has also felt compelled to destroy it. By the early 1980s, Hughes appears to have been visited by an almost masochistic desire to expose his complicated dealings with Plath's literary remains. He has even gone so far as to remind readers that the book lying completed on Plath's desk at the time of her death had been "carefully ordered."

Her husband destroyed: it was as a result of his own testimony that the person most responsible for the ongoing publication of Sylvia Plath's writings came to be seen as also working to suppress them. But this was not always the case. In summarizing the outpouring of attention generated by the appearance of the 1965 *Ariel,* Perloff reminds us that "no one doubted that *Ariel* was indeed *Ariel;* no one, that is, raised the issue of whether or not Plath's book, as published by Faber & Faber in London and Harper & Row in New York, reflected the poet's own stated wishes." By the time the world became aware of the existence of those wishes, Plath's fame had been established, and it was a fame resting largely on a volume shepherded into print by her husband. As Elaine Feinstein writes in her biography of Hughes, Plath's "worldwide fame was entirely posthumous."

It was not only after her death that Hughes worked on behalf of Plath's poetry. In *The Other "Ariel,"* Linda Bundtzen provides many examples of the support given. During her work in the Smith College archive, for instance, Bundtzen found "lists of poem subjects assigned by Hughes," with "Plath's annotations or dots by many of them, indicating that she had tried" to act on Hughes's suggestions. Bundtzen reads Hughes's behavior more as interference than assistance and cites one poem in particular in support of her interpretation: "If 'The Rabbit Catcher' is about marriage, it is also about the way marriage enthralls a woman's creativity. In the first draft of this poem, Plath's efforts to disenthrall herself from marital constraints are part of the writing process. Hughes, was, after all, more than a husband; he was also her poetic mentor. Their marriage was a collaboration of two writers, but an unequal one, in which Hughes's early success ensured his dominant position."

Hughes can only be understood as "dominant" over Plath in that he survived her. During the seven years of their marriage, it was just as possible to see Plath as the dominant figure. While *The Savage God,* published in 1971, quickly became, in the words of Janet Malcolm, the "foundation text of the Plath legend," Alvarez also managed to convey that "the balance of power" had, by the summer of 1962, "shifted for the time being to her." One wonders whether a unique kind of power had not always resided with Plath. She had begun publishing at the age of eight; Hughes did not see his first poem in print until 1956, when he was twenty-six. Friend Lucas Meyers remembered that "it was Sylvia who got Ted's first book, *The Hawk in the Rain,* to the Harper contest, which it won, establishing him." Clark reports that Plath "helped him choose the final poems for *The Hawk in the Rain,* and would limit his revisions for the Faber edition." Whatever may have happened between Plath and Hughes, she never lost her belief in him as a poet. On the day she wrote "Daddy," October 12, 1962, Plath told a friend about her continuing admiration for her husband's work: "The one thing I retain is love for & admiration of his writing, I know he is a genius, and for a genius there are no bonds & no bounds. I feel I did discover him, worked to free him for writing for six years."

"Despite its bitter end," Heather Clark writes,

> Plath and Hughes's experimental, creative marriage was progressive for its time. In the mid-forties, most women abandoned professional aspirations when they married. Yet Hughes prodded Plath, sometimes to exhaustion, to become a better poet. He created exercises for her, made elaborate charts, hypnotized her, exhorted her to concentrate—all to access the inner depths of consciousness where he thought the raw poetic material was buried. Plath, too, constantly prodded Hughes to be more productive. He published very little at Cambridge University before he met Plath; after graduation he drifted, worked odd jobs, and hardly qualified as a minor poet. Plath changed that. She acted as his agent, sending out his manuscripts and entering contests for him. Within a year of their meeting, he was on his way to becoming the most famous young poet in England. He later acknowledged that he owed his literary career to her. She would have gone on writing and publishing if they had never met; he might not have. Without Plath's ambition at his back, as he wrote in a late poem, "I'd be fishing off a rock / In Western Australia."

"We work and walk about," Hughes wrote to his brother in May 1957, "and repair each other's writings."

By their fruits ye shall know them. In the years Plath and Hughes spent together, remarkable books were written or published: *The Colossus and Other Poems* (1960), *The Bell Jar* (1963), *Ariel* (1965), *Winter Trees* (1971), *Crossing the Water* (1971), *Johnny Panic and the Bible of Dreams* (1977), *The Journals of Sylvia Plath* (1982), *The Hawk in the Rain* (1957), *Lupercal* (1960), *Recklings* (1966), *Wodwo* (1967), children's books, and a host of plays for stage and radio. However the Plath-Hughes marriage may have ended, it was experienced by both poets as a boon to their creativity. "By their fruits ye shall know them" appears in a chapter in the New Testament that opens with the admonition "Judge not, that ye be not judged."

Writing after the appearance of *The Collected Poems,* Helen Vendler said something remarkable: "The one thing that recommends Plath to us most strongly now is her ability to change her mind when she saw a new truth." Plath "changed her mind, when it was necessary, in a violent way," Vendler continues, "repudiating her previous position with all the force of her daunting energy. She had no Keatsian capacity for maintaining two contrary truths at once." Plath's poetry does invite readers into a place of force, and the wind blowing through it can be unbalancing. As new truths about Plath continue to surface, however, and as readers are thereby encouraged to change their minds about the force and meaning of her work, we can perhaps learn from Plath's example to muster on her behalf a measure of negative capability. When it comes to understanding the poetic collaboration she enjoyed with her husband, one by now overlaid with six decades of presuppositions, perhaps the most that can be hoped for, in the words of Frieda Hughes, is to contribute to the work of "restoring the balance."

EIGHT

"Have Sure Tried"
HEMINGWAY'S UNFALTERING CAREER

"Are there any more books to be published?" Fidel Castro asked the question while visiting the Finca Vigía at Mary Hemingway's invitation in the summer of 1961. After her husband's suicide in July, Mary had returned to the Hemingway home in Cuba to retrieve private effects and, especially, her husband's surviving manuscripts. During the visit, Mary showed Castro some "hand-corrected galley proofs." "I'm told there are unfinished manuscripts," he remarked, "and that you will bring them out if there are instructions to that effect."

Castro's question was prophetic. By the time he asked it, Mary and her friend Valerie Hemingway had recovered the manuscript of *The Garden of Eden,* more than a thousand pages of what would become *Islands in the Stream,* and a "rambling African novel/diary," Valerie Hemingway remembers, "that would be published as *True at First Light* in 1999." *A Moveable Feast* might have filled out the record of the yet-unpublished books Mary found in the Finca and in a bank vault in Havana but for the fact that Hemingway had brought the manuscript to the United States a year earlier. As Valerie Hemingway goes on to relate, during the following decades each of these works was "reconstructed by editors especially chosen to shape the working drafts into coherent, saleable novels of reasonable length."

And yet—because Ernest Hemingway published only one novel, a novella, some long articles in *Life* magazine, and a handful of short stories after his return from the battlefields of France in 1945, he has often been viewed as a writer suffering a late-life decline, a "faltering career," as Robert E. Fleming puts it. Yet the modest record of publication in the postwar years does not tell the whole story. The major projects embarked upon after 1945 were not two but seven and are listed here in their order of publication:

1950 *Across the River and into the Trees*
1952 *The Old Man and the Sea*
1964 *A Moveable Feast*, edited by Mary Hemingway and Harry Brague (reedited in 2009 as *"A Moveable Feast": The Restored Edition*, by Seán Hemingway)
1970 *Islands in the Stream*, edited by Mary Hemingway, Charles Scribner Jr., and Carlos Baker
1985 *The Dangerous Summer*, edited by Michael Pietsch
1986 *The Garden of Eden*, edited by Tom Jenks
1999 *True at First Light*, edited by Patrick Hemingway (reedited in 2005 as *Under Kilimanjaro*, by Robert W. Lewis and Robert E. Fleming)

This chronology obscures as much as it reveals: while the sequence of books appeared in print across a span of more than fifty years, the several works were generated during the last fifteen years of Hemingway's life. In looking back on this period of Hemingway's career, Malcolm Cowley can therefore observe that "one is astonished to learn how much patient work he accomplished."

Except for the first two titles on the list, however, Hemingway himself did not consider the other projects finished. The act of finishing called "publication" was a posthumous fate, an intervention accomplished by the various editors listed here. Their editions were quarried out of the vast trove of manuscripts, letters, photographs, and all sorts of memorabilia that Mary Hemingway donated to the John F. Kennedy Library in 1968. In bringing forward new Hemingway volumes, these editors have sometimes managed to shape works of great beauty and power.

Hemingway's late-life work—and this is especially true of the posthumously published books—accomplishes something impressive indeed: a prolonged act of confession and Last Judgment. The confessions made and the self-judgments rendered, often in displaced ways, are of Hemingway's performance as a husband and a father. As early as the 1936 *Green Hills of Africa*, he had come to understand that he had often not acted "as a good man should" (64).

At the heart of the self-judgment being rendered in the writing of the postwar years is Hemingway's recognition of a pattern of replacement. Hadley, Pauline, Martha, Mary—it is one thing to leave one woman and then to find another partner, but in Hemingway's case, the replacing of one wife always began before the prior marriage had ended. He came to see this as a recurring process. As he wrote in a passage found in the restored edition of *A Moveable Feast*, "If you deceive and lie with one person against another you will eventually do it again" (219). Hemingway poses the question looming over the late career, and therefore over his final assessment of whether or not he had been a good man, in a sentence written in the 1950s and found in *Under Kilimanjaro*: "I wondered about how many true loves to which you were faithful, until you were unfaithful, a man could have" (382).

The issue of keeping faith is handled with a light touch in *True at First Light*. Hemingway began working on this account of his second safari late in 1954, and Patrick Hemingway produced an edition of his father's "African Journal" in 1999. Near the end of the resulting narrative, Hemingway describes himself meditating on his elected sequence of wives. As the man everyone calls Papa lies alone in his tent—his "one legal wife," Miss Mary, is away in Nairobi—he believes he has acquired a new "religion" so that "I could decide what was a sin and what was not" (281). His thoughts recur to Miss Pauline, the first replacement wife, now two years dead, and to "another wife," Martha Gellhorn, who replaced Pauline but who has "been reclassified so that she did not hold that rank nor category." As the African Imaginary into which Hemingway believes he has entered comes to a climax, he thinks that because of his obvious "fortunes," the African elders assume "I must have at least twelve" wives, including Miss Marlene Dietrich, who "was supposed to be working for me in a small amusement Shamba I owned called Las Vegas."

In passages like this, Hemingway deploys hyperbole to finesse the question of how "a good husband" ought to behave (39). And yet he has also exposed himself to critique by deciding to reemploy, in 1954, the man who twenty years earlier had acted as the white hunter on Hemingway's first African safari. To seek out Philip Percival as a guide a second time involved Hemingway in a long-standing, somewhat invidious comparison, given that in *Green Hills of Africa*, Percival serves as Pauline's "ideal": "brave, gentle, comic, never losing his temper, never bragging, never complaining except in a joke, tolerant, understanding, intelligent, drinking a little too much as a good man should, and, to her eyes, very handsome" (64). Against such a paragon, no one could compete; in May 1935, when the first chapters of *Green Hills* began to be serialized in *Scribner's Magazine,* Hemingway offered a list of "The People in the Book," one including "Mr. Hemingway—A braggart" (259). Not only does he represent himself in *Green Hills* as shooting badly throughout the safari and envying his companions' trophies, but he describes this Mr. Hemingway as breaking into a "highly-righteous" diatribe about Pauline's too-tight boots or becoming "irritable, righteous, pompous" about her difficulties with a camera shutter (94, 120). In his first safari book, Hemingway began the work of taking a good hard look at himself, an effort that only intensified in the postwar years.

It may seem in *True at First Light* as if Hemingway has returned to Africa to learn more about the hunt, but actually the deepest study proposed is the "incalculable casualties of marriage" (92). Yet an effort necessarily involving self-judgment never really gets off the ground. Instead, the pleasures and difficulties of living with one woman take a backseat to the narrator's belief that he can be married to two women at once. He fantasizes a marriage to Debba, a young African woman, and it appears he does manage to sleep with her while Miss Mary is away in Nairobi. Hemingway's fourth wife treats the infatuation with a restrained tolerance; there is no reckoning involved. Papa seems somewhat dazed by his good luck. "Here I was with a wife that I loved and who loved me and tolerated my errors and referred to this girl as my fiancée, tolerating because I was in some ways a good husband and for other reasons of generosity and kindness and detachment and wanting me to know more about this country than I had any right to know" (39).

The pattern of replacement that this episode was to underscore, however, still needed further scrutiny. When Hemingway stopped work on his African book in early 1956, the manuscript had reached a length of 843 pages. In the following year, he began work on both *The Garden of Eden* and *A Moveable Feast.*

The early lies and deceptions played out with Hadley and Pauline lie at the heart of the self-indictment Hemingway pursues in these valedictory works. The adventure of loving two women, handled so gingerly in *First Light*, grows more complex in *The Garden of Eden* and becomes the central tragedy acknowledged in *A Moveable Feast*. The only way out of the dilemma he faced in his mid-twenties was to replace one woman with another: Hemingway's divorce from Hadley became final on April 14, 1927, and he married Pauline Pfeiffer not four weeks after that. As Hemingway writes in the closing paragraphs of the 1964 edition of his Paris memoir: "The husband has two attractive girls around when he has finished work. One is new and strange and if he has bad luck he gets to love them both" (210).

The phrase *bad luck* cloaks an admission in a disavowal, casting Hemingway's act of betrayal as an event that has somehow merely befallen him. In offering the reader a number of previously unpublished passages, the 2009 restored edition of *A Moveable Feast* creates a far different picture. These are passages in which Hemingway, in looking back on his treatment of Hadley and Pauline, confesses to a "terrible remorse" (219). This feeling builds to a climax in the final chapter of the 1964 version of the memoir. It is remorse that overcomes Hemingway as he returns to Shruns after being with Pauline in Paris and sees Hadley "standing by the tracks as the train came in" (210). When it comes to the deepest emotion compelling Hemingway's last judgment, however, *First Light* appears to be a missed chance at acknowledgment, especially given the fact that, in Africa, Hemingway's "lawful wedded wife" actively participates in his fantasy of plural marriage (89). The tone of "comic irony" that Rose Marie Burwell discerns throughout *First Light* preempts any serious reflection on the serious issues toward which the narrative gestures. But the book does succeed in drawing attention toward a keyword in the Hemingway lexicon—*bed*—a word given pride of place in the book's final chapter.

As the chapter opens, Miss Mary has returned from her trip away: "We were in bed and it was quite cold and I lay curled against the tent side of the cot and it was lovely under the sheet and the blankets." Husband and wife listen to the hyenas near the tent and to the lion roaring off to the north:

> "I wish we did not have to ever leave Africa," Mary said.
> "I'd like never to leave here."
> "Bed?" (310)

Mary Hemingway's one-word answer to her husband has the evocative power of a refrain. It is sounded in crucial moments in the books Hemingway published while he was alive, and it continues to act as a vehicle of thought and feeling in the posthumously published books as well. For Hemingway, the word *bed* is a synecdoche for many things: home, marriage, commitment. It is at once a destination and a destiny, a shared place his men want to get back to and never leave, and a place, once had, as Hemingway can see all too well, as he looked back, that will be abandoned.

Hemingway's "habit of picturing . . . bedroom scenes," as Jake Barnes calls them (381), begins early on and surfaces with special poignancy in the late career. Hemingway's love for the word *bed* and all that can happen there may well go back to "Western Wind," which exemplifies his idea of poetry, as Hemingway wrote to Ernest Walsh, before including the following version of the poem in a 1926 letter:

> O western wind, when wilt thou blow
> That the small rain down can rain?
> Christ, that my love were in my arms
> And I in my bed again!

In four lines, the poem describes the Hemingway predicament. Not to have is the beginning of desire—obvious enough. But the corollary is that *to have is the end of desire.*

Hemingway alludes to "Western Wind" both in *A Farewell to Arms* and in *Islands in the Stream*. Frederic Henry engages in an extended riff on the poem during the retreat from Caporetto: "If there were no war we would probably all be in bed. In bed I lay me down my head. Bed and board. Stiff as a board in bed. Catherine was in bed now between two sheets. . . . Maybe she was lying thinking about me. Blow, blow, ye western wind. Well, it blew and it wasn't the small rain but the big rain down that rained. . . . Christ, that my love were in my arms and I in my bed again. That my love Catherine. That my sweet Catherine down might rain. Blow her again to me" (171–72). Here, during the retreat, Frederic finds himself wanting Catherine Barkley because he is separated from her. But when their romance begins and he has her in his arms, Frederic feels distanced from desire, "seeing it all ahead like moves in a chess game" (22).

The game metaphor pervades their subsequent meetings; then, when Helen Ferguson tells him that Catherine "couldn't see you this evening," Frederic feels quite differently. "I had treated seeing Catherine very lightly, . . . but when I could not see her there I was feeling lonely and hollow" (35). Now, not having her, Frederic wants the wind to blow Catherine back. "God knows I had not wanted to fall in love with her," Frederic says to himself, after being reunited with Catherine in Milan (81). After a series of separations and reunions, he has fallen for her nevertheless:

> She came in the room and over to the bed.
> "Hello, darling," she said. She looked fresh and young and very beautiful. I thought I had never seen any one so beautiful.
> "Hello," I said. When I saw her I was in love with her. (80)

Given that a good man ought to provide a woman with a warm and comfortable bed, it is remarkable that so many of Hemingway's men fail to do so. Frederic's worst failure in this regard occurs on the last night he and Catherine spend together before he returns to the front at Gorizia. After kissing her in the street, he says, "Let's go some place" (131). They end up in a hotel room resembling a bordello, with many mirrors and red plush. Catherine does not look happy.

In *Across the River and into the Trees,* Colonel Cantwell and Renata also find themselves without a suitable room and are required to make love in a gondola. The pattern begins in "Up in Michigan," a story written in 1922 and one Hemingway had hoped to place at the opening of *In Our Time.* Liz Coates is forced to experience her initiation into sex with none of the comforts of a bed: "The hemlock planks of the dock were hard and splintery and cold and Jim was heavy on her and he had hurt her" (128). Throughout Hemingway's career, bed remains the longed-for but all too often elusive "good place" (Trogdon 270). This phrase first appears in "Big Two-Hearted River" and is repeated in *The Sun Also Rises, A Farewell to Arms,* and *Islands in the Stream.*

A man can also love "too many beds," a problem approached obliquely in *The Old Man and the Sea.* Santiago appears to be one of Hemingway's solitaries, a man profoundly alone. Yet one of the novella's moving passages acts out a drama of fidelity that evokes, by counterexample, the hidden history of Santiago's married life. Well before he catches his giant fish, Santiago recalls the day he hooked a female marlin. She makes her stricken attempts to escape, and "all the time the male had stayed with her" (49). The verb *stayed* gets repeated three times in the ensuing description: "He had stayed so close the old man was afraid he would cut the line with his tail . . . the male fish had stayed by the boat. . . . He was beautiful, the old man remembered, and he had stayed" (50).

Santiago has not stayed with his wife. She is mentioned only once, when Santiago admits to himself that looking at her photograph makes him lonely, so he keeps it hidden on a shelf under a clean shirt. Unlike the male marlin who stays with his female partner, Santiago has left his wife's bed. "Bed is my friend," he thinks to himself, as he nears the harbor (120). In the Kennedy Library manuscript, Hemingway had written four more sentences after this one, sentences he then crossed out: "Why did I never love bed when I had her? You did, he thought. But then you loved too many beds. But beds were all the same and the sea is a greater whore than all."

Manuscript evidence suggests, then, that Hemingway considered and rejected the idea that *The Old Man and the Sea* was to allow for the surfacing of the themes of Santiago's promiscuity or of marriage and its betrayals. Those themes again surface in *Islands in the Stream* but only after the novel's powerful opening movement, in which Hemingway attempts his most extended treatment of the pleasures and dangers of fatherhood.

When we first meet painter Thomas Hudson in *Islands in the Stream*, he is "still in love with the first woman he had been in love with" (14). He has, nevertheless, married for a third time. In part 2 of the novel—the year is 1943—Hudson's first wife suddenly turns up while he is drinking in a bar in Havana. They kiss as soon as they meet. "I want a big, big bed," she tells him (304). After they make love, she asks him about his third wife. "Why did you marry her, Tom?" He replies, "Because you were in love," and thus unavailable (308). Serial marriage is here revealed to be a drama of replacement in which Hudson continues to fail at the role of "the Faithful Husband" (305), a failure reenacted in this very scene.

Here the theme of marriage and its betrayals is demoted, however, behind Hemingway's attempt to explore the pleasures and dangers of fathering. As the novel opens, Thomas Hudson's third wife is away, somewhere in the Pacific, and Hudson and his writer friend Roger Davis are waiting for

Hudson's sons to arrive for their annual summer visit to Bimini. Hudson has three boys: Young Tom is his son by his first wife, David and Andrew are the sons of his second.

In giving his main character three male children, Hemingway set up a strong parallel with his own life. One son, John Hadley Nicanor, was born to Hadley, while two sons, Patrick and Gregory, were born to Pauline. Hadley ended up raising Hemingway's oldest son, and Patrick and Gregory were often off with a nanny while Pauline traveled with her husband. Over the years, Hemingway spent much of his time away from his sons, although when at home in Key West or Havana or out in Montana in the fall, he did indulge them with long and exciting vacations. "It will be wonderful to have them," Roger says to Thomas Hudson, soon before the boys arrive (55). And he seems to be right, given the Edenic conditions for swimming, for fishing, for listening to their father's stories about Paris, for savoring cook Eddy's potato salad. It is a fantasy of men without women leading a full and happy life.

Reynolds Price judges part 1 of the novel Hemingway's "finest sustained fiction" and detects in it a turn toward human relations that Hemingway had "previously avoided—parental devotion, filial return." Yet in making his claim, Price may well have overlooked the 1933 "Fathers and Sons." As is often the case in the postwar writing, in the "Bimini" section of *Islands in the Stream*, Hemingway seizes the opportunity to revisit an earlier publication to expand upon its concerns—in this case, how a man might become a good father.

"Fathers and Sons" opens with Nick Adams driving through country not his own but still "good to drive through and to see" and remembering his father as sound on fishing and shooting as he was "unsound on sex" (488, 490). The two pieces of "direct sexual knowledge" passed along to Nick from his father were about buggery and mashing, although each term goes unexplained except for mashing being described as "one of the most heinous of crimes" (491). Nick still loves to hunt and fish and registers his gratitude to his father "for bringing him to know it"; as "for the other, that his father was not sound about, all the equipment you will ever have is provided and each man learns all there is for him to know about it without advice" (490).

Nick still carries with him the originating trauma at the center of "Indian Camp," where his father exposed him to a premature initiation into the facts of life. In this uncanny, early short story, a preadolescent Nick is required to be present at a bloody, noisy birth and at a bloody, strangely quiet death. That is one way to educate a child: to throw him into things. This failed scene of instruction, located at the beginning of Hemingway's first full-length book, is meant to serve as a counterexample. Concerned always with how to do something well, Hemingway also understands that any transmission of direct knowledge is a matter of timing and tact. Otherwise, the lesson will be botched.

And this is why, in "Fathers and Sons," as Nick drives on and remembers back, he does not directly answer the voice that suddenly interrupts his reverie. "What was it like, Papa, when you were a little boy and used to hunt with the Indians?" (497). It is Nick's son, riding next to him in the car. Nick is "startled" by the question; "he had felt quite alone but this boy had been with him." Given the fact that no mention of "this boy" has previously been made in the story, the reader may be startled as well.

One reason Nick proceeds to answer his son's questions only indirectly is because he has been remembering having sex with Trudy Bolton in the woods. Taking his own advice about giving advice, Nick does not share any of these memories with the boy. But by way of Nick's internal monologue, Hemingway does share them with the reader. Thus, the son's question "But what were they like to be with?" is followed by this: "'It's hard to say,' Nick Adams said. Could you ever say she did first what no one has ever done better and mention plump brown legs, flat belly, hard little breasts," and so on (497)?

None of what is here shared with the reader does Nick choose to "mention" to his son. The combination of tactful omission and frank admission makes a number of points about Hemingway's understanding of the ethics of "education" (491), to quote a word used earlier in the story. First, education begins in actual lived experience. Second, while what has been learned from experience can be passed along, it is best to do so when the listener is fully prepared to receive the imparted knowledge. There are also certain kinds of experience that may remain incommunicable, and each person learns all there is to know about them without advice.

In "The Short Happy Life of Francis Macomber," Hemingway returned to the question of educating boys. White hunter Robert Wilson thinks about "the great American boy-men" who "stay little boys so long.... Sometimes all their lives" (33). Hemingway, however, does allow his title character to grow up: after running from a lion, Macomber is given a second chance to stand and face a wild animal. In Macomber's case, as Wilson reflects to himself, it had "taken a strange chance of hunting" for him to "come of age" (33, 32). The experience has "made him into a man" (33). The belief that a boy can be turned into a man by exposing him to ordeals has a long list of adherents. The issue becomes more complicated, however—and as Hemingway's life was eventually to reveal—when a male child has no desire to be fashioned toward such an outcome.

Thomas Hudson exposes one of his sons to two ordeals. In the first of these scenes, Hudson allows his boys to swim too close to the real ocean, and "the biggest hammerhead he had ever seen" suddenly materializes, headed straight toward David (88). Hudson shoots his rifle and misses; it is Eddy, however, who uses a machine gun to stop the shark only thirty yards from the boy. "My fault," Eddy says, "I was born here" (90). Hudson responds: "We were all responsible" (91). A good father accepts blame but is also careful not to expose his children to needless harm. While Hudson acknowledges his mistake, he also goes on to repeat it.

In the second threat scene, David hooks a huge swordfish. The fight with the fish goes on at incredible length before the leader goes slack. Everyone on the boat ministers to David, who swears to fight the fish "until I die" (115). Tom worries that the fight might "kill him" (116). Andrew, the younger of the two sons Hudson had with the second wife, only angers his older brother when he asks him about gaffing the fish. In the fourth hour of the fight, Hudson looks at David and sees where "his heels showed the blood that had run down from the soles of his feet" (131). But no one stops the fight. "We have to think about how he feels," Hudson says to the concerned Tom (132). "If David catches this fish he'll have something inside him for all his life and it will make everything easier."

The aesthetic rather than the ethical question raised by the novel's threat scenes has to do with preparations of effect. Phrases like *until I die* and *kill him* are only the most obvious words through which Hemingway gathers the incidents in "Bimini" toward the sense of an ending. It is therefore shocking but not surprising when Hemingway decides to kill off two of the boys only a few days after the three sons leave the island. The message comes by way of a radio form: "YOUR SONS DAVID AND ANDREW KILLED WITH THEIR MOTHER

IN MOTOR ACCIDENT NEAR BIARRITZ" (193). After this catastrophe, painter Thomas Hudson comes to think of his work "as the one thing that he must not lose" if he is to last (195).

This will not be the last shock Hudson must endure. Seven years after the loss of his two youngest sons, Hudson is living in Cuba. With his new wife away, he kills time drinking at the Floridita. Well into part 2, he is joined by a friend, Ignacio. The men tease and drink and gamble, and then Ignacio says:

> "I've known you and your boy Tom for years. By the way how is he?"
> "He's dead."
> "I'm so sorry. I didn't know." (257)

Nor did the reader.

When it comes to managing reader response, Hemingway usually prefers to prepare us for our losses. In the opening chapter of *A Farewell to Arms*, for instance, the phrase *gone with child* signals, in a very literal way, what will eventually happen to Catherine Barkley (4). *In Islands in the Stream*, however, no amount of forecasting can protect the reader against the sheer scale of the accumulating losses. The boys' deaths feel unearned. The killing off of the sons before they reach maturity serves purposes that reach well beyond the exigencies of the novel's plot. It allows the father in the novel, as well as the author of it, to avoid the challenge of having to represent and therefore to adjust to the kinds of people Tom and David and Andrew might eventually have become. Sudden disappearance serves Hemingway as a preemptive strike against loss as well as a veiled admission that the temptation a good man must avoid, as he watches his children grow older, is not replacement but disappointment.

And disappointment is to be the portion of the youngest son. Soon after the three boys arrive on Bimini, Hemingway has their father engage in a summary view. Andrew, "the smallest boy," "was a copy of Thomas Hudson, physically, reduced in scale and widened and shortened. . . . He was a devil too, and deviled both his older brothers, and he had a dark side to him that nobody except Thomas Hudson could ever understand. Neither of them thought about this except that they recognized it in each other and knew it was bad and the man respected it and understood the boy's having it" (57). Gregory Hemingway recognized himself in the portrait of Andrew, later using Hudson's description of his smallest boy as an epigraph to his 1976 *Papa: A Personal Memoir*.

"That nobody else . . . could ever understand"—it is a lovely idea, this kind of generous capacity for comprehension of a son. But as so often in late Hemingway, his prose posits an "ideal" its author will fail to live up to.

Fifty years later to the day of the death of his mother, Pauline, in Los Angeles in 1951, Gregory Hemingway died in the Miami-Dade Women's Detention Center. The two deaths were linked by more than the fact of a shared date. Pauline's death was directly connected to the challenges she and her ex-husband faced in confronting the gender dysphoria manifested by their youngest son. Here is the entry from Brewster Chamberlin's *The Hemingway Log*:

> September 30 (Sunday): From San Francisco, Pauline arrives in Los Angeles to investigate why the police have arrested the nineteen-year-old Gregory and "To keep the Hemingway name out of the newspapers as well as to cure Gregory's disturbance," which is rather a quaint way of putting it; she stays with her sister in the house Virginia shares with her lover Laura Archera. In drag, Gregory has gone into the women's restroom in a movie theater; the problem is not drugs, as some sources indicate. At some point that evening, EH and Pauline engage in a shouting, tear-drenched, angry telephone exchange the exact nature of which is unknown, but EH probably attacks his ex-wife, blaming her for Gregory's troubles.
>
> October 1 (Monday): At 3:00 a.m., Pauline dies at the age of fifty-six of blocked arteries, hypertension, and a rare tumor of the medulla that secretes massive amounts of adrenaline, causing extreme high blood pressure that drops suddenly, resulting in sufficient shock to kill her, in Saint Vincent's Hospital.

In 1951, neither Ernest nor Gregory was aware of the actual cause of Pauline's death, and each believed it was the result of shock on the operating table. It was only in 1960 that Gregory, now a student in medical school, requested an autopsy report and learned of the tumor of the adrenal gland.

When Gregory visited his father in the November after his mother's passing and said, about his arrest in Los Angeles, "It wasn't so bad, really, Papa," Hemingway replied, "Well, it killed your mother." In this exchange, no mention is made of the father's angry phone call to Gregory's distressed mother, an event as likely to precipitate shock as the arrest itself.

In *Running with the Bulls: My Life with the Hemingways*, Valerie Hemingway, Gregory Hemingway's third wife, gives a moving account of the end of her ex-husband's life. In a phone call made to her on October 1, 2001, their son Edward informed Valerie that "his dad had died in a woman's prison that morning." She soon learned that "Greg had been picked up in a disoriented state early one morning while walking home from a party. He was booked for 'indecent exposure.' He had been naked but carrying a dress and high-heeled shoes." Five days after being arrested, "he was found dead of heart disease in his cell."

Valerie Hemingway concludes her memoir with a kind of elegy: "All his life Greg fought a losing battle against a crippling illness. He lacked the critical early help because his parents were unable or unwilling to accept his condition, nor could he come to terms with it himself for a long time. He took up the study of medicine in the hope that he himself might find a cure, or at least a solace. Failing, he developed an alternate persona, a character into which he could retreat from the unbearable responsibilities of being his father's son, and of never ever measuring up to what was expected of him, or to what he expected of himself."

The difficulties Hemingway experienced in accepting his youngest son's struggles with identity cast a poignant light on the sexual experimenting so central to the action of *The Garden of Eden*. Because *Eden* contains sex scenes involving role reversal, as well as a wife's attempts to fashion herself and her husband so as to look alike, the novel has been read as Hemingway's attempt to move beyond the strict binaries of gender. Even though protagonist David Bourne accedes to his wife Catherine's will to change, he does so with a good deal of ambivalence and with no small amount of remorse. The two parties to the Bourne marriage act out a kind of unresolved psychomachia that may represent a tension within their author as well as between themselves.

As the novel opens, David and Catherine Bourne are honeymooning in the South of France. Almost immediately, she makes her arresting confession: "I'm hungry already and we haven't finished breakfast" (5). Through this character, Hemingway explores the further question of whether his story, too, is a tragedy of appetite. Something in the nature of human longing goes unassuaged, and the unending search for the next good place, or the next good wife, gives evidence of the trouble. A novel that begins as a romance in which food and drink and sex and warmth are immediately available quickly devolves into a sense of the already over, as if the experience of a perfect beginning cries out for the breakage of a fall.

Catherine is especially desirous of choreographing bedroom scenes. The first such scene, which Hemingway treats with customary reticence, happens early on. Catherine has promised her husband "a big surprise," something "dangerous," but once David sees her "waiting for him in bed," the prose cuts away from any further detail and comes to rest on an "afterwards" (11). In their second bedroom scene, which ends chapter 1, there is no cutting away. The room has gone dark, and "the top sheet was gone from the bed" (16): "He had shut his eyes and he could feel the long light weight of her on him and her breasts pressing against him and her lips on his. He lay there and felt something and then her hand holding him and searching lower and he helped with his hands and then lay back in the dark and did not think at all and only felt the weight and the strangeness inside and she said, 'Now you can't tell who is who can you?'" (17). David turns out to be less pleased than undone by the experience; as he lies next to his wife in the afterwards, he finds himself saying "goodbye Catherine goodbye my lovely girl goodbye and good luck and goodbye" (18). "What can there be," he soon asks himself, "that will not burn out in a fire that rages like that?" (21). And the answer comes: the changes on which Catherine Bourne insists unfold with such velocity that her story can only end in the fire that consumes her husband's pages even as she engineers her own replacement with Marita and incinerates her marriage.

Through Catherine, Hemingway explores the nature of an appetite not unlike his own. Even as he writes his heartbreaking last books and even as he maintains the discipline of a writing life, he also sees that his way of living is consuming him. Catherine Bourne is Hemingway's most daring self-character, for it is Hemingway who was also a nonstop experimenter, a man with unappeasable hungers who liked the feel and look of a woman's short hair, a husband who enjoyed varying his sexual routines with the woman he called "Miss Mary," and who, like the honeymoon couple who enjoy darkening their skins and talk about going to Africa, dreamed during his second safari of marrying an African woman and of becoming formally inducted into the Wakumba tribe. Catherine also hopes to induct her husband, David, into "dark things" (67), experiences lying well beyond the prescribed canons of identity. This is the "dark side" that Thomas Hudson claims to recognize and respect in his son Andrew, although not a side of his son Gregory that Hemingway was himself able to recognize and to respect.

Catherine Bourne has a hunger for *more*. During the same years in which Hemingway was creating her, he directly addressed his own experience of hunger in *A Moveable Feast*. Most of *Eden* was written in 1958 and 1959, during the same period in which Hemingway was working on his Paris memoir. *A Moveable Feast* ends with the dissolution of Hemingway's first marriage and his admission of his love for Pauline Pfeiffer. Because *The Garden of Eden* reimagines Hemingway's 1927 honeymoon with Pauline in the Camargue, it can be read as a sequel to the Paris memoir. Taken together, the two books offer Hemingway's final take on the costs and pleasures of replacement.

Hemingway's appetites are on display in the memoir's opening pages and are given full expression in chapter 6, "A False Spring." In chapter 1, "A Good Café on the Place St.-Michel," Hemingway likens the replacement of one partner with another to an act of "transplanting" (5), as when a self, like a plant, has become root-bound and needs more space in which to grow. What takes place in "A Good Café" is, however, only an imaginary transplanting. As Hemingway writes at his table, a girl comes in, and he finds himself "disturbed" by her. "I've seen you beauty, and you belong to me now," he thinks to himself, "whoever you are waiting for. You belong to me and all Paris belongs to me and I belong to this notebook and this pencil." Then Hemingway goes back to his writing. When he looks up, "she had gone. I hope she's gone with a good man, I thought" (6).

In imagining himself as part of a triangle involving a "pretty" girl and a good man, the twenty-five-year-old Hemingway anticipates his eventual fate. In 1933, eight years after Ernest replaced Hadley with Pauline, his first wife married Paul Mowrer, "a much finer man than I ever was or ever could be." The finer man was also, in Thomas Hudson's phrase, a Faithful Husband.

"You write with the most terrible nostalgia anyone has ever had," Marita says to David Bourne, in a portion of the manuscript of *Eden* that Tom Jenks chose to cut from his edition of the novel. *A Moveable Feast* appears to have been written out of a similar emotion, with the man who is composing his memoir, like Thomas Hudson, giving continual evidence of still being in love with his first wife. In an essay about the persistence of desire, J. Gerald Kennedy has powerfully invoked Hemingway's unending love for Paris, for Hadley, and "his continuing longing for that lost world." "I hope Hadley understands," Hemingway wrote in one of the "Fragments" that can be found at the end of the restored edition. "She is the heroine and the only person who had a life that turned out well" (229). In the 1964 edition of *Feast*, Hemingway can say about his first wife: "I loved her and I loved no one else and we had a lovely magic time when we were alone. I worked well and we made great trips, and I thought we were invulnerable again, and it wasn't until we were out of the mountains in the late spring, and back in Paris that the other thing started again" (210–11).

The restored edition follows the word *again* with another sentence, one not quoted in Mary Hemingway's version of the memoir. "Remorse was a fine thing and with a little luck and if I'd been a better man it might have saved me for something worse probably instead of being my true and constant companion for the next three years" (218–19). "Finer man ... good man ... better man"—Hemingway may understand the appeal of these phrases, but he is unable to apply them to himself.

The word *remorse* does not appear in "A False Spring," the sixth chapter of *A Moveable Feast*, but the emotion is powerfully registered there nevertheless. Ernest and Hadley have returned to Paris after having luck at the racetrack. A good lunch is followed by a walk through the Tuileries, where they begin to play "Do you remember?" (56). As the phrase gets repeated, the two young marrieds recall hiking over the St. Bernard Pass, a fruit cup at Biffi's in the Galleria, an inn at Aigle where Hadley read in the garden while Ernest fished. As the memories cascade, they take on the tone of an old couple looking back on a long marriage rather than of two young people still in the process of setting out on one.

After all their "talking and walking," Ernest and Hadley find themselves standing on a bridge near the Louvre. Ernest asks if is she is hungry again, and they decide to go to Michaud's for "a truly grand dinner." As they stand looking in at the restaurant window, Ernest wonders "how much of what we had felt on the bridge was just hunger. I asked my wife and she said, 'I don't know, Tatie. There are so many sorts of hunger. In the spring there are more. But that's gone now. Memory is hunger'" (56–57).

Memory is hunger. What might memory be hungry for? *A Moveable Feast* unfolds as a book hungry for a past irrevocably lost through choices its narrator has long since made. But this is the wisdom of an old man looking back. In "A False Spring"—and this despite the playing of the remembering game—the young Hemingway in the book is looking forward into an unknown future that the older man writing his story has painfully lived out. And just as "there is never any ending to Paris," a claim made on the last page of the 1964 version of the memoir (211), so there is never any ending to the hunger Hemingway feels as he stands on the bridge and to the hunger he feels again in the final paragraphs of "A False Spring." As he lies beside his wife in bed, he recalls the "wonderful meal at Michaud's":

> When we had finished and there was no question of hunger any more the feeling that had been like hunger when we were on the bridge was still there when we caught the bus home. It was there when we came in the room and after we had gone to bed and made love in the dark it was there. When I woke with the windows open and the moonlight on the roofs of the tall houses, it was there. I put my face away from the moonlight into the shadow but I could not sleep and lay awake thinking about it. We had both wakened twice in the night and my wife slept sweetly now with the moonlight on her face. . . . Life had seemed so simple that morning when I had wakened and found the false spring and heard the pipes of the man with his herd of goats and gone out and bought the racing paper.
>
> But Paris was a very old city and we were young and nothing was simple there, not even poverty, nor sudden money, nor the moonlight, nor right and wrong, nor the breathing of someone who lay beside you in the moonlight. (57–58)

All this happens well before "an unmarried young woman becomes the temporary best friend of another young woman who is married, goes to live with the husband and wife and then unknowingly, innocently and unrelentingly sets out to marry the husband" (209).

Feeling caught in a similar situation, David Bourne says to himself, "Do not start blaming who you love nor apportioning blame" (132). He says this as he looks down into the sea and tries to "think clearly" about what it means to "love two women." A passage not appearing in the 1964 *A Moveable Feast* but now available as a result of the editing in the restored edition shows Hemingway in a more self-blaming mood: "For the girl to deceive her friend was a terrible thing but it was my fault and blindness that this did not repel me. Having become involved in it and in love I accepted all the blame for it myself and lived with the remorse" (219).

This frank acceptance of blame is a welcome discovery, although Hemingway had perhaps already begun to apportion blame in the bedroom scene at the end of "A False Spring." "It was there . . . it was there . . . it was there"— by way of these repetitions, the thereness of the young husband's feeling that had been like hunger remains present in a way he cannot deny. He has everything a Hemingway man could want—food, a room in Paris, lovemaking, and a wife sleeping sweetly in his bed. He could have said then what he said earlier in the chapter: "I thought that was all we needed" (53). Yet it is not enough.

As he lies next to Hadley at the end of "A False Spring," in perhaps his greatest bedroom scene and in one of the last such scenes he was ever to write, Hemingway comes close to understanding his part in the outcomes of his life. The conclusion is strangely impersonal. How he will end up has little to do with the women in his bed; in his imaginings they were to prove, in any case, replaceable. No, the problem is here articulated as a kind of undefinable, unassuageable hunger and was *in him*, and from the beginning. Learning to live with this hunger, or failing to learn how to do so, is a crucial variable in the career of a good man.

"The feeling that had been like hunger" is built in—and not to the writer alone. As Hemingway admits in *A Moveable Feast*, "I found that many of the people I wrote about had very strong appetites and a great taste and desire for food, and most of them were looking forward to having a drink" (101). For over a century now, Hemingway has been eliciting and cultivating such appetites in his readers as well. In his case, the feeling that had been like hunger most often found its focus on the woman who was next to him in bed. As a supreme scientist of desire, and even as he was losing the faculties that allowed him to experience the feeling, Hemingway in his late work exposed himself to a hunger of memory that reveals how difficult it is to want what we have.

What we thought we had, in the year Hemingway's life ended, was plentiful enough: five novels, a novella, over fifty short stories, a play, a spoof of Sherwood Anderson, a novelized memoir of hunting in Africa, a study of bullfighting in Spain. Then, three years after Hemingway's death, the posthumously edited books began to appear. If the myth of the faltering career can ever be laid to rest, we must acknowledge the full story of Hemingway's continuing labor, even as we recognize how an unending process of recovery has made readers hunger for more. And despite this embarrassment of riches, we may still be confronted with the sometimes inordinate nature of our expectations for any writer's career. Writers are too often held accountable for what they did not do rather than valued for what they have actually accomplished. There is a pretension in such disappointment, a failure to dignify the struggle involved in any writing life. Hemingway kept at it, and he worked harder than we knew. "Am working on the last one," he wrote to his editor at Scribner's from Ketchum, Idaho, in February 1961. By the "last one," he meant the final chapter of *A Moveable Feast*. "Try to only think from day to day and work the same but things have been rough and are rough all over." He worried whether the transcriber of his manuscript could read his handwriting. And then he added: "This is all being done under difficulty but it is being done. . . . Have sure tried."

NINE

Ralph Ellison's Labor of Love

After a friend sent me the just-published edition of *The Selected Letters of Ralph Ellison* in December 2019, I found myself unable to stop reading it. Edited by John F. Callahan and Marc C. Connor, the volume delivers a strangely compelling mixture of outrage and erudition. It is, above all, a story of the longing for culture and of how, after achieving a writing life, a young man who had no money for shoes at Tuskegee succeeded in transforming himself into what we used to call "a man of letters."

The Selected Letters also tell another story. Even before the 1952 publication of *Invisible Man*, Ellison had begun work on a second novel. He labored away on the project for over four decades and produced thousands of pages, but he died without shepherding them into a novel form. "The longer the book remained unfinished," a sympathetic Stanley Crouch can write, "the more excruciating the pain. And for a long time, sadly, he lived with a constant, debilitating sense of having failed."

But a second novel was eventually published. *Juneteenth* appeared in 1999 and was followed by a much more expansive treatment of Ellison's literary remains in the 2010 *Three Days before the Shooting*.... These posthumous editions convert any sense of Ellison's having failed into a hard-won if belated form of success.

In each of its published forms, the plot of Ellison's second novel opens with the arrival of Reverend Alonzo Hickman in Washington, DC, and the shooting of Senator Adam Sunraider on the Senate floor. Memories spiraling out of these events reveal the senator to have been raised by Hickman in an all-Black community in rural Georgia. Given the name Bliss, the boy of "indeterminate race" was trained to be a preacher until he disappeared, became a filmmaker and con artist, and then emerged as a racist politician from New England (4). He is shot by Severen, a young man he managed to engender along the way.

Juneteenth consists of 353 pages. The main body of *Three Days* runs to 459 densely printed ones. But the 2010 volume is more than twice that long and is divided into three parts. Part 1 contains what I am calling the main body of the novel: books 1 and 2 and "Bliss's Birth." Part 2 offers "three computer sequences" left behind by Ellison (486). "Although many of the characters, episodes, and even entire passages remain unchanged from Books I and II and earlier typewritten drafts dating back to the 1950s," editors Callahan and Adam Bradley conclude that "what Ellison produced on the computer nonetheless comprises a separate body of work" (488). This section of the volume takes up 499 pages. The 130 pages of part 3 offer a selection of Ellison's notes on the novel as well as reprintings of the eight excerpts from the project published during Ellison's lifetime. Massive as the volume may be, its contents represent only a selection of what Ellison left behind. As Timothy Parrish points out in *Ralph Ellison and the Genius of America*, "Even the 1,101 closely printed pages contained in *Three Days* do not make up the complete manuscript, and one can well imagine other editors coming up with different versions."

"I have dropped the shuck," Ellison wrote to his friend Albert Murray on May 14, 1951. Ellison had finished *Invisible Man*—it was published on April 14, 1952. "Fanny is well and glad it's finished, I'm back at 608 Fifth trying to get started on my next novel. (I probably have enough stuff left from the other if I can find the form." The parenthesis with which Ellison's letter ends was left unclosed—the future was open-ended. The pages with which his second novel ought to end also conclude with a defining act of punctuation. As Reverend Hickman looks back on the story told in a section of the novel called "Bliss's Birth," he has this to say in its closing sentences: "Who knows, His ways are strange ways, Hickman. Maybe it was all His plan, you had to be what you were then in order to lead his flock. It took all of that to come to this, and little Bliss was the father to the man and the man was also me..." (481). Two things stand out here: "It took all of that to come to this"; and the final ellipsis. Given that Ellison's project remains self-reflexive throughout, *all of that* can be read as referring to the entire reading experience leading up to this moment. The *this* is the ending of the novel, which will or will not, depending on a reader's experience, feel fully earned. The ellipsis, on the other hand, gestures toward an awareness that the search inaugurated in "Bliss's Birth" has not yet ended and may never end.

Neither of the posthumously published versions of Ellison's second novel concludes with "Bliss's Birth" and the words I have quoted from it. Instead, *Juneteenth* ends with the wounded Senator Sunraider seeming "*to hear* the sound of Hickman's consoling voice, calling from somewhere else." In *Three Days*, book 2 ends with Miss Maud looking for her righteous bridegroom and her three little babies: "Tell me, darlin's, that pretty soon my righteous bridegroom is going to come tripping down the hall with the pretty blue carpet on the floor and that the little pink roses will still be up there on the *wall*paper! Aaah, tell me, tell me!" (455).

Callahan and Bradley argue that Ellison's second novel "doesn't end so much as stop" (xxvii). Given the endings provided in their edited versions of the novel, the claim is fair enough. But the entire chapter called "Bliss's Birth" generates a sense of rising intensity that also generates the sense of an ending. And the chapter is conveniently positioned in *Three Days* to perform the work I am calling upon it to do: appearing as it does just after the conclusion of book 2 (and therefore after Miss Maud's words quoted earlier), readers of the edition need only to *keep reading* through the next twenty-two pages, and they will have the experience of a satisfying and fitting conclusion.

I am proposing, then, a reediting of Ellison's second novel. In order to make the case for my choice of an ending, it is necessary to go back, back to the story of how the novel began, and to follow the workings of Ellison's imagination as he made his way through the forty years left to him after the publication of *Invisible Man*.

Some six months after announcing he had dropped the shuck, Ellison again wrote to Murray: "One thing both of us can be sure of is that whether our books are miscarriages or what not, this kind of labor of love is never lost, not completely lost, because just the effort to do what has never been done before, to define in terms of the novel that which has never been defined before is never completely lost. Hell, besides I'm trying to organize my next book." Writing is here conceived as a labor of love. In referring to his novels as if they were children, some brought to birth and some not, Ellison has begun to apprehend that his artistic struggle was also to become his novel's central theme. Fearing that his novel might miscarry, he organized it around the experience of raising and losing a child. Thus it is that his 1954 Guggenheim application opens with the sentence: "My projected novel will be concerned with the problem of identity in America, dramatized in terms of a young man's search for his father." In the end, more searching is done by the father than by the son, but which generation would prove more prodigal is largely beside the point.

Ellison ended up searching as long and hard for his novel as either Hickman or Bliss ever search for each other. In a letter dated February 1, 1954, he found himself "in my old agony again trying to write a novel. I've got some ideas that excite me and a few scenes and characters, but the rest is coming like my first pair of long pants—slow as hell." In April 1955, he told Paul Engle, "I am involved with a novel which I hope to finish by 1956." Writing from the American Academy in Rome, almost a year later, he complained to a boyhood friend about "working on a novel and it's beating me to my d.b.a. but that's the usual way with me—a book's like a bad case of constipation, and I guess some would say that that's the way mine read." By the following summer, Ellison was telling Stanley Edgar Hyman about "still having trouble in giving the book the dramatic drive I feel it needs.... Just learned that the kid preacher's name, Bliss, means rapture, a yielding to experience."

In the summer after that, Ellison was again linking the act of writing to the process of giving birth. As he told a friend at Knopf: "About the novel I'll only say that some of the scenes are molto outrageous. If only I didn't require the gestation period of an elephant to bring forth my odd mice! Next time I'll play it *New Yorker* smart, I'll write the first and last scenes and let the reader guess the development." The reference to beginnings and endings, along with the early admission to Murray about the struggle "to organize" his material, was a reminder to Ellison that above all, as he had written in 1951, he needed to "find the form."

Over the years, Ellison continued to make reference to his work-in-progress. Only a few months before his death, in the spring of 1994, Ellison said to David Remnick: "The novel has got my attention now. I work every day, so there will be something very soon."

Of the theories that attempt to explain why Ellison proved unable to give his novel an ending, three make good sense.

The first has to do with a fire. In early 1967, the Ellisons bought a country house in Plainfield, Massachusetts. "Oh, how beautiful it is," Fanny wrote to a friend, "wild flowers, birds and acres & acres of woods we've not even had time to explore." Less than a year later, on November 4, as Fanny and Ralph returned to the house from errands in the nearby town of Adams, they saw black smoke coming out of the roof. By the time the local fire brigade arrived, the house was gone.

At first, Ellison minimized the loss. "I lost part of my manuscript—the revisions over which I had labored [in] the summer and valuable notebooks." By the following October, he told a reporter about losing 365 pages, "a neatly symbolic figure," writes Arnold Rampersad, "to which he would cling for many years." By 1974, in response to an article in the *New York Times* about slowpoke American writers, Ellison wrote, "When you lose 365 pages of a novel, you just can't reclaim the subtleties, the abstract ideas, the rhythm, even punctuation, and you undergo a traumatic experience, even though you tell yourself you don't."

A second theory about finishing has to do with Ellison becoming a public man. Vaulted into fame after the publication of *Invisible Man*, he was suddenly in demand as a civic statesman. The subsequent record of Ellison's travels to speaking engagements and various consultancies is downright dizzying. Universities such as Virginia and Princeton dangled job offers, and Ellison eventually accepted a faculty position at New York University. During the Johnson administration, Ellison became a frequent visitor at the White House. He joined virtually every board he was invited to join: the National Council on the Arts, the American Academy of Arts and Sciences, the Century Association, the board of the Kennedy Center, the Colonial Williamsburg Foundation. And he took an active part in each of these organizations. But that work took time. "When you get institutionalized," as his admirer James Alan McPherson was to write, "you become an extension of the institution and you are constantly called upon to justify yourself in those terms."

Perhaps the most persuasive explanation for Ellison's not finishing has to do with the momentum of history itself. His second novel was to be situated in the early 1950s; in a note to himself, Ellison imagined that the "action takes place on the eve of the Rights movement" (973). Then came *Brown v. Board of Education,* the rise of massive resistance, the determination of Rosa Parks, and the pilgrimage of Martin Luther King Jr. After the killings began in the 1960s, Ellison recognized "that the assassination in his novel carried potential meanings he was not sure he wanted to allow." "Part of what's taken so long," Ellison told *Playboy* in 1982, "is that so many things have changed so fast in our culture that as soon as I thought I had a draft that brought all of these things together, there would be another shift and I'd have to go back and revise all over again." As Parrish concludes, Ellison "seems to have begun the novel out of despair that America would ever recognize blacks as 'equal.' Then, with history's sudden boomerang into 'equality' for blacks, the book may have seemed to Ellison to be out of time with the times."

Support for Parrish's claim can be found in an interview conducted by Arnold Rampersad with another African American novelist: "Toni Morrison would observe that this story was 'not really a story anybody needed to hear again.' She went on: 'Ellison had tried to revive the senile "tragic mulatto" genre. Faulkner had done it already and about as well as it could have been done.... If Ellison had turned it out quicky after *Invisible Man,* that would have been fine.' But for all practical purposes, 'the story was dead.'" In 2004, the year in which this interview took place, Morrison would only have had access to the severely edited *Juneteenth.* She might well have felt differently about Ellison's project after the 2010 publication of *Three Days before the Shooting....*

However out of synch Ellison may have been with the times, during his lifetime he did arrange to publish eight excerpts from the gestating whole:

"And Hickman Arrives" (1960)
"The Roof, the Steeple and the People" (1960)
"It Always Breaks Out" (1963)
"Juneteenth" (1965)
"Night-Talk" (1969)
"A Song of Innocence" (1970)
"Cadillac Flambé" (1973)
"Backwacking, a Plea to the Senator" (1977)

All but a few of these excerpts, usually heavily revised, found a place in the main body of *Three Days* as it appears in the 2010 edition, and they are printed in full at the back of the volume.

Callahan has recounted the experience of editing *Juneteenth* in an article appearing in 2002. After publishing a scholarly article on Ellison in the late 1970s, Callahan had been the recipient of an appreciative letter from Ellison himself. Ralph and Fanny and John soon became friends, and Callahan would go on to become the major editor of Ellison's unpublished work. It was Callahan who helped Fanny rearrange the New York apartment when Ellison insisted on dying at home, and he also oversaw the funeral arrangements after Ralph's death.

Soon thereafter, Fanny invited Callahan into her husband's study. There he found "stacks of printout, scraps of notes, jottings on old newspapers and magazine subscription cards, and several neat boxes of computer disks." There were also thick black binders of typescripts and "folder after folder of earlier drafts painstakingly labeled according to character or episode." After sorting through the remains, Callahan determined that "the center of Ellison's saga" was the Hickman-Sunraider relationship. He proceeded to put together the book he called *Juneteenth*.

The core of *Juneteenth* roughly corresponds to book 2 in *Three Days before the Shooting*.... In an afterword to *Juneteenth*, Callahan had this to say: "Of the potential 'three volumes' Ellison had referred to in 1970 but not yet finished, Book II had come to constitute an all but complete novel. Except for a very few, very brief passages written in the early 1990s, the novel is not Ellison's most recent effort, but it is the most ambitious and latest, freestanding, compelling, extended fiction in the saga. Moreover, it contains the story and relationship of the two principal characters at the heart of the work Ellison had set his sights on and described over the years."

However freestanding he perceived book 2 to be, Callahan also made some additions to it. He interpolated four of the already-published excerpts—"And Hickman Arrives," "The Roof, the Steeple and the People," "Juneteenth," "Night-Talk"—as well as the modest addition of a paragraph from "Cadillac Flambé." But Callahan's most consequential editorial decision was to include "a thirty-eight-page manuscript" referred to as "Bliss's Birth" and to position it as the penultimate chapter 15 (457).

Callahan concludes his afterword to *Juneteenth* with a promise: "A subsequent scholar's edition will document my corrections and include sufficient manuscripts and drafts of the second novel to enable scholars and readers to follow Ellison's some forty years of work on his novel-in-progress." *Three Days* is that volume, although it is not clear that it manages to "find the form."

For Ellison, finding a form would have involved settling on an ending. As he argues in *Shadow and Act*, a fiction of any length requires a mastery of the "structural unities of *beginning, middle,* and *end.*" Learning how to proportion and to pace these three essential parts is the novelist's work. But as Ellison told John Hersey in 1982, when it came to his second novel, he "was never satisfied with how the parts connected" (xix).

Ellison knew a true ending when he saw it. In "Twentieth-Century Fiction and the Mask of Black Humanity," Ellison takes considerable pains to counter Hemingway's claims about the ending of *Huckleberry Finn.* Hemingway had said that readers should "stop where the N–– Jim is stolen from the boys. That is the real end. The rest is just cheating." In making this claim, Ellison argues, "Hemingway missed completely the structural, symbolic and moral necessity for that part of the plot in which the boys rescue Jim." Ellison knew that Tom and Huck's frustrated and frustrating attempts to "set a free n–– free"—to liberate an already manumitted Jim from the smokehouse—were accurately predictive of the redundant and never-quite-finished order of business in which well-meaning persons kept trying and failing to bring about the promised Emancipation.

The supreme test of the novelist, as Ellison came to understand it, is the capacity to manage narrative time. It is essential to "put a detail in its proper place in an action," Ellison told an audience in 1976. If the novelist is successful, "you have the arousal, the tension, the friction, and satisfaction of most expectations" (190). "This is a *peripeteia,*" Ellison wrote in one of his notes on the second novel (972); he was thinking hard, as he imagined the possibility of an ending, about expectation and reversal. Yet although he had generated more than enough working parts, Ellison remained unsure about how they might be most powerfully "connected."

In *Three Days,* Bliss, now a filmmaker, faces a continuity problem of his own whenever he attempts to edit a movie. At the end of a day's shooting, "there would be nothing more than a jumble of scenes" (279). "You mean you piece it together?" Bliss is asked by the girl he is courting (277). "That's the idea," Bliss responds. In the face of the "rambling impressions" produced by a day's shooting, Bliss's partner is of little help (279). "Donelson ached to reverse time, I yearned to master it, or so I told myself." So Bliss takes the day's jumble and makes a followable shape: "I edited a series of shots, killing time." Bliss's will to impose continuity on a day's "rushes" serves as an exemplum of the challenges Ellison faced as he worked to edit his daily efforts into shape. But the problem of continuity was to remain, one perhaps overdetermined by the pressures Ellison may have felt as he attempted to be true to the disruptions experienced by his people during the ongoing American experiment.

In mastering form, as Ellison wrote in his response to a critique by Irving Howe, it was essential not to betray content: "If I am to fulfill the writer's basic responsibilities to his craft, then surely I must insist upon the maintenance of a certain level of precision in language, a maximum correspondence between the form of a piece of writing and its content." The content driving his second novel was, in a word, *integration*. In 1969, Ellison admitted, "I am stuck with integration, because the very process of the imagination . . . is nothing if not integrative."

Ellison's second novel thereby turns upon a profound irony: While, in America, integration of Black and white bodies has already long since occurred, and at the most intimate physical level, those bodies continue to be artificially segregated by both law and custom. To capture this irony, Ellison settled upon the formal device of the "claiming scene." ("Concentrate on *scene*," Ellison wrote to himself, in one of his notes on his work in progress [974].) These scenes reenact both the historical fact of touching across the color line along with the cultural and psychological inhibitions—Jim Crow, family or race pride, hysterical possessiveness, Oedipal longings and competitions—that work to separate rather than to join.

Each of the three claiming scenes in books 1 and 2 of *Three Days* deals with the provenance of a child. Where has the child come from, and to whom does it belong? Where, above all, can fathers earn and find a place to stand in the "cyclonic whirl" of American family life (89). As Welborn McIntyre thinks to himself, "In this country a man is exceptionally lucky if he is able to recognize the child he rears as his own" (88–89). These claiming scenes thereby dramatize a personal and a national crisis of recognition and thereby prepare readers to experience "Bliss's Birth" as the novel's promised end.

"Bliss's Birth" is a title written in Ellison's hand on the first page of thirty-eight typewritten pages dated "1965." Callahan and Bradley argue that Ellison's notes about these pages indicate an intention "to place them somewhere in Book II" (457). Accordingly, the two editors position these pages directly after the concluding page of their version of book 2, which is where, it turns out, they actually belong. But this fourth and most compelling claiming scene can only accomplish a "satisfaction of most expectations" because of Ellison's careful preparations of effect.

The first claiming scene occurs during a flashback experienced by Welborn McIntyre in chapter 9 of book 1. Ellison chooses McIntyre as the narrator of book 1 of *Three Days* because as a white reporter, he stands at a considerable distance from the shooting he has witnessed and is assigned to report upon. His cluelessness turns out to be a strange kind or resource, granting him permission to ask awkward questions and to expose himself to serious embarrassments as he pursues his "involvement in Hickman's idea-quest" (976).

"Shortly before the war," McIntyre tells us, "back when I still thought of myself as a champion of 'social significance' . . . I met while attending a dance held in a famous Harlem hall now destroyed, a young girl, a Negro" (101). Her name is Laura Johnson. As Welborn and Laura become a couple, their social circle comes to look upon them as representing a future in which "the wounds, outrages, and inequities which haunted contemporary society would be resolved by transcendent love."

But Laura becomes pregnant. Welborn finds himself "torn between my love, my sense of honor, and the fierce new aspect which the future revealed, now that I would have a dark wife and child perhaps as dark" (102). He becomes so upset that he cannot eat. Welborn determines nevertheless "to do the manly thing" and to marry the mother of his child (103).

Laura's mother then intervenes. In an interview with Welborn, she begins by telling him, "Laura didn't tell me that you were white" (106). When he announces the plan to marry, the mother explodes: "You have got to do *what!* With *my* daughter—boy, who do you think you're talking to?" (108). After commanding Laura to come upstairs, the mother launches into her tirade: "You mean to stand there and talk to me about loving this peckerwood—you, my own daughter? Loving him when even if he ain't a foreigner, he's probably the kind who sucks a black woman's tit from the minute he's born and lets her change his didies and feeds him and teaches him his manners and protects him, and then, when he's fourteen and feeling himself, he calls her a 'n—– bitch' and proceeds to hop on top of the first young black gal he can get to catch his devilment" (109).

Mrs. Johnson leaves the room and returns with a shotgun. "My legs flowed toward the woman with the shotgun and stopped, seeing her turn aside, her face grim as I pressed myself past" (110). Laura cries out to him in protest. But—"I left."

Welborn recognizes that the mother has provided him with "an easy solution to my problem" (110). He also feels to have lost "some precious but untenable vision of life." And he then recognizes a more bitter fact about Mrs. Johnson: "She preferred to have her daughter bear the burden of white bastardy rather than accept me as a son-in-law" (111).

As Welborn stumbles away from the Harlem apartment, his mind keeps "anticipating the outcome of our affair, screaming to me of the paradox that although ended, cut off, severed, it could never end" (115). It cannot end because it has engendered a child. "What would become of the part of me," he wonders, "that would be taken south to grow up in a lowly and alien section of the land?" His mind then moves from anguish to regret. "If only I had been more careful!" He begins to think of his unborn child as "bomb-like," a fertile seed extending itself into the distant future, "completely out of control." "I wanted desperately to stop it."

Like all of Ellison's claiming scenes, the story of Laura and Welborn carries with it the aura of interracial romance. The violence and eloquence of the mother's response to such a romance drains the situation of pathos and renders it almost comic. Even as the mother of a pregnant girl enacts a parody of the shotgun wedding, a number of hard truths are revealed, truths that remain fundamental in the upcoming prefiguring scenes. The first is the sometimes passionate but often casual and even careless longing of American bodies to cross the color line. The second is the possessive power of parental love, a power expressed by way of the repetition of the words *my* and *own*. The third is the tenuous standing of the father function when it comes to laying claim to a child.

In the second claiming scene, in book 2, Bliss is lying in his coffin. We have already learned that as a boy Bliss was recruited by Hickman to play his part in resurrection spectacles staged during religious revivals. Bliss is trained to wait in the coffin until the opportune moment and then to rise up and ask, "Why hath Thou forsaken me?" (252). He has also thereby been called upon to reenact the Western tradition's central agony of the abandoned son.

On the occasion in question, a redheaded woman turns up. She runs toward Bliss's coffin, yelling: "He's mine, mine! That's Cudworth, my child. My baby. You gypsy n——s stole him, my baby" (338). Bliss can see that "Yes, she is white." "Who's Cudworth?" he wonders, and then he realizes "Me, she means me" (339).

In the ensuing melee, as the white woman lifts Bliss out of the coffin, she is met by a congregation of Black women "hallowed with wrath" (341). Bliss finds himself suspended between the redheaded woman who holds his head and the sisters who have seized his arms and legs. Bliss and Hickman are now sharing this reverie, and Hickman is carried back to a time when Black women were charged with mothering a white woman's child. He thinks about "when women found that the only way they could turn over the responsibility of raising a child to another woman was to turn over some of the child's love and affection along with it" (342). Hickman sees that the Black women hanging on to Bliss "had helped raise somebody else's baby and loved it." "That situation," he concludes, "must make a child's heart a battleground."

And now here, in his church, Hickman witnesses a white woman "moving out of her territory and bursting into theirs." He knows that "down there her kind always wins the contest in the end—for the child, I mean—with ours being doomed to lose from the beginning and knowing it. They have got to be weaned—our women, I mean, the nursemaids. And yet, it seems to make their love all the deeper and tenderer." "Comes the teen time," Hickman reflects, these white children grow deaf to their nursemaid's lullabies and "cast out the past and start out new" (343). "They just don't recognize no continuance of anything after that: not love, not remembrance, not understanding, sacrifice, compassion—nothing." In imitation of this pattern, Bliss will eventually allow himself to be claimed by the white world. The Black congregation may succeed in wresting him back from the redheaded woman, but as Hickman concludes, "I left you in some of the sisters' hands and you misbehaved" (350). Bliss, so skilled at imposing continuity on pieces of film, grows up to pass as white and embraces the discontinuous life.

Hickman's recollection of the claiming scene with the redheaded woman exposes a history of attachment and repudiation leading to a developmental catastrophe for America's white children. Nursed by a Black "mammy" and then returned to the privilege of being white, they "learn how to *spurn* love" (343). But they have also experienced what it is to love and touch across the color line.

Profound as these repudiations may be, Ellison means to remind us that the discontinuities forced upon Black children under slavery were far more traumatic than anything a white suckling might have experienced. Often forcefully separated from their birth parents, slave children had no choice in the matter of how they might respond to a form of weaning far more violent than anything Hickman imagines in the second claiming scene.

Bliss may appear to be a boy of indeterminate race—as Mrs. Proctor says, "He don't show no sign in his skin or hair or features" of being Black (363)—but the sisters of Hickman's congregation claim him as one of theirs nevertheless. After he has been successfully reclaimed, Bliss listens to "the dark down labyrinthine ways of gossip" as Mrs. Proctor and Body's mother attempt to reconstruct the motivations of the redheaded woman (357). Their central assumption is that while Bliss's long-lost mother may be white, his father is Black, although this only leads to a further question about the redheaded woman: "Who in this lowdown South ever heard of a white *woman* claiming anything a black man had something to do with?" (363).

So much for the second claiming scene. In the argument I am making about what might be called Ellison's "hidden form," the third claiming scene, positioned at the end of book 2, has the function of leading directly into the climactic revelations in "Bliss's Birth." The scene takes place at Jessie Rockmore's Washington, DC, apartment.

Rockmore's three-story house is filled with memorabilia, a kind of crazy museum of the American past. When Hickman and a friend arrive at the scene—they are looking for the brother of one of Hickman's parishioners—they find themselves caught up in something resembling a bad traffic stop. In a "hall that was filled with men and women dressed in nightclothes" (436)—Rockmore rents out space to Black lodgers—two white policemen are engaged in some sort of raid on the premises. There has been a rumor of bootlegging.

Then Miss Maud turns up. "We all know that you're just burning to get brutal with us," she screams at the police (436). She proceeds to engage in an indictment of police methods and assumptions. All the Man has to do, she argues, is to find himself in a tight situation and the police "set about *terrorizing* him until he can make him own up to being responsible for whatever he charges him with doing" (442).

Maud's analysis of the guilt-inducing nature of police power forwards the novel's search for a credible source of authority—a true father principle—in American life. Early on in book 1, when McIntyre finds Hickman praying over the wounded Sunraider, he poses a question: "Why on earth would you weep for a man who is known, who is *notorious* for hating your people?" (70). The answer can come only through a reading of the novel ahead, but the impatient reporter insists that "the nation must have answers" now (71). Hickman responds: "They're the same old answers, son: Cain and Abel, the prodigal son and his father." In listening to Hickman, McIntyre realizes he has been "allowed to hear the voice of a mysterious authority" (72), although it is an authority having little to do with the kind being exercised by the power located on Capitol Hill.

The answer to McIntyre's question, Hickman indicates, lies at the heart of family life, and as McIntyre will go on to speculate: "Hasn't it been said that at some point each and every son wills his father's death? And isn't a nation a larger, more intricate form of family, and thus, like most families, thronged with dark, mysterious yearnings?" (74). The practice of democracy, Ellison's fable means to demonstrate, begins at home, and he had argued as much in the speech given when accepting the 1953 National Book Award: "The way home we seek is that condition of man's being at home in the world, which is called love, and which we term democracy."

But what if an entire people have not been invited to experience America as a home? The national failure of fathering can be traced back to the founding itself, where "Washington and Jefferson and Franklin" agreed to the inclusion in the Constitution of the Three-Fifths Clause and invented the Senate as a concession to the anxieties of major slaveholding states (282). "The democratic dream of our fathers" was betrayed, McIntyre comes to realize, from the very beginning (77). Hence, McIntyre thinks to himself, there arose the American habit of assassination: "Couldn't it be, McIntyre, that everyone in this country harbors a deeply repressed compulsion to shoot senators?" (74).

In Ellison's version of American history, Lincoln embodies contradiction at the source. In book 2, during a prolonged vigil at the Lincoln Memorial, Hickman focuses on the "look" of sadness on Lincoln's face (419). He sees in the look the expressed pain over all that Lincoln was unable to accomplish. There was, above all, "Lincoln's divided attitude toward the slaves" (422). "Maybe it's the confusion in the heart which makes history in the first place," Hickman reasons (423). "Maybe Abraham Lincoln doubted that freedom would work even if there was no black and white problem to deal with, and so he preferred not to think about it while he had a war to win." When it came to reestablishing the Union, "some say he didn't see a place for us in it." Still and nevertheless, and even though Lincoln "failed and he knew that he could only take one step along the road that would make us free" (419), "you"—and here Hickman engages in direct address to a statue in the same way as when a son might speak to a parent—"you're one of the few who ever earned the right to be called 'Father'" (420).

While the right to be called father begins at home, that burden and privilege extends all the way to the figure enshrined in the Lincoln Memorial. Hickman's reflections in the shadow of the statue touch upon one of Ellison's central themes, "that helpless, American, most democratic yearning which seeks ever to effect some sense of personal connection between the self and historical events" (86). In order to highlight these connections, Ellison stages his third claiming scene against the backdrop of Rockmore's assembled lithographs and photographs of everyone from Robert E. Lee to Crazy Horse to Jack Johnson.

The third claiming scene begins in earnest when Miss Maud starts to unpack her dream. "Gentlemen, last night I dreamed that I had given birth to three sweet little babies. That's right! One of them was black and one was white and one was 'riney red" (448). But "you ain't even married!" yells one of her listeners. "And don't I know it," Miss Maud yells back, but "My bridegroom shall cometh!" Was her giving birth without a husband any worse, she asks "than it would be if one of you gentleman was to give a woman a baby without marrying her, without letting her be a mother?" (449). "Is it any worse than it would be if a woman was to give *you* a baby that you didn't know she was going to give you?" (450).

For Hickman, Maud's questions about origin and legitimacy begin to take "on a note of personal significance" (450). He also has been given a baby he did not expect to receive, and he has tried to raise it as best he could. But he has also lost that child. Thus it is that as he listens to Maud, Hickman becomes "suddenly aware of the distorted surfacing of a story so intimately a part of him that for years it had existed in his consciousness less as a structure of events than as an emotion." "Reluctant to reveal itself," the story is also intent on "reassembling itself" (451, 452). It is the story of "Bliss's Birth," and it is the climactic ending to *Three Days before the Shooting . . .*, an ending for which the claiming scenes have fully prepared us.

"And I named him Bliss," the chapter begins (459). The opening conjunction reaches back toward a piece of text with which it can be connected up. Callahan and Bradley speculate that after the Plainfield fire, as Ellison "set to work 'reconstructing,'" he had reached a "narrative fork . . . where Book II" arrives at the scene "at Jessie Rockmore's townhouse" (xx). But as he continued to revise, "it is not at all clear that he took the action further, let alone resolved on an ending" (xxi). "Bliss's Birth" works beautifully, however, as the next and final step to be taken after Ellison reached the fork in his narrative.

It works, in part, because in it Ellison delivers his most powerful claiming scene, one in which a man who has not engendered a child is required to deliver it and to raise it. Ellison made sure to have echoes of the prior claiming scenes firmly in place: "He first was mine," Hickman thinks to himself, in the chapter's second paragraph, and further along, he will say, "I had been claimed" (477).

The twenty-two pages comprising "Bliss's Birth" in *Three Days* unfold as an interior monologue in which Hickman recalls his adopted son's violent beginnings as he sits by the bedside of that now wounded son. The memory opens with a twenty-six-year-old Hickman in a lamplit room feeling the weight of a rifle across his knees. He is waiting for the last act, waiting for the men who have lynched his brother, Robert, and therefore killed his mama too. Instead of being attacked by a guilty and avenging posse, a lone woman comes to his door. It is the white woman who had pointed at Robert and cried "rape."

"There's not much time, she said" (461). There is not much time because she is seven months pregnant. She also has nowhere else to go, having spared the life of her actual lover by fingering Robert but having burned all her bridges to the white community in the process. "Whose is it, then?" Hickman asks her (466). Her answer: "All I can tell you is that it wasn't your brother." The biological father, described by the woman as "someone more precious to me than myself," will remain unidentified (465).

Hickman has to decide what he will do. He thinks about burning down the house and killing himself, the woman, and the unborn child. But he also begins to imagine *her*. "But to who else could she go, Hickman?" he asks himself (467). As he continues to pose big questions—as in "Do you think . . . I'd let you put me in the position of trying to act like Christ?" (468)—he finds himself being drawn into something. "You didn't know it at the time but when you started talking she had shifted out of your hands and put you into hers." Then the contractions set in, and Hickman finds himself "helpless before the rhythm of those pains."

He delivers the baby. "And him not even brown so that I could have made some sensible meaning out of her coming here to me; just nothing definite, just baby-mouse-red and wrinkled up like a monkey with a strawberry rash" (470). This is Bliss, the indeterminate, a child who will be loved despite his lack of a verifiable identity.

The woman now makes her final demand: "I came to give you back your brother. . . . Take him and keep him and bring him up as your own" (473). "Let him share your Negro life," she urges. Acting almost as if in a daze, Hickman finds himself assenting: "Maybe the baby *could* redeem her and me my failure of revenge and my softness of heart, and help us all" (475). In that moment, Hickman decides to give the child a name. "I'll call him Bliss, because they say that's what ignorance is."

As he looks back, Hickman can see one thing: "That was the end of the old life for me" (475). There will be no more of "the hard, young, wasteful living" (480). Hickman begins again to follow his music and follows it "right into the pulpit at last." He finds sanctuary in a Black congregation, "where all babies could grow without too much questioning as to where they came from" (477). He has been changed by what he has begun to feel: "I had been claimed by then and they loved him."

Why, after all this, does Bliss decide to leave and disappear? To this question, the novel gives no easy answer. As Bradley argues in *Ralph Ellison in Progress*, "Bliss/Sunraider remains a central character in Ellison's fiction through most of the transcripts, though he is matched, and finally eclipsed, in importance by Hickman." In the end, Bradley concludes, Bliss "has been reduced largely to a plot device, less character himself than motivation for the actions of others." Bliss can fade in importance because the central concern of the novel is *the effect on the parent* of the experience of raising a child. "I raised you," Hickman says to the wounded Bliss (302). Raising, not engendering—fatherhood as Ellison conceives it has little to do with biological origins.

In the winter of 2023, an old friend emailed to say her daughter was dying; alcohol and cancer had taken their toll. When Katie and I were able to talk on the phone, we remembered people from high school and spoke in particular of her husband, Tim, who had died almost thirty years earlier, in his midforties. He had been my best friend, and as Katie's second husband, he had helped to raise the children of her first marriage.

When it came to talking about the love of children, I mentioned a Japanese phrase for that love, "darkness of the heart." Katie liked the sound of that and then said how that love seemed to involve a "humiliation." Yes, I agreed, something like that is often involved, but I wanted to suggest another word, one a little less pejorative: "Maybe it's more like a humbling." And Katie replied: "A humbling, yes, I guess that's right."

"This kind of labor of love is never lost." These were Ellison's words to Albert Murry as he looked back on the activity of writing his first novel. He had thereby learned how it feels to make something and then to send it out into a world that may well refuse to love it. However unfinished the labor of love may turn out to be, it is the experience of loving that is transformative, as the last words of "Bliss's Birth" suggest. As he sits by his son's bedside, Hickman reminds himself that the Lord's ways are strange ways: "Maybe it was all His plan, you had to be what you were then in order to lead his flock. It took all of that to come to this, and little Bliss was the father to the man and the man was also me . . . ." With these words, Ellison finishes his second novel.

"The child is father to the man" is usually taken to mean that an older, mature self grows out of (is "fathered by") a younger less mature self. But Ellison is taking the claim quite literally. A child is father to the man by requiring its own father—*through the act of fathering*—to grow up. And any achieved maturity that might result, as is so evident while Hickman browses through time, involves a humbling: So much can and too often does go wrong in the work of raising a child. God himself may be humbled before the demands of a plan in which a father has asked so much of a dutiful son that he can cry out, as Bliss is taught to do, "My God, my God, why hast thou forsaken me?"

But do the last words in "Bliss's Birth" work as an ending? Callahan and Bradley argue that book 2 of *Three Days* "seems to break off in midair" (3), and it does end with the somewhat unsatisfying demand being made by Miss Maud's "tell me, tell me!" "Bliss's Birth" concludes, on the other hand, with "and the man was also me . . . ." The story being told does not break off—it fades out. Here a simple mark of punctuation does what is needed. The ellipsis is perfectly expressive of the case about parenting Ellison has been trying to make throughout. The work of raising a child is never done—not as long as one is alive—just as being transformed by that activity from child to man is never complete.

A nation, too, struggles to grow up, and if that nation is a democracy, the achieved maturity of its civic life depends upon the capacity for indiscriminate loving care. Hence, the conflation of the words *love* and *democracy* in Ellison's lovely and already-quoted definition: "The way home we seek is that condition of man's being at home in the world, which is called love, and which we term democracy." The achievement of this love, as Lincoln once said, is "the work we are in."

When Ellison chose to assign Hickman the difficult but potentially rewarding work of acting as a substitute parent, he drew upon his own complex fate. In *Shadow and Act*, he recalls his voracious reading as a boy and "the vicarious identification and empathetic understanding which it encouraged." These feelings were "due, in part, perhaps to the fact that some of us were fatherless—my own father had died when I was three—but most likely it was because boys are natural romantics. We were seeking examples, patterns to live by, out of a freedom which for all of its being ignored by the sociologists and subtle thinkers, was implicit in the Negro situation. Father and mother substitutes also have a role to play in aiding the child to help create himself." If democracy is a political order in which every adult is called upon to act as a father or a mother, then it can only achieve its full promise if each of its citizens is willing to extend love to other people's children whether they are lovable or not and to assist in the raising of those children regardless of where they come from. The work we are in turns out to be a labor of love. Ellison's final ellipsis therefore invites readers to enter a contemplative space—does it perhaps register as a sigh?—in which they can take the time to reflect on their own experiences as citizens or parents as they live out the inevitably humbling consequences of their labors of love.

Afterword
LITERATURE AND RE-DREAMING

Each chapter in this book attempts to recover a particular historical drama surrounding writing that has not been and probably never will be left alone. My focus has been on work left either unedited or unfinished and therefore unpublished at an author's death. But even authors who have made considerable efforts to achieve "career closure" while still alive can find themselves subject to dramatic posthumous revisitings and reopenings.

In my introduction, I made passing reference to the *New York Edition* of Henry James. In this "*act* of re-appropriation," as James styles it in the "Author's Preface" to *The Golden Bowl*, he attempted to assert parental control over all that he had written and to give it a final, self-approved form (xiv). The first of the twenty-four volumes of the edition appeared in 1907. By the time James was finished with his labor of love, he had decided to exclude *Washington Square* and *The Europeans* from the official procession and to rewrite passages and sentences with such care as even to worry over "the position of a comma" (xxiii). The prefaces he provided his chosen sequence were later gathered into a volume called *The Art of the Novel*.

"To revise," James maintains, "is to see, or to look over, again" (xvi). For years, his "only law" had been "to get and to keep finished and dismissed work well behind one" (xiv), but now, at the age of sixty-four, having consented to "re-read in their order my final things," he finds himself prompted to apply a little "splash of soap-and-water" to some of his more "awkward infants" (xv).

As in the word *re-read,* when the prefix *re-* appears in the "Author's Preface," James usually sets it off from its root word with a hyphen. The two-letter prefix thus assumes the status of a refrain. The eighteen different *re-* words deployed by James include "re-perusal" (xiii) "re-presentation," and a final "re-dreaming" (xxii). James may have hoped that his late life act of "return" might work to prevent any "vulgarly irresponsible re-issue of anything" (xiii, xv). But there is a momentum built into the deployment of *re-* that time cannot resist. The looking over of something *again* opens it to "the reviving and reacting vision" of those who come after (xxi). James admits as much when he characterizes his edition as extending "an earnest invitation to the reader to dream again in my company and in the interest of his own larger absorption of my sense" (xxii).

This re-dreaming by readers who come after has taken ambitious form in *The Cambridge Edition of the Complete Fiction of Henry James.* The edition fills thirty-four volumes. A general editor's preface lays out some guiding principles: "This edition aims to represent James's fictional career as it evolves.... Consequently it does not attempt to base its choices on the principle of the 'last lifetime edition,' which in the case of Henry James is monumentally embodied in the twenty-four volumes of the NYE [*New York Edition*]." The choice is to honor James's initial impulses rather than his final wishes: "The *CFHJ* [the *Cambridge Edition*], as a general rule, adopts rather the text of the first published edition of a work." James might have been anticipating such a reversal in the preface to *The Wings of the Dove:* "One's plan, alas, is one thing and one's result another" (xiii).

For those inclined to lament the ignoring of James's late attempt at "making my brood more presentable" (xv), it may be useful to remember that even the Word of God has undergone a hailstorm of translation and revision, and with some thoughts about the unending "re-dreaming" of these words, I would like to conclude.

For readers of the Bible in English, the high point of the process of re-dreaming Holy Scripture was the creation of the King James Bible. The men assembled to do this work saw themselves as coming after. In their preface, they write, "Wee neuer thought from the beginning, that we should neede to make a new Translation, nor yet to make of a bad one a good one ... but to make a good one better, or out of many good ones, one principall good one." *Many good ones,* they write. Had the English divines been afforded world enough and time, they could have cited "good" versions of the Bible reaching back through Coverdale, Tyndale, Luther, Erasmus, Wyclif, Jerome, the Evangelists, the creators of the Septuagint, and all the way to the Hebrew scribes long since lost to history whose work of composition had traditionally been credited to Moses himself.

Some forty-seven scholars worked for seven years to bring the King James Bible into being. In their "Epistle Dedicatory," they recall for the King "how convenient it was, that out of the Original Sacred Tongues, together with comparing of the labours, both in our own, and other foreign Languages, of many worthy men who went before us, there should be one more exact Translation of the holy Scriptures into the *English Tongue*." The phrase *one more* here consorts uneasily with the word *exact* and was to prove predictive of an ongoing impulse to keep translating that resulted, during the centuries to come, in so many English takes on the biblical text as to produce one with the oxymoronic title of the "Revised Standard Version."

Christian readers of the New Testament, and regardless of whichever version of the text they may choose to prefer, are beneficiaries of a radical act of amendment. The very book that many believe to be the *new* good news was itself added to a book an earlier group of believers never thought of as *old* and had deemed sufficient and complete. A Christian reading of the Bible as a whole, especially one that accepts the second testament as somehow fulfilling the first, is a profoundly revisionary act. It models an approach to textual authority in which something new has the power to change the understanding of something old. Insofar as the making of the Bible can be said to have a verifiable history, it is the story of its afterlife.

For a student of literature in English, the most formidable attempt to revise Holy Scripture took place in an epic poem. Milton's *Paradise Lost* pursues many "Things unattempted yet in prose or rhyme" (1.16), but the central attempt is to retell the Genesis story in blank verse while somehow remaining true to both the spirit and the letter of the often-translated original. It is fair to say that Milton succeeded in giving Adam and Eve—not to speak of Christ and Satan and even God himself—such rich inner lives as to have enhanced his base text beyond anything any other writer in English has ever been able to imagine or to attempt.

Milton anticipates James's and Faulkner's fascination with the work of the *re-*: He sees that everywhere in the story he is retelling, things keep happening *again*. Books 7 and 8 of *Paradise Lost* are devoted to the story of how God made the world, and the poem requires two books in order to tell the story because the Old Testament commences with two versions of the Creation story; it is as if our most canonical text cannot quite decide how it ought to begin and so tells the story twice.

Genesis 1 presents the Creation from God's perspective, and in it, the two genders are made simultaneously but are given no names—"male and female created he them." Genesis 2 presents the Creation from the human perspective. After Adam is made from the dust of the ground, he is given a name and a task and a prohibition—but he has no partner. As God contemplates his Creation, a realization occurs: "And the Lord God said, It is not good that the man should be alone; I will make an help meet for him." God resolves to create "Woman," so called "because she was taken out of man."

Book 7 of *Paradise Lost* retells Genesis 1. "Let us make now man," the Eternal Father says to his Son, "in our image." The angel Raphael is relating the story to Adam and so continues: "Male he created thee, but thy consort / Female for race." By *race*, Milton means that two genders, here created simultaneously, are required in order to generate the "race of worshippers" that Adam and Eve will eventually produce (7.630).

In book 8, Milton retells Genesis 2. He also preserves the idea of Eve as an amendment—as a second thought. He accomplishes a major revision of Genesis 2, however, by making it seem as if the idea of Woman originated with Adam.

Adam wakes up, begins to name things, intuits his source in "some great Maker," (8:278), falls asleep, dreams of being transported into paradise, and wakes to find his dream true. A "conversation" (8. 419) with the "Author of all this" soon follows (8. 317). Adam is invited to name the animals and praises his Author for "all this good" (8. 361). Then he renders his critique: "but with me / I see not who partakes" (8.383–64). Adam feels lonely. He is again put to sleep, Eve emerges out of his dream, and he wakes "To find her" (8.479). Adam's response to his Author: "This turn hath made amends"

(8.491). But God has already admitted that he has been conducting a little seminar: "Thus far to try thee, Adam, I was pleased." He proceeds to say that "I, ere thou spak'st / Knew it not good for man to be alone" (8.444–45). God has been acting, that is, like the good teacher who allows the students in the room to develop their own ideas of what might be good for them. Even as God writes his Book, it turns out that the characters being created in it can solicit revisions from their Author. To return to the passage from Faulkner quoted in my introduction, in book 8 of *Paradise Lost*, Milton re-dreams the story of the creation of Eve as "a happy marriage of speaking and hearing" in which two voices overpass to love.

James once wrote that "it is ever the second doing, for me, that is *the* doing." God might seem to agree. The Creation is imagined by Milton as a second thought, although it is Satan who articulates the point as he prepares to invade Eden a second time:

> O Earth, how like to Heav'n, if not preferred
> More justly, seat worthier of gods, as built
> With second thoughts, reforming what was old.
>
> (9.99–101)

Second thoughts: the earth is a repair job. Remembering the War in Heaven and how his rebellion "thinner left the throng" of God's adorers (9.142), Satan interprets the making of the earth as an act of revenge:

> he to be avenged,
> And to repair his numbers thus impaired
> ....
> Determined to advance into our room
> A creature formed of earth.
>
> (9.143–49)

Earlier in the poem, God has also used the word *repair*. But he engages in his reparation because he likes to make rather than to break things: "I can repair / That detriment," he tells his Son, "and in a moment will create / Another

212 • Afterlife

world" (7.152–55). The world we know is then made. But the Creation, as the stories told in the Bible proceed to reveal, remains radically unfinished and subject to revision until such time as the Author of all things has perfected his final text and put an end to any further re-dreaming. Then there will be not flood but fire:

>   Meanwhile
> The world shall burn, and from her ashes spring
> New Heav'n and Earth, wherein the just shall dwell,
> And after all their tribulations long
> See golden days.
>
> (3:333–37)

NOTES

INTRODUCTION

1 "Publication – is the Auction": the quotation is from poem 788 in R. W. Franklin's variorum edition of *The Poems of Emily Dickinson*.
1 an "after-life": Dupee, 201.
2 "the distinguished thing": Ibid., 250.
2 "A parted ev'n just between twelve and one": *The Norton Shakespeare* (1997), 1471. All quotations from Shakespeare are from this edition unless otherwise indicated.
2 *a Table of green*: Ibid., 1471.
2 "the justly admired emendation": M. Mack, *Alexander Pope*, 428.
2 "the hope of the reader": Johnson, *Johnson on Shakespeare*, 8:704.
3 In the search for "some one text": Greg, "The Rationale of the Copy-Text," 22.
3 "We are not to regard the 'goodness'": Ibid., 15.
3 "the guidance of some particular early text": Ibid., 29.
3 "the tyranny of the copy-text": Ibid., 26.
3 "Wherever there is more": Ibid., 29.
3 "it is impossible to exclude individual judgement": Ibid., 26.
4 "the present edition is an exhibition": Mumford, "Emerson behind Barbed Wire," 3.
4 "twenty different diacritical marks": Ibid., 4.
4 "someone in the academic world": Wilson, "The Fruits of the MLA," 10.
4 by "the editing factories": Parker in Scafella, 17.
5 "grounds of self-incrimination": Ibid., 18.
5 "It is often said that textual criticism": Tanselle, 35.
5 "not just a set of books": quoted in Fritz.
5 "scrupulous and intelligent": Ibid.
6 "our nation's cultural heritage": Library of America website, https://loa.org.
6 conclusion that "the Library of America": W. Franklin, 187.

6 "I'm down on MLA": Robert S. Levine, email to the author, October 16, 2021.
6 "times have changed": Levine, "Editing Melville's *Pierre*," 169.
7 "none of the texts I have edited": Polk, *Children of the Dark House*, 5–6.
7 "transmission histories": McGann, *A Critique of Modern Textual Criticism*, xxi.
7 "search for the single unitary utterance": Ibid., xv.
8 "The peculiarity of being": Didion, "Last Words," 76–77.
8 "You think something is in shape": Ibid., 78.
8 "Have material arranged as chapters": Hemingway, *Ernest Hemingway: Selected Letters*, 916.
8 "without a final chapter": Hemingway, *"A Moveable Feast": The Restored Edition*, 10.
8 "I failed to complete the pieces": Hemingway in Brenner, 215.
9 "Concentrate on *scene*": Ellison, *Three Days before the Shooting...*, 974.
9 a scene "left out": Pope, 105–6.
10 "'And now,' Shreve said": Faulkner: *Novels, 1936–1940*, 261.
11 "fall far short": Jacobs, *Incidents in the Life of a Slave Girl*, 1.

1. *KING LEAR* AND THE HOPE OF THE READER

Numbers in parentheses are taken from *The Norton Shakespeare*, edited by Stephen Greenblatt et al. (New York: Norton, 1997).

13 "shocked by Cordelia's death": *Johnson on Shakespeare*, 8:704.
13 "run through the whole": Clark, *The History of "King Lear,"* in *Shakespeare Made Fit*, 295.
13 "Cord. Now comes my Trial": Ibid., 302.
14 "I wrong'd Him too": Ibid., 371.
14 "a Heap of Jewels": Ibid., 295.
14 to bring "the true text": C. H. Shattuck, 112.
14 "The metamorphoses the text has undergone": Wells, "*The History of King Lear*": Oxford World's Classics, 60.
14 "always makes us anxious": Johnson, 7:83.
14 "one event is concatenated with another": Ibid., 7:75.
14 we "are hurried irresistibly along": Johnson, 8:703.
14 "incidentally enforced" his "moral": Ibid., 8:704.
15 "expectation in preference to surprise": Coleridge, 77.
15 "A happy ending!": Lamb in Kermode, *"King Lear": A Casebook*, 45.
15 "*King Lear* is a fiction": Kermode, *The Sense of an Ending*, 39.
15 process of editorial "amendment": Johnson, 7:105.
15 "The fact that Quarto precedes Folio": G. W. Williams, 346.
16 "collated the old copies": Johnson, 7:94.

16	they serve as "independent witnesses": Wells, "*The History of King Lear*": Oxford World's Classics, 6–7.
16	"the two texts presented here": Bevington, 509.
17	what he called a "base text": Wells, 3, 7.
17	*Lear* "necessarily incorporates a number": Ibid., 8.
17	"should govern the procedure": Greg, *The Editorial Problem in Shakespeare*, ix.
17	"The aim of a critical edition": Ibid., x.
18	"interpreted this as 'spies'": Johnson, 8:700.
18	possessed of "*Negative Capability*": Keats, *John Keats: Selected Letters*, 41–42.
19	"It was a convention": Bate, *The RSC Shakespeare*, 2008.
21	Edgar "seems to me": Eliot, *The Letters of T. S. Eliot*, 2:361.
22–23	"singularly obtuse": Orgel in *King Lear. The Complete Pelican Shakespeare*, xli.
23	"the use of rhymed couplets": Wells, 49.
23	he "is dominated by his wife": Kirschbaum, 38.
24	"Shakespeare has deliberately made": Ibid., 34.
24	Albany "has a markedly increased": Ibid., 45.
24	in "the opening movements": Urkovitz, 86.
24	"Albany abruptly emerges as a character": Ibid., 92.
25	"Each time the audience is led": Ibid., 120–21.
25	"Albany's pattern of delay": Ibid., 113.
25	"perfectly consistent with Albany's character": Ibid., 125.
26	"In *parrhesia*": Foucault, *Fearless Speech*, 12.
26	"says what he *knows*": Ibid., 14.
26	This "practice of telling the truth": Foucault, *The Courage of Truth*, 5.
26	sincerity of the speaker is "his *courage*": Ibid., 12.
27	"It is true that, in some sources, Cordelia ends": Fraser in *King Lear*, Signet Classic (1963), 193.
27	"thy loving daughter": *King Lear*, Signet Classic, 210.
27	the "avoidance of love": Cavell in Kermode, "*King Lear*": *A Casebook*, 245.
27	a "preposterous idea": Sandy Mack, email to the author, November 10, 2011.
29	"I should need / Colours and words": Wordsworth, *The Prelude* (1805), 11:309–11.
30	"It is as if speech itself": Granville-Barker, 305.
31	"This scene," Pope wrote: Pope, *The Works of Shakespear: Volume the Sixth*, 105–6.
31	"Kent and a Gentleman": M. Mack, "*King Lear*" *in Our Time*, 9.
32	"*feeling with* is what the play demands": Adelman, 4.
32	"to be so ashamed": Zak, 55.
33	the "relatedness" Maynard Mack views: M. Mack, "*King Lear*" *in Our Time*, 115.
34	"All the miracles of the play": Adelman, 20.
34	"Of all Shakespeare's heroines": Bradley in Adelman, 27.
34	"the feeling that what happens to such a being": Ibid., 32.
35	"Let him, that is": Johnson, 7:111.

2. WORDSWORTH, THE LOVED ONE, AND THE MAKING OF *THE PRELUDE*

Numbers in parentheses are taken from William Wordsworth, *The Prelude: The Four Texts (1798, 1799, 1805, 1850)*, edited by Jonathan Wordsworth (New York: Penguin, 1995). Citations from Wordsworth's shorter poems and essays are taken from William Wordsworth, *The Major Works*, edited by Stephen Gill (New York: Oxford, 1984).

38 "the earliest extant drafts": de Selincourt, "Early Readings in *The Prelude*," 866.
38 "compact and rounded whole": W. Wordsworth, *The Prelude: The Four Texts*, x.
39 "in a simpler and more concentrated form": Ibid., 570.
39 "remembering back": Hemingway, "Now I Lay Me," *The Short Stories*, 365.
39 "great and cresive self": Emerson, "Experience," *Essays and Lectures*, 487.
41 "This is the only incident": Moorman, *William Wordsworth, A Biography: The Early Years*, 13.
41 "the truest memory of early childhood": Onorato, 205.
41 "The child did *not* cry": Ibid., 216.
42 "it is only in retrospect": Ibid.
42 "could name no moment": Gosse, 59.
43 a "cumbersome" addition: W. Wordsworth, *The Prelude*, 1799, 1805, 1850, 568.
43 "revisions are normally—not always": Ibid., 567.
44 "against the fact that things may come": Weiskel, 180.
45 "We parted from Coleridge": D. Wordsworth, *The Grasmere and Alfoxden Journals*, 95.
46 "Do not make loving": Moorman, *William Wordsworth, A Biography: The Early Years*, 553.
46 "I half dread that concentration": Ibid., 552.
46 "from my forefinger where I had worn it": D. Wordsworth, *The Grasmere and Alfoxden Journals*, 126.
46 "the two men running": Ibid.
47 "She and Wordsworth": Moorman, *William Wordsworth, A Biography: The Early Years*, 179.
47 "for a couple of hours": D. Wordsworth, *The Grasmere and Alfoxden Journals*, 69.
47 "They discoursed, no doubt": Moorman, *William Wordsworth, A Biography: The Early Years*, 555.
47 "we resolved to see": D. Wordsworth, *The Grasmere and Alfoxden Journals*, 82.
48 "We walked by the sea-shore": Ibid., 124.
48 "there is no more": F. Wilson, *The Ballad of Dorothy Wordsworth*, 201.
48 "On Sunday the 29th": D. Wordsworth, *The Grasmere and Alfoxden Journals*, 125.
48 "On Monday 4th October": Ibid., 126.
48 "When we are there": Wilson, *The Ballad of Dorothy Wordsworth*, 47.
48 "He was capable of abandoning": Blank, 83.

48 "surviving family decided to suppress": Moorman, *William Wordsworth, A Biography: The Later Years*, 182.
49 "So passed the time": "Vaudracour and Julia," *Wordsworth: Poetical Works*, 97.
51 "the closer Wordsworth became to someone": Wilson, *The Ballad of Dorothy Wordsworth*, 72.
52 "What is lonely": Bradley, *Oxford Lectures on Poetry*, 142.
53 "violence of Affection": Wilson, *The Ballad of Dorothy Wordsworth*, 36.
53 "because in you . . . I fondly view": Moorman, *William Wordsworth, A Biography: The Early Years*, 74.
53 "drop the concept of an ideal single text": Stillinger, 200.
54 Wordsworth's "love for Mary": Moorman, *William Wordsworth, A Biography: The Early Years*, 548.
54 "These new letters show": Darlington, 20.
54 "peaceful rather than stimulating": Moorman, *William Wordsworth, A Biography: The Early Years*, 78.
54 "Every hour of absence": Darlington, 26.
54 "a letter for myself": Ibid., 39.
55 "a thousand kisses": Ibid., 42.
55 "thy limbs as they are stretched": Ibid., 27.
55 "William's French family": Ibid., 24.
55 "slipped easily and naturally": Moorman, *William Wordsworth, A Biography: The Early Years*, 317.
55 "I fancied that we should have seen": Darlington, 61–62.
55 "Few people much mind": Wilson, *How to Survive the "Titanic,"* 270.

3. ENDING *GREAT EXPECTATIONS*

All quotations from *Great Expectations* unless otherwise indicated are taken from the Norton Critical Edition edited by Edgar Rosenberg.

59 "soul error": R. Shattuck 71.
62 doing "double duty": Meckier in Bloom, *Charles Dickens's "Great Expectations,"* 194.
62 "The theme" of *Great Expectations:* Daleski, 210.
62 "At this stage in his development": Ibid., 241.
63 "No amount of fire": Fitzgerald, *The Great Gatsby*, 101.
63 "some idea of himself": Ibid., 117.
64 "Pip's first visit to Miss Havisham's": J. H. Miller, 264.
64 "On this day he makes": Ibid.
65 Dickens's reader "is placed in much the same position": Quoted in Hammond, 239.
65 "wish for something awful": Flint in Jordan, *The Cambridge Companion to Charles Dickens*, 46.

66 *"readerly* expectations": Bradbury, 18.
66 "The expectation process": Meckier in Bloom, *Charles Dickens's "Great Expectations,"* 183–84.
67 "wisp of incest": Brown in Bloom, *Charles Dickens's "Great Expectations,"* 50.
73 "a father's last will": Sadrin, *Parentage and Inheritance*, 13.
76 "extraordinary gift for hope:" Fitzgerald, 6.
77 "Some natural tears": *Paradise Lost,* book 12, lines 645–49. All quotations from the poem are taken from the Modern Library edition of 2007, edited by William Kerrigan et al.
78 "a Victorian Adam and Eve": *Great Expectations,* Oxford World's Classics, xxxii.
79 "Abundant recompense": Wordsworth, *Major Works,* 134.
82 "a novel of returns": Dickens, *Great Expectations,* Oxford World's Classics, xiv.
82 "the first object he notices": Sadrin, *Great Expectations,* 225.

4. HARRIET JACOBS AND THE ORDEAL OF RECEPTION

All quotations from *Incidents in the Life of a Slave Girl* are taken from the Harvard University Press edition of 1987, edited by Jean Fagan Yellin, unless otherwise indicated.

86 not turn on a "scene of violence": Houston Baker in *Reading Rodney King / Reading Urban Uprising,* 38.
86 proceeds by way of the "undertell": Foreman in Garfield and Zafar, 77.
86 "too orderly" and "too melodramatic": Blassingame, *The Slave Community,* 373.
86 Goldsby writes, "that, because of the literary stylings": Goldsby in Garfield and Zafar 12.
87 readers contact "Mrs. Jacobs": Jacobs, *Incidents in the Life of a Slave Girl* (Norton Critical Edition), 165.
87 "simple and attractive": Ibid., 162.
87 "invaluable friend": Yellin, *Harriet Jacobs,* 183.
87 "made a call on Washington St.": Ibid., 184.
87 "In the mid-1800s": Clifford, 1.
87 published "the first full-length argument": Moland, xii.
88 "I have thought that I wanted": Yellin, *Harriet Jacobs,* 135.
89 "abridged, and struck out": Ibid., 141.
90 "Even before her death": Ibid., 261.
90 "an unreliable story listener": Stepto, 304.
90 "Naturally," William L. Andrews writes, "Jacobs would like": Andrews, 248–49.
93 "the sexual abuse of Linda": Garfield in Garfield and Zafar, 109.
93 "bind fragile reader and slave-author": Ibid., 110.
93 "to invade the ear": Ibid., 109–10.
93 "unreliability" in literary texts: Stepto, 309.

94 "there hangs over the book a kind of sadness": Auden in *Huck Finn among the Critics*, 134.
94 "*Now, old Jim, you're a free man*": Twain, *Mississippi Writings*, 894.
94 "chained . . . again": Ibid., 904.
94 "Ef it wuz *him*": Ibid., 894–95.
94 "When I got to where I found the boy": Ibid., 904–5.
95 "all that trouble and bother": Ibid., 909.
95 "what was most intriguing about black slave narratives": Garfield and Zafar, 30.
96 "Between Jacobs and Flint": Andrews, 277.
97 "Is it possible that they shared": Yellin, *Harriet Jacobs*, 28.
97 "competition between the master and slave": Andrews, 277.
98 "an excess of maternal feeling": Morrison, *Conversations with Toni Morrison*, 252.
99 her "best thing": Morrison, *Beloved*, 322.
99 "the freedom to love": Du Bois, 370.
99 It involves "two figures": Ibid., 383.
99 "To get to a place": Morrison, *Beloved*, 162.
100 "kind, benevolent face": Jacobs, *Incidents in the Life of a Slave Girl* (Norton Critical Edition), 197–98.
100 "it was generally held that the work was a fiction": Yellin, *Harriet Jacobs*, 262.
100 "The same love of liberty": Stanton and Anthony, 324.
100 "And so she vanished": Yellin, *Harriet Jacobs*, 261.
101 "It was but natural": Brawley, 39.
101 "plucked Jacobs out of invisibility": Andrews, 267.
101 "the 'editing' of Lydia Maria Child": Loggins, 228.
101 "were offered as 'told to' accounts": Bontemps, xv.
102 "fictitious names to all places and persons": Teller, x.
102 "In spite of Lydia Maria Child's insistence": Blassingame, *The Slave Community*, 274.
102 "Much is gained and not much is lost": Blassingame, *Slave Testimony*, xvii.
102 "accuracy," "reliability," and "the ring of truth": Ibid., xvi, xxiii, xxxix.
103 "pivotal authentication of self": Fox-Genovese, 392.
103 "the new feminist criticism": Yellin, *Harriet Jacobs*, xvi.
103 "accepted academic opinion": Ibid.
103 "recalled seeing at the Schomburg Collection": Ibid., xvii.
103 "clutch of letters involving Harriet Jacobs": Ibid.
104 "I ordered copies of the letters": Ibid.
104 "the style of *Incidents*": Yellin in *The Slave's Narrative*, 268.
104 "editing Jacobs's letters": Ibid., 277.
105 "When I was in New York": Sterling, 77.
105 "The spelling I believe was every word correct": Ibid., 77–78.
105 "the death of the grandmother": Yellin, *Harriet Jacobs*, 125–26.
105 "If I was not so tied down": Sterling, 80.

107 "the appearance of Jacobs's letters": Jacobs, *Incidents in the Life of a Slave Girl* (Norton Critical Edition), 204.
107 "having solved the puzzle": Yellin, *Harriet Jacobs*, xvii.
107 "The canonical nature of the Harvard edition": Goldsby in Garfield and Zafar, 14.
107 "What is striking here": Moland, 350.
108 A work of literature "is credited": Johnson, *Johnson on Shakespeare*, 7:77.
108 *How it felt to me:* Didion, *Slouching towards Bethlehem*, 134.

5. THE DICKINSON WARS

All quotations from Dickinson's poems are taken from the Franklin variorum unless otherwise indicated.

109 "Then Vinnie came to me": Bingham, 401.
110 the poems "would never sell": Ibid.
110 "cryptographic proportions": Sewall, 1:216.
110 "the poems were having a wonderful effect": Bingham, 402.
110 It is "safe to say": Sewall 1:218–19.
110 "some of her mistakes": Bingham, 402.
110 "I wish I were a Hay": Franklin, *The Editing of Emily Dickinson*, 22–23.
111 "I died for Beauty": Ibid., 22.
111 "over fifty had been changed": Ibid., 25.
111 "The 1896 volume has more titles": Ibid., 86.
111 Todd "extended" the editorial practices: Ibid.
112 "Here the two allies often met": Bianchi, *Emily Dickinson Face to Face*, 26.
112 *war between the houses:* Sewall, 1:258.
112 "I want to know anything": Ibid., 257.
112 the "bias is clear": Ibid., 252.
112 stealing "a kiss": Hart and Smith, *Open Me Carefully*, 7.
112 "Sue – you can go": Ibid., 68.
112 "the differences expressed in this letter": Ibid., 69.
113 "a family quarrel of endless involutions": Sewall, 1:195.
113 "Dear Toddy": Walsh, 25.
113 "She appreciates me completely": Ibid., 38.
113 "sides are still taken": Sewall, 1:162.
113 "It was in 1946": Ibid., xii.
113 "indispensable to the project": Ibid.
114 "Sue, the alien element": Ibid., 196.
114 "I went to see Vinnie": Bingham, 339.
114 "no legal validity": Gordon, 285.
114 "If Mrs. Austin Dickinson discovered it": Bingham 355.
114 "misrepresentation and fraud": Ibid., 350.

114 "on the meadow adjacent": Gordon, 290.
114 "Did Miss Vinnie ever talk to you": Sewall, 1:260.
114 "At this point publication stopped": Bingham, vii.
115 she "put all the manuscript materials": Sewall, 1:234.
115 "a bewildering series of editions": Franklin, *The Editing of Emily Dickinson*, xvi.
115 "Martha was determined": Habegger, 603.
115 "In some poems dashes are sprinkled": Todd and Bingham, *Bolts of Melody*, ix.
116 "The variorum tried": Franklin, *The Editing of Emily Dickinson*, 117.
116 "Emily Dickinson is supposed to have cherished": Bishop quoted in Morris, 143.
116 "Certainly in that first witchery": Bianchi, *The Life and Letters of Emily Dickinson*, 47.
116 Charles Wadsworth as "the unquestionable choice": Gelpi quoted in Habegger, 421.
116 "The legend of a broken heart": Bingham, 97.
117 question of Emily Dickinson's "lover": Morris, 72.
117 "explanatory value": Ibid., 73.
117 "Almost no one would dispute": Smith, *Rowing in Eden*, 129.
117 "the sisters-in-law's desire": Ibid., 25.
117 "attempting to create a female counterculture": Pollack, 61.
117 "fabulated a romantic tale": Ibid., 63.
117 "overt professions of homosexual love": Ibid., 62.
117 "conceived as the alternative to her disappointed love": Ibid., 79.
117 "Lesbianism, for Dickinson": Ibid., 80.
117 "Dickinson 'published' herself": Smith, *Rowing in Eden*, 4.
117 "Poetry Workshop": Ibid., 155.
117 "induction requires more than one example": Habegger, 368.
118 evidence of a "rift": Sewall, 2:440.
118 "Sue and Emily's regular and intimate exchanges": Smith, *Rowing in Eden*, 157.
118 "to make a cohesive book": Hart and Smith, xxi.
118 "manuscripts that editor Thomas W. Johnson did not link": Ibid., xxii.
118 "The letter-poem": Ibid., xxv.
118 "enclosing poems in letters": Mitchell, 166.
118 "the first literary scholar": Franklin, *The Poems of Emily Dickinson*, 1:6.
119 "seeks to intrude minimally": Ibid., 1:27.
119 "the creation of sixteen dash types": Crumbley, x.
119 "for simplicity," to "show all these 'pointings'": Hart and Smith, xxiv.
119 "to even the long and short dashes": Smith, *Rowing in Eden*, 65.
119 "While any handwritten text must suffer": Cameron, *Lyric Time*, 14.
119 "a consistent system": Lindberg-Seyersted, 196.
119 "served a multitude of purposes": Vendler, *Dickinson*, 21.
120 Dickinson's "surviving manuscript texts urge us": McGann, *Black Riders*, 38.
120 "Her calligraphy influences her": Howe, 153.

120 "The sly producer shapes her letters": Smith, *Rowing in Eden*, 85.
120 In her "experimental edition": Werner, *Emily Dickinson's Open Folios*, 55.
120 "this edition is about undoing": Ibid., 13.
120 "The drafts and fragments": Ibid., 5.
120 "the least intrusive of modern technologies": Mitchell, 23.
120 "the problem of blank spaces": Ibid., 50.
120 "an Accu-Spec II": Ibid., xv.
121 "It is my conviction": C. Miller, 7.
121 "moment or stage in a work's presentation": Ibid., 10.
121 poems can "be read without any yearning": Christensen, 148.
121 "to move away from a heroic narrative": Ibid., 15.
121 "This is an expensive and exclusive edition": Ibid., 88.
121 "the black and white photography": Ibid., 89.
121 "dissipation of certainty": Mitchell, 29.
121 "when a writer whose paradigm": Ibid., 30.
122 "perpetuate familiar assumptions": Perlow, 239.
122 Harvard "acquired claims to the manuscripts": Franklin, *The Poems of Emily Dickinson*, 1:6.
122 "Harvard's claims of ownership": Perlow, 248.
122 "The President and Fellows": Werner et al., *The Gorgeous Nothings*, 253.
122 "does not offer a schedule": Perlow, 248.
123 "Wild nights – Wild nights!": Franklin, *The Poems of Emily Dickinson*, 1:300.
123 "Longing, we say": Hass, *Praise*, 4.
124 "One poem only I dread a little to print": Bingham, 127.
124 "Though some readers take this as an image": Habegger, 590.
124 "The speculation that the speaker of the poem": Vendler, 94.
125 "Rowing in Eden –": Smith, *Rowing in Eden*, 66.
125 "eye-catching stanza of five lines": Ibid., 65.
125 "The manner of notation": Blackmur quoted in Christensen, 49.
125 "a reproduction of the manuscript": Levine et al., *The Norton Anthology of American Literature, 1820–1865*, 10th ed., 1518–19.
125 "The Poems' will ever": Bingham, 86.

6. FAULKNER REVISES

Unless otherwise indicated, all quotations from works by Faulkner are taken from the volumes published by the Library of America. The Noel Polk Editorial Papers from the Library of America and Random House Editions of William Faulkner are identified as MSS 13902 and are held in the Albert and Shirley Small Special Collections at the University of Virginia. Permission to quote from them is gratefully acknowledged.

127	"This novel, in both its manuscript and typescript versions": Blotner in *William Faulkner Manuscripts 5*, 1:viii.
127	"Faulkner had discovered the shape": Wyatt, *Prodigal Sons*, 90.
128	"Between 1927 and 1932": Polk, *Children of the Dark House*, 40.
129	"Faulkner was in the final stages": Blotner, *Faulkner: A Biography*, 1:556.
129	"Five lengthy sequences underwent relocation": Ibid., 1:556–57.
129	the finish date: "29 September 1927": Ibid., 1:557.
129	"I have written THE book": Faulkner, *Selected Letters of William Faulkner*, 38.
129	"It's too bad you don't like Flags in the Dust": Ibid., 39.
129	"It is with sorrow in my heart": Blotner, *Faulkner: A Biography*, 1:559.
129	"diffuse and non-integral": Ibid., 560.
129	"got going" on a new novel: Faulkner, *Selected Letters of William Faulkner*, 40.
129	"some children being sent away": Blotner, *Faulkner: A Biography*, 1:567.
130	"When Faulkner wrote about the novel's composition": Ibid., 1:570.
130	"One day I seemed to shut a door": Ibid.
130	"I have been trying": Faulkner, *Selected Letters of William Faulkner*, 40.
130	"Will you please try": Blotner, *Faulkner: A Biography*, 1:570.
130	"I don't think he can cut his work": Ibid., 1:581.
131	"I said, 'A cabbage'": "William Faulkner's Essay on the Composition of *Sartoris*" in Kinney, 119–20.
132	"the analysis of BW's deletions": Blotner, *Faulkner: A Biography*, "Notes," 86.
132	"the typescript which Faulkner retained": Blotner, *William Faulkner Manuscripts 5*, 1:x.
132–33	"Harcourt Brace & Co bought me from Liveright": Faulkner, *Selected Letters of William Faulkner*, 41.
133	"mingled admiration and doubts": Blotner, *Faulkner: A Biography*, 602.
133	"You're never going to publish": Ibid., 603.
133	"My copies of SARTORIS": Faulkner, *Selected Letters of William Faulkner*, 42.
133	"*The Sound and the Fury* is an apt title": Sundquist, 22.
134	"extensive cutting job": Faulkner, *Flags in the Dust* (1974), viii–ix.
134	"a sort of composite": Ibid., ix.
134	"remembered that her late father had spoken": Ibid., x.
134	"This typescript," we are informed: Faulkner, *Faulkner: Novels, 1926–1929*, 1173–74.
134	"In 1973 Random House published an edition": Faulkner, *Flags in the Dust* (2006), 406.
135	"there are more than seventeen hundred variants": Hayhoe in Kinney, 241.
135	"Day's apparent misunderstanding of the nature of the text": Ibid., 238.
135	"has stated that she did not ask Day": Ibid., 240.
136	Railton locates "three manuscript pages": Railton, *Digital Yoknapatawpha*.

138 "dreams of a world": Sartre in Kinney, 144.
138 "Faulkner had basically lined up": Porter, 38.
140 "lugubrious preoccupations": Polk, *Sanctuary*, 297.
140 "*Flags in the Dust*, Sundquist argues,": Sundquist, 7.
140 material about Benbow, "revisions": Ibid., 8.
141 "some of the Benbow material": Polk, *Children of the Dark House*, 42.
141 "The guiding principle behind Faulkner's revision": Polk, *Sanctuary*, 300.
141 Horace's "modified stream-of-consciousness": Ibid., 300–301.
141 "the germ of my apocrypha": *Faulkner in the University*, 285.
142 "This feeling that an ancestor's actions": Irwin, 61.
145 "internalized other": Williams, *Shame and Necessity*, 84.

7. PLATH AND THE RABBIT CATCHER

147 "It was a place of force": Plath, *Ariel: The Restored Edition*, 7.
147 "the awful daring of a moment's surrender": Eliot, *The Complete Poems and Plays*, 49.
147 in the Plath canon "it is also the poem": Rose, 135.
149 "The failure in vision": Perloff in *Poems in Their Place*, 318–19.
150 The poem makes "explicit reference": Ibid., 319.
150 "In June 1962, my father began an affair": *Ariel: The Restored Edition*, xiii.
150 the affair "was discovered": Plath, *The Letters of Sylvia Plath*, 2:790.
150 "nothing had happened to harm": Stevenson, 245.
150 Ted "was sympathetic to the simple economics": Bundtzen, 43.
150 "of a mind stirred": Malcolm, 128.
150 a "scenario" of Plath's suicide: Ibid., 124.
150 "perusing the first draft": Ibid., 128.
150 to use one of Hughes's words, as "documentary": Ibid., 129.
151 "the morning we set out": T. Hughes, *Birthday Letters*, 111.
151 with the "two babes": Ibid., 183.
151 "who have turned, in their sleep": Ibid., 182.
151 "You saw baby-eyed / Strangled": Ibid., 145.
151 "In those snares / You'd caught": Ibid., 146.
152 "small, ranked waves / Washing": Ibid., 80.
152 "'Like a lariat,' you said": Ibid., 81.
153 "current of attraction": Stevenson, 243.
153 "partly a cry for help": Ibid., 244.
153 "Yet nothing had happened": Ibid., 245.
153 "incessant dialogue": Middlebrook in Helle, 255.
153 "developmental growth spurts that go on occurring": Ibid., 264.
153 "his life as an artist": Ibid., 265–66.
153 "Plath had finally outgrown the usefulness": Ibid., 266.

153 "Plath's textual body is also hopelessly entangled": Bundtzen, 7.
153 "saw a late draft of the text": Rose, xii.
153 Rose's "interpretation of one poem": Ibid., xiii.
154 "Most crudely," Rose writes: Ibid., 138.
154 products of "a mind": Ibid., 141.
154 "The logic of blame": Ibid., 68.
154 "blame belongs to no one": Ibid., 58.
154 "Extraordinary, this need": Lessing, 336–37.
155 "What we are seeing": Ibid., 336.
155 "My focus is on writing": Rose, xi–xii.
155 "Like the child caught up": Ibid., 98.
155 "in the Plath-Hughes debate": Malcolm, 177.
156 "Previous biographies have focused": Clark, xix.
156 "no blame is apportioned": Ibid., 720.
156 "In 'Daddy' and 'Lady Lazarus'": Clark, *The Grief of Influence*, 153.
156 "help from Olwyn Hughes": Stevenson, ix.
157 "neatly arranged in a black binder": Clark, 895.
157 "the best poetry critic": Ibid., 831.
157 "These were the poems": Ibid., 764.
157 "the muse has come": Plath, *The Letters of Sylvia Plath*, 882.
158 "The poems in this volume": T. Hughes, *Winter Trees*, 7.
158 attempting "to set everything": Plath, *Sylvia Plath: The Collected Poems*, 15.
158 "The *Ariel* eventually published": Ibid., 15.
158 "Sylvia Plath's own prepared collection": Ibid., 295.
159 "In 1981 my father published": Plath, *Ariel: The Restored Edition*, xvii.
159 "replaces the attack on him": Bundtzen, 17.
159 "realizing perhaps . . . that the mood and 'story'": T. Hughes, *Winter Pollen*, 204.
160 "The question must remain": Bundtzen, 159.
160 The two *Ariels* "have a plot": Perloff, 311.
161 "begins with the birth": Ibid., 313.
161 In the 1965 *Ariel*, "on the other hand": Ibid., 313–14.
162 "integrated collections": Miner in *Poems in Their Place*, 40.
162 "Timber-trees, promiscuously growing": Jonson, 117.
162 "In the States": T. Hughes, *Winter Pollen*, 166.
162 "concern for certain people": Ibid., 167.
162 "Was the whole book simply unacceptable": Ibid., 166–67.
163 "perhaps Sylvia Plath's publishers will eventually give": Perloff, 330–31.
163 "This edition of *Ariel*": Plath, *Ariel: The Restored Edition*, xi.
163 Other "last-minute changes of mind": Brain in Helle, 18.
163 "should only be regarded as Plath's latest draft": Ibid., 20.
163 "to narrativize the circumstances": Ibid., 19.

163 "the more we try to establish": Ibid.
163 "Few poets have disclosed": T. Hughes in Alexander, 152.
163 "Sylvia Plath's poetry, like a species": Ibid., 153.
163 it is "in the last entries": Ibid., 153–54.
164 "Her writing here (as in her poems)": Ibid., 157.
164 "the terror is encountered head on": Ibid., 162–63.
164 "Sylvia Plath's journals exist": Ibid., 152.
164 "I destroyed": Plath, *The Journals of Sylvia Plath*, xiii.
165 "no one doubted that *Ariel* was indeed *Ariel*": Perloff, 309.
165 "worldwide fame was entirely posthumous": Feinstein, 163.
165 "lists of poem subjects": Bundtzen, 49.
165 "foundation text of the Plath legend": Malcolm, 20.
165 "the balance of power": Alvarez, 12.
165 "it was Sylvia": Stevenson, 314.
165 "helped him choose the final poems": Clark, 484.
166 "The one thing I retain": Ibid., 778.
166 "Despite its bitter end": Ibid., xxv.
166 "We work and walk": Ibid., 491.
167 "The one thing that recommends Plath": Vendler in Alexander, 4.
167 "restoring the balance": *Ariel: The Restored Edition*, xviii.

8. "HAVE SURE TRIED"

Page numbers in parentheses are taken from the following works by Hemingway, and Hemingway citations in the notes are given by title alone.

Ernest Hemingway: Selected Letters, 1917–1961, edited by Carlos Baker (New York: Scribner, 1981).

"*A Farewell to Arms*": *The Hemingway Library Edition*, edited by Seán Hemingway (New York: Scribner, 2012).

The Garden of Eden (New York: Scribner, 1986).

Manuscript of *The Garden of Eden*, ser. 1.2, box MS46, item 422.1, folder 21, Ernest Hemingway Collection, John F. Kennedy Presidential Library and Museum, Boston.

Green Hills of Africa (New York: Scribner, 1935).

"Green Hills of Africa: Part I," *Scribner's Magazine*, May 1935, 257–68.

In Our Time. See Trogdon.

A Moveable Feast (New York: Scribner, 1964).

"*A Moveable Feast*": *The Restored Edition*, edited by Seán Hemingway (New York: Scribner, 2009).

The Letters of Ernest Hemingway, vol. 3: *1926–1929*, edited by Rena Sanderson, Sandra Spanier, and Robert W. Trogdon (New York: Cambridge University Press, 2015).

The Old Man and the Sea (New York: Scribner, 1952).

Manuscript of *The Old Man and the Sea*, ser. 1.1.15, box MS27, item 190, folder 2, Ernest Hemingway Collection. John F. Kennedy Presidential Library and Museum, Boston.

The Short Stories of Ernest Hemingway (New York: Scribner, 1954).

The Sun Also Rises; see Trogdon.

Trogdon, Robert W., ed. *Hemingway: The Sun Also Rises and Other Writings, 1918–1926* (New York: Library of America, 2020).

True at First Light (New York: Scribner, 1999).

Under Kilimanjaro, edited by Robert W. Lewis and Robert E. Fleming, (Kent, OH: Kent State University Press, 2005).

168 "Are there any more books": V. Hemingway, 186.
168 "rambling African novel/diary": Ibid., 178.
168 "reconstructed by editors especially chosen": Ibid., 213.
169 a "faltering career": Fleming, 104.
169 "one is astonished to": Cowley, 105.
172 "comic irony": Burwell, 135.
173 "O western wind, when wilt thou blow": *Letters*, 3:314.
175 "Why did I never": Manuscript of *The Old Man and the Sea*, ser. 1.1.15, box MS27, item 90, folder 2, p. 105.
176 "finest sustained fiction": Price, 137.
176 Hemingway had "previously avoided": Ibid., 138.
180 "September 30 (Sunday)": Chamberlin, 283–84.
181 "It wasn't so bad": Dearborn, 544.
181 "his dad had died": V. Hemingway, 294.
181 "he was found dead": Ibid., 295.
181 "All his life Greg fought": Ibid., 296–97.
183 "a much finer man": *"A Moveable Feast": The Restored Edition*, 219.
183 "You write with the most terrible nostalgia": Manuscript of *The Garden of Eden*, ser. 1.2, box MS46, item 422.1, folder 21, p. 4.
184 "his continuing longing for that lost world": Kennedy, 212.
187 "Am working on the last one": *Ernest Hemingway: Selected Letters*, 916–18.

9. RALPH ELLISON'S LABOR OF LOVE

All numbers in parentheses refer to pages in the 2010 edition of *Three Days before the Shooting . . . .*

188 "The longer the book remained unfinished": Rampersad, 551.
189 "Even the 1,101 closely printed pages": Parrish, 13.
189 "I have dropped the shuck": Ellison, *Selected Letters*, 291.
190 "to *hear* the sound": Ellison, *Juneteenth*, 348.
190 "One thing both of us can be sure of": Ellison, *Selected Letters*, 296.
191 "My projected novel will be concerned": Ibid., 371.

191 "in my old agony again": Ibid., 347.
191 "I am involved with a novel": Ibid., 378.
191 "working on a novel": Ibid., 402.
191 "still having trouble in giving the book": Ibid., 447.
191 "About the novel I'll only say": Ibid., 473.
192 "The novel has got": Rampersad, 563.
192 "Oh, how beautiful it is": Ibid., 436.
192 "I lost part of my manuscript": Ibid., 443.
192 "When you lose 365": Ibid., 493.
192 "When you get institutionalized": Ibid., 425.
193 "that the assassination in his novel": Parrish, 80.
193 "Part of what's taken": Rampersad, 533.
193 "seems to have begun": Parrish, 77.
193 "Toni Morrison would observe": Rampersad, 359.
194 "stacks of printout, scraps": Callahan, "The Making of Ralph Ellison's *Juneteenth*," 178.
194 "Of the potential 'three volumes'": Ellison, *Juneteenth*, 366.
194–95 "A subsequent scholar's edition": Ibid., 368.
195 "structural unities of *beginning*": Ellison, *Shadow and Act*, 174.
195 "stop where the N-- Jim is stolen": Ibid., 34.
195 "set a free n-- free": Twain 909.
195 "put a detail in its proper place": Rampersad, 512.
196 "If I am to fulfill": Ellison, *Shadow and Act*, 125.
196 "I am stuck with integration": Posnock, *The Cambridge Companion to Ralph Ellison*, 15.
201 "The way home we seek": Rampersad, 271.
204 "Bliss/Sunraider remains": Bradley, *Ralph Ellison in Progress*, 126.
206 "the work we are in": Lincoln, 687.
206 "the vicarious identification and empathetic understanding": Ellison, *Shadow and Act*, xv.

AFTERWORD

Numbers in parentheses, unless otherwise indicated, refer to the "Author's Preface" to *The Golden Bowl* in Henry James's *New York Edition*. Readers interested in the creation of the edition can consult Philip Horne, *Henry James and Revision: The New York Edition* (Oxford: Clarendon, 1990); or David McWhirter, ed., *Henry James's New York Edition: The Construction of Authorship* (Cambridge: Cambridge University Press, 1995).

208 "career closure" while still alive: Millgate, 2.
209 "This edition aims to represent": *The Sacred Fount: The Cambridge Edition of the Complete Fiction of Henry James*, xiii.

BIBLIOGRAPHY

Adelman, Janet. *Twentieth Century Interpretations of "King Lear."* Englewood Cliffs, NJ: Prentice-Hall, 1978.
Alexander, Paul, ed. *Ariel Ascending: Writings about Sylvia Plath.* New York: HarperCollins, 1985.
Alvarez, A. *The Savage God: A Study of Suicide.* London: Weidenfeld & Nicolson, 1971.
Anderson, Charles. *Emily Dickinson's Poetry: Stairway of Surprise.* New York: Holt, Rinehart and Winston, 1960.
Andrews, William L. *To Tell a Free Story: The First Century of Afro-American Autobiography, 1760–1865.* Urbana: University of Illinois Press, 1986.
Bevington, David. "Determining the Indeterminate: The Oxford Shakespeare." *Shakespeare Quarterly* 38, no. 4 (Winter 1987): 501–19.
Bianchi, Martha Dickinson. *Emily Dickinson Face to Face: Unpublished Letters with Notes and Reminiscences.* Boston: Houghton Mifflin, 1932.
———. *The Life and Letters of Emily Dickinson.* Boston: Houghton Mifflin, 1924.
———. *The Single Hound: Poems of a Lifetime.* Boston: Little, Brown, 1914.
Bingham, Millicent Todd. *Ancestors' Brocades: The Literary Debut of Emily Dickinson.* New York: Harper & Brothers, 1945.
Blank, G. Kim. *Wordsworth and Feeling: The Poetry of an Adult Child.* Madison, WI: Fairleigh Dickinson University Press, 1995.
Blassingame, John W. *The Slave Community: Plantation Life in the Antebellum South.* New York: Oxford University Press, 1972.
———. *Slave Testimony: Two Centuries of Letters, Speeches, Interviews, and Autobiographies.* Baton Rouge: Louisiana State University Press, 1977.
Bloom, Harold, ed. *Charles Dickens's "Great Expectations": Modern Critical Interpretations.* Philadelphia: Chelsea House, 2000.

Blotner, Joseph. *Faulkner: A Biography.* Vols. 1 and 2. New York: Random House, 1974.

Bontemps, Arna. *Great Slave Narratives.* Boston: Beacon Press, 1969.

Bradbury, Nicola. *Charles Dickens's "Great Expectations."* New York: Simon & Schuster, 1990.

Bradley, A. C. "King Lear." *Shakespearean Tragedy.* London: Macmillan, 1904.

———. "Wordsworth." *Oxford Lectures on Poetry.* Bloomington: Indiana University Press, 1961.

Bradley, Adam. *Ralph Ellison in Progress: From "Invisible Man" to "Three Days before the Shooting . . . ."* New Haven: Yale University Press, 2010.

Brain, Tracy. "Unstable Manuscripts: The Indeterminacy of the Plath Canon." In Helle, *The Unraveling Archive: Essays on Sylvia Plath.*

Brawley, Benjamin. *The Negro in Literature and Art in the United States.* New York: Duffield & Company, 1929.

Brenner, Gerry. *A Comprehensive Companion to Hemingway's "A Moveable Feast": Annotation to Interpretation.* Lewiston, NY: Edwin Mellen Press, 2000.

Brown, Carolyn. "*Great Expectations:* Masculinity and Modernity." In *Charles Dickens's "Great Expectations": Modern Critical Interpretations,* edited by Harold Bloom. Philadelphia: Chelsea House, 2000.

Bundtzen, Linda. *The Other "Ariel."* Amherst: University of Massachusetts Press, 2001.

Burwell, Rose Marie. *Hemingway: The Postwar Years and the Posthumous Novels.* New York: Cambridge University Press, 1996.

Callahan, John F. "The Making of Ralph Ellison's *Juneteenth.*" *Columbia: A Journal of Literature and Art,* no. 36 (2002): 175–89.

Cameron, Sharon. *Choosing Not Choosing: Dickinson's Fascicles.* Chicago: University of Chicago Press, 1992.

———. *Lyric Time: Dickinson and the Limits of Genre.* Baltimore: Johns Hopkins University Press, 1979.

Cavell, Stanley. "The Avoidance of Love." In Kermode, *"King Lear": A Casebook.*

Chamberlin, Brewster. *The Hemingway Log: A Chronology of His Life and Times.* Lawrence: University Press of Kansas, 2015.

Christensen, Lena. *Editing Emily Dickinson: The Production of an Author.* New York: Routledge. 2013.

Clark, Heather. *The Grief of Influence: Sylvia Plath and Ted Hughes.* New York: Oxford University Press, 2011.

———. *Red Comet: The Short Life and Blazing Art of Sylvia Plath.* New York: Knopf, 2020.

Clark, Sandra, ed. *Shakespeare Made Fit: Restoration Adaptations of Shakespeare.* London: Everyman, 1997.

Clifford, Deborah Pickman. *Crusader for Freedom: A Life of Lydia Maria Child.* Boston: Beacon Press, 1992.

Coleridge, Samuel Taylor. *The Literary Remains of Samuel Taylor Coleridge.* Vol. 2. Edited by Henry Nelson Coleridge. Frankfurt: Outlook Verlag, 2018.

Cowley, Malcolm. "A Double Life, Half Told." *Atlantic,* December 1970, 105–8.

Crumbley, Paul. *Inflections of the Pen: Dash and Voice in Emily Dickinson.* Lexington: University Press of Kentucky, 1997.

Daleski, H. M. *Dickens and the Art of Analogy.* London: Faber, 1970.

Darlington, Beth, ed. *The Love Letters of William and Mary Wordsworth.* Ithaca: Cornell University Press, 1981.

Dearborn, Mary V. *Ernest Hemingway: A Biography.* New York: Knopf, 2017.

De Selincourt, Ernest. "Early Readings in *The Prelude*." *Times Literary Supplement,* November 12, 1931, 866.

Dickens, Charles. *Great Expectations.* Norton Critical Edition. Edited by Edgar Rosenberg. New York: Norton, 1999.

———. *Great Expectations.* Oxford World's Classics. Oxford: Oxford University Press, 2008.

———. *Little Dorrit.* Oxford World's Classics. Oxford: Oxford University Press, 2008.

———. *The Mystery of Edwin Drood.* Oxford World's Classics. Oxford: Oxford University Press, 2009.

Dickinson, Emily. *The Poems of Emily Dickinson.* Edited by Thomas H. Johnson. Cambridge: Belknap Press of Harvard University Press, 1955.

———. *The Poems of Emily Dickinson: Variorum Edition.* Edited by R. W. Franklin. 3 vols. Cambridge: Belknap Press of Harvard University Press, 1998.

Didion, Joan. "Last Words." *New Yorker,* November, 9, 1998, 74–80.

———. *Slouching towards Bethlehem.* New York: Farrar, Straus & Giroux, 1968.

Donaldson, Scott, ed. *The Cambridge Companion to Ernest Hemingway.* New York: Cambridge University Press, 1996.

Du Bois, W. E. B. *Du Bois: Writings.* Edited by Eric Foner, Nathan Huggins, and Henry Louis Gates Jr. New York: Library of America, 1986.

Dupee, F. W. *Henry James.* New York: Doubleday, 1956.

Eliot, T. S. *The Complete Poems and Plays: 1909–1950.* New York: Harcourt Brace Jovanovich, 1971.

———. *The Letters of T. S. Eliot.* Vol. 2: *1923–1925.* Edited by Valerie Eliot and Hugh Haughton. New Haven: Yale University Press, 2009.

Ellison, Ralph. *Conversations with Ralph Ellison.* Edited by Maryemma Graham and Amrajit Singh. Jackson: University Press of Mississippi, 1995.
———. *Juneteenth.* Edited by John F. Callahan. New York: Random House, 1999.
———. *The Selected Letters of Ralph Ellison.* Edited by John F. Callahan and Marc C. Conner. New York: Random House, 2019.
———. *Shadow and Act.* New York: Random House, 1964.
———. *Three Days before the Shooting . . . .* Edited by John F. Callahan and Adam Bradley. New York: Random House, 2010.
Emerson, Ralph Waldo. "Experience." *Emerson: Essays and Lectures.* Edited by Joel Porte. New York: Library of America, 1983.
Faulkner in the University. Edited by Frederick L. Gwynn and Joseph L. Blotner. 1958. Reprint, Charlottesville: University of Virginia Press, 1995.
Faulkner, William. *Flags in the Dust.* Edited by Douglas Day. New York: Random House, 1973.
———. *Flags in the Dust.* Edited by Noel Polk. New York: Random House, 2006.
———. *Sanctuary.* New York: Cape & Smith, 1931.
———. *Sanctuary: The Original Text.* Edited by Noel Polk. New York: Random House, 1981.
———. *Sartoris.* 1929. Reprint, New York: Random House, 1956.
———. *Selected Letters of William Faulkner.* Edited by Joseph Blotner. New York: Random House, 1977.
———. "William Faulkner's Essay on the Composition of *Sartoris.*" Edited by Joseph Blotner. *Yale University Library Gazette* 4, no. 3 (January 1973): 121–24. (A copy of the essay can be found in Kinney [118–20].)
———. *William Faulkner Manuscripts 5: Flags in the Dust,* vols. 1–2. Introduced and arranged by Joseph Blotner. New York: Garland, 1987.
———. *William Faulkner: Novels, 1926–1929.* Edited by Joseph Blotner and Noel Polk. New York: Library of America, 2006. (This volume contains *Flags in the Dust.*)
———. *William Faulkner: Novels, 1930–1935.* Edited by Joseph Blotner and Noel Polk. New York: Library of America, 1985.
———. *William Faulkner: Novels, 1936–1940.* Edited by Joseph Blotner and Noel Polk. New York: Library of America, 1990. (This volume contains *Absalom, Absalom!* and *The Unvanquished.*)
Feinstein, Elaine. *Ted Hughes: The Life of a Poet.* New York: Norton, 2003.
Fitzgerald, F. Scott. *"The Great Gatsby," "All The Sad Young Men" & Other Writings 1920–1926.* Edited by James L. W. West III. New York: Library of America, 2022.

Fleming, Robert E. *The Face in the Mirror: Hemingway's Writers*. Tuscaloosa: University of Alabama Press, 1994.

Flint, Kate. "The Middle Novels: *Chuzzlewit, Dombey,* and *Copperfield*." In Jordan, *The Cambridge Companion to Charles Dickens*.

Foucault, Michel. *The Courage of Truth: The Government of Self and Others*. New York: Palgrave Macmillan, 2011.

Foucault, Michel, and Joseph Pearson. *Fearless Speech*. Los Angeles: Semiotext(e) 2001. (Lectures delivered at UC Berkeley in the fall of 1983.)

Fox-Genovese, Elizabeth. *Within the Plantation Household: Black and White Women of the Old South*. Chapel Hill: University of North Carolina Press, 1988.

Franklin, John Hope. *From Slavery to Freedom: A History of Negro Americans*. New York: Knopf, 1947.

Franklin, R. W. *The Editing of Emily Dickinson: A Reconsideration*. Madison: University of Wisconsin Press, 1967.

———. *The Manuscript Books of Emily Dickinson*. 2 vols. Cambridge: Belknap Press of Harvard University Press, 1981.

———. *The Poems of Emily Dickinson: Reading Edition*. Cambridge: Belknap Press of Harvard University Press, 1999.

———. *The Poems of Emily Dickinson: Variorum Edition*. 3 vols. Cambridge: Belknap Press of Harvard University Press, 1998.

Franklin, Wayne. "The 'Library of America' and the Welter of American Books." *Iowa Review* 15, no. 2 (Spring–Summer 1985): 176–94.

Fraser, Russell, ed. *King Lear*. Signet Classic. New York: Penguin Putnam, 1963.

Fritz, Meaghan. "'The coiled fish of the sea': A Brief History of the Northwestern-Newberry Edition of *The Writings of Herman Melville*." Northwestern University Press blog, November 22, 2017. https://nupress.northwestern.edu/blog/2017/11/22.

Garfield, Deborah M., and Rafia Zafar, eds. *Harriet Jacobs and Incidents in the Life of a Slave Girl*. New York: Cambridge University Press, 1996.

Gay, Peter. *Education of the Senses: Victoria to Freud*. Vol. 1. New York: Oxford University Press, 1984.

Gelpi, Albert J. *Emily Dickinson: The Mind of the Poet*. Cambridge: Harvard University Press, 1965.

Gordon, Lyndall. *Lives Like Loaded Guns: Emily Dickinson and Her Family's Feuds*. New York: Viking, 2010.

Gosse, Edmund. *Father and Son*. 1907. Reprint, Oxford: Oxford University Press, 2009.

Granville-Barker, Harley. *Prefaces to Shakespeare.* Vol. 1. Princeton: Princeton University Press, 1946.

Greg, W. W. *The Editorial Problem in Shakespeare: A Survey of the Foundations of the Text.* 2nd ed. Oxford: Clarendon Press, 1951.

———. "The Rationale of the Copy-Text." *Studies in Bibliography* 3 (1950–51): 19–36.

Habegger, Alfred. *My Wars Are Laid Away in Books: The Life of Emily Dickinson.* New York: Random House, 2001.

Hammond, Mary. *Charles Dickens's "Great Expectations": A Cultural Life, 1860–2012.* Farnham, England: Ashgate, 2015.

Hart, Ellen Louise, and Martha Nell Smith. *Open Me Carefully: Emily Dickinson's Intimate Correspondence to Susan Huntington Dickinson.* Ashfield, MA: Paris Press, 1998.

Hass, Robert. *Praise.* New York: Ecco Press, 1979.

Helle, Anita, ed. *The Unraveling Archive: Essays on Sylvia Plath.* Ann Arbor: University of Michigan Press, 2007.

Hemingway, Ernest. The Ernest Hemingway Collection. John F. Kennedy Presidential Library and Museum, Boston.

———. *Ernest Hemingway: Selected Letters, 1917–1961.* Edited by Carlos Baker. New York: Scribner, 1981.

———. *"A Farewell to Arms": The Hemingway Library Edition.* Edited by Seán Hemingway. New York: Scribner, 2012.

———. *The Garden of Eden.* New York: Scribner, 1986.

———. *Green Hills of Africa.* New York: Scribner, 1935.

———. "Green Hills of Africa: Part I." *Scribner's Magazine,* May 1935, 257–68.

———. *Hemingway: "The Sun Also Rises" & Other Writings, 1918–1926.* Edited by Robert W. Trogdon. New York: Library of America, 2020.

———. *In Our Time.* See Trogdon.

———. *The Letters of Ernest Hemingway, 1926–1929.* Vol. 3. Edited by Rena Sanderson, Sandra Spanier, and Robert W. Trogdon. New York: Cambridge University Press, 2015.

———. Manuscript of *The Garden of Eden.* Series 1.2, box MS46, item 422.1, folder 21. Ernest Hemingway Collection. John F. Kennedy Presidential Library and Museum, Boston.

———. Manuscript of *The Old Man and the Sea.* Series 1.1.15, box MS27, item 190, folder 2. Ernest Hemingway Collection. John F. Kennedy Presidential Library and Museum, Boston.

———. *A Moveable Feast.* New York: Scribner, 1964.

———. *"A Moveable Feast": The Restored Edition.* Edited by Seán Hemingway. New York: Scribner, 2009.

———. *The Old Man and the Sea.* New York: Scribner, 1952.

———. *The Short Stories of Ernest Hemingway.* New York: Scribner, 1954.

———. *The Sun Also Rises.* See Trogdon.

———. *True at First Light.* New York: Scribner, 1999.

———. *Under Kilimanjaro.* Edited by Robert W. Lewis and Robert E. Fleming. Kent, OH: Kent State University Press, 2005.

Hemingway, Gregory. *Papa: A Personal Memoir.* Boston: Houghton Mifflin, 1976.

Hemingway, Valerie. *Running with the Bulls: My Life with the Hemingways.* New York: Ballantine, 2004.

Howe, Susan. *The Birth-Mark: Unsettling the Wilderness in American Poetry.* Hanover, NH: Wesleyan University Press, 1993.

Huck Finn among the Critics: A Centennial Selection. Edited by M. Thomas Inge. Frederick, MD: University Publications of America, 1985.

Hughes, Ted. *Birthday Letters.* New York: Farrar, Straus & Giroux, 1998.

———. *Winter Pollen: Occasional Prose.* New York: Picador, 1995.

Irwin, John T. *Doubling and Incest / Repetition and Revenge: A Speculative Reading of Faulkner.* Baltimore: Johns Hopkins University Press, 1975.

Jacobs, Harriet A. *Incidents in the Life of a Slave Girl.* Edited by Jean Fagan Yellin. Cambridge: Harvard University Press, 1987.

———. *Incidents in the Life of a Slave Girl.* Norton Critical Edition. Edited by Nellie Y. McKay and Frances Smith Foster. New York: Norton, 2001.

———. *Incidents in the Life of a Slave Girl.* Edited by Walter Magnes Teller. New York: Harcourt Brace Jovanovich, 1973.

James, Henry. *The Golden Bowl.* Vol. 23 of *The New York Edition of Henry James.* 1909. Reprint, New York: Augustus M. Kelley, 1971.

———. *The Sacred Fount. The Cambridge Edition of the Complete Fiction of Henry James.* 1901. Edited by T. J. Lustig. Cambridge: Cambridge University Press, 2019.

———. *The Wings of the Dove.* Vol. 19 of *The New York Edition of Henry James.* 1909. Reprint, New York: Augustus M. Kelley, 1971.

Johnson, Samuel. *Johnson on Shakespeare.* Yale Edition of the Works of Samuel Johnson. Vols. 7 and 8. Edited by Arthur Sherbo. New Haven: Yale University Press, 1968.

Jonson, Ben. *The Complete Poetry of Ben Jonson.* Edited by William B. Hunter Jr. New York: Norton, 1963.

Jordan, John O., ed. *The Cambridge Companion to Charles Dickens.* Cambridge: Cambridge University Press, 2001.

Keats, John. *Keats: Selected Letters.* Oxford World's Classics. Edited by Robert Gittings. Oxford: Oxford University Press, 2009.

Kennedy, J. Gerald. "Hemingway, Hadley, and Paris: The Persistence of Desire." In Donaldson, *The Cambridge Companion to Ernest Hemingway.*

Kermode, Frank. *The Sense of an Ending: Studies in the Theory of Fiction.* New York: Oxford University Press, 1967.

———, ed. *Shakespeare: "King Lear": A Casebook.* 1969. Rev. ed. London: Macmillan, 1992.

Kinney, Arthur F., ed. *Critical Essays on William Faulkner: The Sartoris Family.* Boston: G. K. Hall, 1985. (George F. Hayhoe's 1975 article appears here, "as especially revised for this volume by the author.")

Kirschbaum, Leo. *Character and Characterization in Shakespeare.* Detroit: Wayne State University Press, 1962.

Kohler, Michelle, ed. *The New Emily Dickinson Studies.* New York: Cambridge University Press, 2019.

Lessing, Doris. *Walking in the Shade: Volume Two of My Autobiography—1949–1962.* New York: Harper, 1998.

Levine, Robert S. "Editing Melville's Pierre: Text, Nation, Time." In *Neither the Time nor the Place: The New Nineteenth-Century Studies,* edited by Christopher Castiglia and Susan Gillman. Philadelphia: University of Pennsylvania Press, 2022.

———. *The Norton Anthology of American Literature.* Vol. B: *1920–1865.* 10th ed. New York: Norton, 2022.

Lincoln, Abraham. *Lincoln: Speeches and Writings, 1859–1865.* Edited by Don E. Fehrenbacher. New York: Library of America, 1989.

Lindberg-Seyersted, Brita. *Voice of the Poet: Aspects of Style in the Poetry of Emily Dickinson.* Cambridge: Harvard University Press, 1968.

Loggins, Vernon. *The Negro Author: His Development in America.* New York: Columbia University Press, 1931.

Mack, Maynard. *Alexander Pope: A Biography.* New Haven: Yale University Press, 1985.

———. *"King Lear" in Our Time.* Berkeley: University of California Press, 1965.

Malcolm, Janet. *The Silent Woman: Sylvia Plath and Ted Hughes.* New York: Knopf, 1994.

McGann, Jerome J. *Black Riders: The Visible Language of Modernism.* Princeton: Princeton University Press, 1993.

———. *A Critique of Modern Textual Criticism*. Charlottesville: University Press of Virginia, 1992.

Meckier, Jerome. "Charles Dickens's *Great Expectations*: A Defense of the Second Ending." In *Charles Dickens's "Great Expectations": Modern Critical Interpretations*, edited by Harold Bloom. Philadelphia: Chelsea House, 2000.

Middlebrook, Diane. "Creative Partnership: Sources for 'The Rabbit Catcher.'" In Helle, *The Unraveling Archive: Essays on Sylvia Plath*.

Miller, Cristanne. *Emily Dickinson's Poems: As She Preserved Them*. Cambridge: Belknap Press of Harvard University Press, 2016.

Miller, J. Hillis. *Charles Dickens: The World of His Novels*. Cambridge: Harvard University Press, 1958.

Millgate, Michael. *Testamentary Acts: Browning, Tennyson, James, Hardy*. New York: Oxford University Press, 1992.

Milton, John. *Paradise Lost*. Edited by William Kerrigan, John Rumrich, and Stephen M. Fallon. New York: Modern Library, 2008.

Mitchell, Domhnall. *Measures of Possibility: Emily Dickinson's Manuscripts*. Amherst: University of Massachusetts Press, 2005.

Moland, Lydia. *Lydia Maria Child: A Radical American Life*. Chicago: University of Chicago Press, 2022.

Moorman, Mary. *William Wordsworth, A Biography: The Early Years, 1770–1803*. Oxford: Oxford University Press, 1965.

———. *William Wordsworth, A Biography: The Later Years, 1803–1850*. Oxford: Oxford University Press, 1965.

Morris, Timothy. *Becoming Canonical in American Poetry*. Urbana: University of Illinois Press, 1995.

Morrison, Toni. *Beloved*. 1987. Reprint, New York: Random House, 2004.

———. *Conversations with Toni Morrison*. Edited by Danielle K. Taylor Guthrie. Jackson: University Press of Mississippi, 1994.

Mumford, Lewis. "Emerson behind Barbed Wire." *New York Review of Books* 10, no. 1, January 18, 1968, 2–4.

The Norton Anthology of English Literature. 3rd ed. Edited by M. H. Abrams. New York: Norton, 1974.

Onorato, Richard. *The Character of the Poet: Wordsworth in "The Prelude."* Princeton: Princeton University Press, 1971.

Orgel, Stephen, ed. *King Lear. The Complete Pelican Shakespeare*. New York: Penguin Putnam, 1999.

Parker, Hershel. "Textual Criticism and Hemingway" in Scafella, *Hemingway: Essays of Reassessment*.

Parrish, Timothy. *Ralph Ellison and the Genius of America*. Amherst: University of Massachusetts Press, 2012.
Perloff, Marjorie. "The Two *Ariels*: The (Re)Making of the Sylvia Plath Canon." In *Poems in Their Place*.
Perlow, Seth. "Textures Newly Visible: Seeing and Feeling the Online Dickinson Archives." In *The New Emily Dickinson Studies*, edited by Michelle Kohler. New York: Cambridge University Press, 2019.
Plath, Sylvia. *Ariel*. 1965. Reprint, New York: Harper & Row, 1966.
———. *Ariel: The Restored Edition*. Foreword by Frieda Hughes. New York: HarperCollins, 2004.
———. *The Collected Poems*. Edited by Ted Hughes. New York: Harper & Row, 1981.
———. *The Journals of Sylvia Plath*. Edited by Frances McCullough; Ted Hughes, consulting ed. New York: Random House, 1982.
———. *The Letters of Sylvia Plath*. Vol. 2: *1956–1963*. Edited by Peter K. Steinberg and Karen V. Kukil. New York: HarperCollins, 2018.
Poems in Their Place: The Intertextuality and Order of Poetic Collections. Edited by Neil Fraistat. Chapel Hill: University of North Carolina Press, 1987.
Polk, Noel. *Children of the Dark House: Text and Context in Faulkner*. Jackson: University Press of Mississippi, 1996.
———. Noel Polk Editorial Papers from the Library of America and Random House Editions of the Works of William Faulkner. Special Collections, University of Virginia, Accession no. 13902.
Pollack, Vivian. *Dickinson: The Anxiety of Gender*. Ithaca: Cornell University Press, 1984.
Pope, Alexander. *The Works of Shakespear in Six Volumes*. Vol. 6 (1723–25). Reprinted in *Warburton's Shakespear* of 1747. New York AMS Press, 1968.
Porter, Carolyn. *William Faulkner*. New York: Oxford University Press, 2007.
Posnock, Ross, ed. *The Cambridge Companion to Ralph Ellison*. New York: Cambridge University Press, 2005.
Price, Reynolds. "For Ernest Hemingway." *A Common Room: Essays 1954–1987*. New York: Atheneum, 1987.
Railton, Stephen. *Digital Yoknapatawpha*. University of Virginia. Added in 2015. https://faulkner.drupal.shanti.virginia.edu/content/hmanuscripts.
Rampersad, Arnold. *Ralph Ellison: A Biography*. New York: Knopf, 2007.
Reading Rodney King / Reading Urban Uprising. Edited by Robert Gooding-Williams. London: Routledge, 1993.
Rose, Jacqueline. *The Haunting of Sylvia Plath*. London: Virago Press, 1991.

Sadrin, Anny. *Great Expectations.* London: Unwin Hyman, 1988.

———. *Parentage and Inheritance in the Novels of Charles Dickens.* New York: Cambridge University Press, 1994.

Sartre, Jean-Paul. "William Faulkner's *Sartoris*" (1938). (A translation of the essay by Melvin Freidman can be found in Kinney 142–46.)

Scafella, Frank. *Hemingway: Essays of Reassessment.* New York: Oxford University Press, 1991.

Sewall, Richard B. *The Life of Emily Dickinson.* 2 vols. New York: Farrar, Straus & Giroux, 1974.

Shakespeare, William. "*The History of King Lear.*" Oxford World's Classics. Edited by Stanley Wells. New York: Oxford University Press, 2000.

———. *The Norton Shakespeare.* Based on the Oxford Edition. Edited by Stephen Greenblatt, Walter Cohen, Jean E. Howard, and Katharine Eisenman Maus. New York: Norton, 1997.

———. *The RSC Shakespeare: William Shakespeare's Complete Works.* Edited by Jonathan Bate and Eric Rasmussen. New York: Modern Library, 2007.

———. *The Tragedy of "King Lear."* New Cambridge Shakespeare. Edited by Jay L. Halio. Cambridge: Cambridge University Press, 1992.

Shattuck, Charles H. "Setting Shakespeare Free." *Journal of Aesthetic Education* 17, no. 4 (Winter 1983): 107–23.

Shattuck, Roger. *Proust's Way: A Field Guide to* In Search of Lost Time. New York: Norton, 2000.

The Slave's Narrative. Edited by Charles T. David and Henry Louis Gates Jr. New York: Oxford University Press, 1985.

Smith, Martha Nell. Dickinson Electronic Archives. https://www.emilydickinson.org

———. *Rowing in Eden: Rereading Emily Dickinson.* Austin: University of Texas Press, 1992.

Stanton, Elizabeth Cady, Susan B. Anthony, and Matilda Joslyn Gage, eds. *History of Woman Suffrage.* Vol. 1. 1881. Reprint, New York: Arno Press, 1969.

Stepto, Robert B. "Distrust of the Reader in Afro-American Narratives." In *Reconstructing American Literary History,* edited by Sacvan Berkovitch. Cambridge: Harvard University Press, 1986.

Sterling, Dorothy: *We Are Your Sisters: Black Women in the Nineteenth Century.* New York: Norton, 1984.

Stevenson, Anne. *Bitter Fame: A Life of Sylvia Plath.* Boston: Houghton Mifflin, 1989.

Stillinger, Jack. *Multiple Authorship and the Myth of Solitary Genius.* New York: Oxford University Press, 1991.

Sundquist, Eric J. *Faulkner: The House Divided.* Baltimore: Johns Hopkins University Press, 1983.

Taggard, Genevieve. *The Life and Mind of Emily Dickinson.* New York: Knopf, 1930.

Tanselle, G. Thomas. *A Rationale of Textual Criticism.* Philadelphia: University of Pennsylvania Press, 1989.

Todd, Mabel Loomis, with Millicent Todd Bingham. *Bolts of Melody: New Poems of Emily Dickinson.* New York: Harper, 1945.

——— . *Letters of Emily Dickinson.* Edited by Mabel Loomis Todd. 1894. Reprint, New York: Harper & Brothers, 1931.

——— . *Poems.* Edited by Mabel Loomis Todd and T. W. Higginson. Boston: Robert Brothers, 1890.

——— . *Poems, Second Series.* Edited by T. W. Higginson and Mabel Loomis Todd. Boston: Robert Brothers, 1891.

——— . *Poems, Third Series.* Edited by Mabel Loomis Todd. Boston: Roberts Brothers, 1896.

Twain, Mark. *Mississippi Writings: "The Adventures of Tom Sawyer," "Life on the Mississippi," "Adventures of Huckleberry Finn," "Pudd'nhead Wilson."* Edited by Guy Cardwell. New York: Library of America, 1982.

Urkovitz, Steven. *Shakespeare's Revision of "King Lear."* Princeton: Princeton University Press, 1980.

Vendler, Helen. *Dickinson: Selected Poems and Commentaries.* Cambridge: Belknap Press of Harvard University Press, 2010.

——— . "An Intractable Metal." In *Ariel Ascending: Writings about Sylvia Plath,* edited by Paul Alexander. New York: HarperCollins, 1985.

Walsh, John Evangelist. *The Hidden Life of Emily Dickinson.* New York: Simon & Schuster, 1971.

Weiskel, Thomas. *The Romantic Sublime: Studies in the Structure and Psychology of Transcendence.* Baltimore: Johns Hopkins University Press, 1976.

Werner, Marta L. *Emily Dickinson: The Gorgeous Nothings.* Edited by Marta Werner, Jen Bevin, and Susan Howe. New York: New Directions, 2013.

——— . *Emily Dickinson's Open Folios: Scenes of Reading, Surfaces of Writing.* Ann Arbor: University of Michigan Press, 1995.

——— . *Radical Scatters: Emily Dickinson's Late Fragments and Related Texts.* Amherst: University of Massachusetts Press, 2005.

Williams, Bernard. *Shame and Necessity.* Berkeley: University of California Press, 1994.

Williams, George Walton. Review of *The Division of the Kingdoms: Shakespeare's Two Versions of "King Lear."* Medieval and Renaissance Drama 2 (1995): 343–50.

Wilson, Edmund. "The Fruits of the MLA I: 'Their Wedding Journey.'" *New York Review of Books* 11, no. 5, September 26, 1968, 8–12.

Wilson, Frances. *The Ballad of Dorothy Wordsworth: A Life.* 2008. Reprint, New York: Farrar, Straus & Giroux, 2016.

———. *How to Survive the "Titanic," or the Sinking of J. Bruce Ismay.* New York: Harper, 2011.

Wordsworth, Dorothy. *The Grasmere and Alfoxden Journals.* Edited by Pamela Woof. Oxford: Oxford University Press, 2008.

Wordsworth, Jonathan. *William Wordsworth: The Borders of Vision.* New York: Oxford University Press, 1982.

Wordsworth, William. *Major Works Including "The Prelude."* Edited by Stephen Gill. Oxford: Oxford University Press, 2008.

———. *The Prelude.* Edited by Ernest de Selincourt. 1926. 2nd ed., revised by Helen Darbishire. Oxford: Oxford University Press, 1959.

———. *The Prelude, 1799, 1805, 1850.* Norton Critical Edition. Edited by Jonathan Wordsworth, M. H. Abrams, and Stephen Gill. New York: Norton, 1979.

———. *The Prelude: The Four Texts (1798, 1799, 1805, 1850).* Edited by Jonathan Wordsworth. New York: Penguin, 1995.

———. *Wordsworth: Poetical Works.* Edited by Thomas Hutchinson and Ernest de Selincourt. London: Oxford University Press, 1974.

Wyatt, David M. *Prodigal Sons: A Study in Authorship and Authority.* Baltimore: Johns Hopkins University Press, 1980.

Yellin, Jean Fagan. *Harriet Jacobs: A Life.* New York: Basic Civitas Books, 2004.

Zak, William F. *Sovereign Shame: A Study of "King Lear."* Lewisburg, PA: Bucknell University Press, 1984.

INDEX

Aaron, Daniel, 6
Adelman, Janet, 32, 34
All the Year Round (journal), 61
Alvarez, Al, 150, 157, 162, 165
   The Savage God: A Study of Suicide, 150, 165
American Literature (journal), 103
Amy Post Family Papers, 104
Anderson, Charles, 119
   Emily Dickinson's Poetry: Stairway of Surprise, 119
Anderson, Sherwood, 187
Andrews, William L., 90, 96–97, 101
Anthony, Susan B., 100
   History of Woman Suffrage, 100
Anti-Slavery Bugle (newspaper), 87
Auden, W. H., 94

Baker, Carlos, 169
Bate, Jonathan, 19
Bates, Arlo, 111
Bevington, David, 16–17
Bianchi, Martha Dickinson, 111–12, 115–16, 122
   Emily Dickinson Face to Face: Unpublished Letters with Notes and Reminiscences, 111–12
   The Life and Letters of Emily Dickinson, 116
   The Single Hound: Poems of a Lifetime, 115
Bingham, Millicent Todd, 112–16, 119, 122
   Ancestors' Brocades: The Literary Debut of Emily Dickinson, 114, 116, 119
   Bolts of Melody: New Poems of Emily Dickinson, 115

Bishop, Elizabeth, 116, 118
   "Crusoe in England," 118
Blackmur, R. P., 125
Blake, William, 7
Blank, G. Kim, 48
Blassingame, John W., 86, 102
   The Slave Community: Plantation Life in the Antebellum South, 86, 102
   Slave Testimony: Two Centuries of Letters, Speeches, Interviews, and Autobiographies, 102
Blotner, Joseph, 127, 130–32
   Faulkner: A Biography, 131
Boni & Liveright, 129–32
Bontemps, Arna, 101
   Great Slave Narratives, 101
Bowers, Fredson, 4, 7
Bradbury, Nicola, 66
Bradley, A. C., 34, 52
Bradley, Adam, 189–90, 197, 203–5
   Ralph Ellison in Progress: From "Invisible Man" to "Three Days before the Shooting . . .," 204
Brague, Harry, 169
Brain, Tracy, 163
   "Unstable Manuscripts: The Indeterminacy of the Plath Canon," 163
Brawley, Benjamin, 101
   The Negro in Literature and Art in the United States, 101
Brown, Carolyn, 67
Brown, John, 87, 89

Bryant, John, 5
Bulwer-Lytton, Edward, 60–61
   A Strange Story, 61
Bundtzen, Linda, 153, 159–60, 165
   The Other "Ariel," 153, 165
Burwell, Rose Marie, 172

Callahan, John F., 188–90, 194–95, 197, 203
Cameron, Sharon, 119, 125
   Lyric Time: Dickinson and the Limits of Genre, 119
Castro, Fidel, 168
Cavell, Stanley, 27–28
Center for Editions of American Authors, 4–7
Center for Scholarly Editions, 4–7
Chamberlin, Brewster, 180
   The Hemingway Log: A Chronology of His Life and Times, 180
Chesterton, G. K., 62
Child, Lydia Maria, 85, 89–91, 100–107
Christensen, Lena, 121
Christian Recorder (newspaper), 87
Clark, Heather, 155–56, 166
   The Grief of Influence: Sylvia Plath and Ted Hughes, 156
   Red Comet: The Short Life and Blazing Art of Sylvia Plath, 155–56
Clifford, Deborah Pickman, 87
Coffin, Joshua, 87
Coleridge, Samuel Taylor, 14–15, 18, 45–46
   "Dejection: An Ode," 45
Coleridge, Sara, 45–46
Collins, Wilkie, 60
Connor, Marc C., 188
Coverdale, Miles, 210
Cowley, Malcolm, 169
Crane, Stephen, 4
Crazy Horse, 202
Crouch, Stanley, 188
Crumbley, Paul, 119
   Inflections of the Pen: Dash and Voice in Emily Dickinson, 119

Daleski, H. M., 62–63
Darbishire, Helen, 28
Darlington, Beth, 54

The Love Letters of William and Mary Wordsworth, 54–56
Day, Douglas, 134–38, 140
de Selincourt, Ernest, 38
Dickens, Charles, 9, 11, 57–84
   David Copperfield, 9, 11, 57–84
   Great Expectations (Norton Critical Edition), 57–84
   Great Expectations (Oxford World's Classics), 78, 80
   Little Dorrit, 79
   The Mystery of Edwin Drood, 73
Dickinson, Austin, 109, 111–14
Dickinson, Edward (Ned), 113
Dickinson, Emily, 1, 2, 7, 9, 11, 89, 109–25
—editions:
   The Poems of Emily Dickinson (1955), 116, 118
   The Poems of Emily Dickinson: Variorum Edition (1998), 116, 118
—poems:
   "I cannot live with You," 117
   "I died for Beauty – but was scarce," 111
   "I wish I were a Hay," 110
   "Publication – is the Auction," 1, 110
   "Safe in their Alabaster Chambers," 111, 117
   "The Sea said," 120
   "Wild Nights," 119, 123–25
Dickinson, Lavinia, 109–114
Dickinson, Susan Gilbert, 109–25
Dickinson, Thomas Gilbert, 113, 118
Dickinson Electronic Archives, 122
Didion, Joan, 8–9, 108
   "Last Words," 8
Dietrich, Marlene, 170
Donne, John, 124
   "A Valediction: Forbidding Mourning," 124
Douglas-Fairhurst, Robert, 82
Douglass, Frederick, 86–87, 101, 103
   Narrative of the Life of Frederick Douglass, 86–87
Du Bois, W. E. B., 99
   The Souls of Black Folk, 99
Dupee, F. W., 1

Eliot, T. S., 21, 147
Elkins, Stanley, 102

Ellison, Fanny, 189, 192, 194
Ellison, Ralph, 7, 9, 11, 188–207
—books:
  Invisible Man, 188–189, 191, 193
  Juneteenth, 188, 193–95
  The Selected Letters of Ralph Ellison, 188
  Shadow and Act, 195, 206
  Three Days before the Shooting . . ., 9, 188, 193–207
—stories:
  "And Hickman Arrives," 193–94
  "Backwacking, a Plea to the Senator," 193
  "Cadillac Flambé," 193–94
  "It Always Breaks Out," 193
  "Juneteenth," 193–94
  "Night-Talk," 193–94
  "The Roof, the Steeple and the People," 193–94
  "A Song of Innocence," 193
Emerson, Ralph Waldo, 4, 139
Emily Dickinson Archive, 122
Emily Dickinson Collection, 122
Engle, Paul, 191
Erasmus, 210
Erskine, Albert, 134

Faber & Faber, 157
Faulkner, William, 6–7, 9–11, 126–46, 193, 212
  Absalom, Absalom!, 9–11, 137–38, 142, 145, 212
  As I Lay Dying, 128
  Flags in the Dust (1973), 134–43
  Flags in the Dust (2006), 128–43
  Light in August, 127, 129
  Mosquitoes, 128
  "An Odor of Verbena," 143–46
  Sanctuary, 128, 141
  Sartoris, 127–46
  Soldier's Pay, 128
  The Sound and the Fury, 127, 129–30, 133, 141–42
  "Twilight," 129
  The Unvanquished, 143–46
  "Vendée," 143, 146
  William Faulkner Manuscripts 5: Flags in the Dust, 127

"William Faulkner's Essay on the Composition of *Sartoris*," 130–32
Feinstein, Elaine, 165
Fielding, K. J., 61
Fitzgerald, F. Scott, 62, 76
  The Great Gatsby, 62, 76
Fleming, Robert E., 169
Flint, Kate, 65
Foreman, P. Gabrielle, 86
Forster, John, 60–61
Foucault, Michel, 26
Fox-Genovese, Elizabeth, 102–3
  Within the Plantation Household: Black and White Women of the Old South, 102–3
Frankenstein (Shelley), 75
Franklin, John Hope, 94
  From Slavery to Freedom: A History of Negro Americans (1947), 94
Franklin, R. W., 111, 115–16, 118–19, 121–25
  The Manuscript Books of Emily Dickinson, 121
  The Poems of Emily Dickinson: Variorum Edition, 116, 118
Franklin, Wayne,
  "The 'Library of America' and the Welter of American Books," 6
Fraser, Russell, 27
Freud, Sigmund, 62

Garfield, Deborah M., 93
Garrison, William Lloyd, 87
Gay, Peter, 113
  Education of the Senses: Victoria to Freud, 113
Gellhorn, Martha, 170
Gelpi, Albert J., 116
Gissing, George, 62
Goldsby, Jacqueline, 86, 107
Gosse, Edmund, 42
  Father and Son, 42
Gould, George, 116
Grand Street (magazine), 163
Granville-Barker, Harley, 30
Greenblatt, Stephen, 15, 27
Greetham, D. C., 7

Greg, W. W., 3, 7, 17
   The Editorial Problem in Shakespeare: A Survey of the Foundations of the Text, 17
   "The Rationale of the Copy-Text," 3
Grimké, Angelina, 87, 95
Grimké, Francis J., 100

Habegger, Alfred, 115, 117, 124
Halio, Jay L., 17
Hall, Mary Lee, 112, 114
Harcourt, Alfred, 130–33
Harcourt Brace & Company, 130–33
Harsnett, Samuel, 27
Hart, Ellen Louise, 112, 118–19
   Open Me Carefully: Emily Dickinson's Intimate Correspondence to Susan Huntington Dickinson, 118–19
Hass, Robert, 123
Hawthorne, Nathaniel, 4, 6
Hayhoe, George F., 135
Hemingway, Edward, 181
Hemingway, Ernest, 2, 8–9, 11–12, 39, 92, 108, 169–87, 195
   Across the River and into the Trees, 169, 174
   "Big Two-Hearted River," 174
   The Dangerous Summer, 8, 169
   A Farewell to Arms, 173–74, 179
   "Fathers and Sons," 176–77
   The Garden of Eden, 2, 8, 168–72, 181–86
   Green Hills of Africa, 170–71
   "Green Hills of Africa: Part I" (serialization), 171
   "Indian Camp," 176–77
   In Our Time, 174
   Islands in the Stream, 169, 173–80
   Manuscript of *The Garden of Eden*, 168, 183
   Manuscript of *The Old Man and the Sea*, 175
   A Moveable Feast (1964), 2, 8, 92, 108, 168, 172, 183–87
   A Moveable Feast: The Restored Edition, 169, 184, 186
   The Old Man and the Sea, 169, 174–75
   "The Short Happy Life of Francis Macomber," 177–78
   The Sun Also Rises, 173–74
   True at First Light, 2, 168–73
   Under Kilimanjaro, 169–70
   "Up in Michigan," 174
Hemingway, Gregory, 176, 179–81, 183
   Papa: A Personal Memoir, 180
Hemingway, Hadley, 170–72, 176, 183–86
Hemingway, John Hadley Nicanor, 176
Hemingway, Mary, 8, 168–73, 182, 184
Hemingway, Patrick, 170, 176
Hemingway, Pauline Pfeiffer, 170–72, 176, 180, 183
Hemingway, Seán, 169
Hemingway, Valerie, 168, 181
   Running with the Bulls: My Life with the Hemingways, 181
Hersey, John, 195
Higgins, John, 27
Higginson, Thomas W., 110–11, 119, 124
Holinshed, Raphael, 27
Horniblow, Margaret, 91
House, Humphry, 59
Howe, Irving, 196
Howe, Susan, 120
Howells, William Dean, 62
Hughes, Frieda, 150–51, 159, 163, 167
Hughes, Nicholas, 151
Hughes, Olwyn, 150, 153, 156
Hughes, Ted, 147, 149–67
   "Astringency," 151
   Birthday Letters, 151–52
   "The Evolution of 'Sheep in Fog,'" 159
   The Hawk in the Rain, 165–66
   Lupercal, 166
   Recklings, 166
   Wodwo, 166
Hurley, Cheryl, 5
Hutchinson, Sara, 45–46
Hyman, Stanley Edgar, 191
Irwin, John T., 142
   Doubling and Incest / Repetition and Revenge, 142

Jacobs, Harriet A., 9, 11, 85–108
   The Deeper Wrong, 107
   Harriet Jacobs Family Papers, 101
   Incidents in the Life of a Slave Girl (Yellin 1987), 85–108

Incidents in the Life of a Slave Girl (Teller 1973), 101–2
Jacobs, John, 91, 97
Jacobs, Joseph, 97
Jacobs, Louisa, 88, 97, 105
James, Henry, 1, 208–9
    The Art of the Novel, 208
    The Cambridge Edition of the Complete Fiction of Henry James, 209
    The Europeans, 208
    The Golden Bowl, 208
    The New York Edition, 1, 208–9
    Washington Square, 208
    The Wings of the Dove, 209
Jenks, Tom, 8, 169, 183
Jerome, Saint, 210
Johnson, Jack, 202
Johnson, Thomas H., 116, 118, 122
Johnson, Samuel, 2, 13–14, 16, 18, 25, 35, 65, 108
Jonathan Cape, 133
Jonathan Cape and Harrison Smith, 133
Jonson, Ben, 161–62
    —books:
    Epigrammes, 161
    The Forrest, 161–62
    Under-wood, 161–62
    —poems:
    "That Women Are but Men's Shadows," 162
    "To Celia," 161
    "To Heaven," 162
    "To Penshurst," 162
    "To Sickness," 162
    "To the Reader," 162
    "To the World," 162
    "Why I Write Not of Love," 161

Keats, John, 18
Kennedy, J. Gerald, 184
Kermode, Frank, 15
King James Bible, 209–12
King, Martin Luther, Jr., 193
Kirschbaum, Leo, 23–24

Lamb, Charles, 15
Lee, Robert E., 202

Lessing, Doris, 154–55
    Walking in the Shade: Volume Two of My Autobiography—1949–1962, 154
Levine, Robert S., 6, 125
    "Editing Melville's *Pierre*: Text, Nation, Time," 6
    The Norton Anthology of American Literature. Vol. B: 1820–1865, 125
Lewalski, Barbara K., 18, 23
Lewis, Robert W., 169
Liberator (newspaper), 87
Library of America, 5–6, 128, 134–35
    Crime Novels, 6
    Reporting Vietnam, 6
Life magazine, 169
Lincoln, Abraham, 201–2
Lindberg-Seyersted, Brita, 119
Liveright, Horace, 129
Loggins, Vernon, 101
    The Negro Author: His Development in America, 101
Lord, Otis Phillips, 116
Lowell, Robert, 157
Luther, Martin, 210

Mack, Maynard, 31, 33
Mack, Maynard (Sandy), Jr., 27
Macready, William Charles, 14
Malcolm, Janet, 150, 155, 165
    The Silent Woman: Sylvia Plath and Ted Hughes, 150, 155
May, Samuel J., Jr., 87
McGann, Jerome J., 7, 120
    A Critique of Modern Textual Criticism, 7
McKerrow, Roland B., 3, 5
McPherson, James Alan, 192
Meckier, Jerome, 62, 77
Melville, Herman, 4–6
    Pierre; Or, the Ambiguities, 6
    The Writings of Herman Melville, 5
Meriwether, James, 135
Meyers, Lucas, 165
Middlebrook, Diane, 153
    "Creative Partnership: Sources for 'The Rabbit Catcher,'" 153

Miller, Cristanne, 121
   Emily Dickinson's Poems: As She Preserved Them, 121
Miller, J. Hillis, 64
Milton, John, 62, 77–84, 210–13
   Paradise Lost, 62, 77–84, 210–13
Miner, Earl, 161
Mississippi Quarterly (journal), 135
Mitchell, Domhnall, 118, 120–21
   Measures of Possibility: Emily Dickinson's Manuscripts, 120
Modern Language Association, 3, 7
   MLA Bibliography, 109
Moland, Lydia, 107
Montaigne, 27
Moorman, Mary, 41, 47, 54–55
Morris, Timothy, 117
Morrison, Toni, 98–100, 193
   Beloved, 98–100, 108
Moses, 210
Mowrer, Paul, 183
Moynahan, Julian, 62
Mumford, Lewis, 4
   "Emerson behind Barbed Wire," 4
Murray, Albert, 189–90, 205

The Narrative of James Williams, 101
Nashe, Thomas, 3
National Anti-Slavery Standard (newspaper), 89
National Endowment for the Humanities, 4, 6
Nell, William C., 87, 103
New York Daily Tribune (newspaper), 88
New York Review of Books (magazine), 5
New York Times (newspaper), 192
Norcom, James, 91, 107
Norcom, Mary, 91
The Norton Anthology of English Literature, 3rd edition, 38

Observer (newspaper), 158, 162
Onorato, Richard, 41–42, 51
Orgel, Stephen, 22

Parker, Hershel, 4–5
   "Textual Criticism and Hemingway," 4
Parks, Rosa, 193

Parrish, Timothy, 189, 193
   Ralph Ellison and the Genius of America, 189
Percival, Phillip, 170
Perkins, Max, 89
Perloff, Marjorie, 149, 161, 163, 165
   "The Two *Ariels*: The (Re)Making of the Sylvia Plath Canon," 161
Perlow, Seth, 110
Phillips, Wendell, 87
Plath, Aurelia, 157
Plath, Sylvia, 7, 9, 11, 147–67
—books:
   Ariel (1965), 147, 156–67
   Ariel: The Restored Edition, 163–67
   The Collected Poems, 158–59, 164
   The Bell Jar, 156, 166
   The Colossus and Other Poems, 163, 166
   Crossing the Water, 166
   Johnny Panic and the Bible of Dreams, 166
   The Journals of Sylvia Plath, 163, 166
   The Letters of Sylvia Plath, 150
   Winter Trees, 158, 166
—poems:
   "The Applicant," 159
   "Ariel," 157, 163
   "The Arrival of the Bee Box," 159
   "Barren Woman," 158
   "A Birthday Present," 157
   "The Bee Meeting," 157, 159
   "Contusion," 160
   "The Couriers," 159
   "Cut," 157
   "Daddy," 157, 162, 166
   "Death & Co.," 157, 163
   "Edge," 158, 160
   "The Jailor," 158
   "Kindness," 159
   "Lady Lazarus," 157, 159
   "Lesbos," 157
   "Magi," 163
   "Mary's Song," 157
   "Morning Song," 157, 159
   "Poppies in July," 159–60
   "The Rabbit Catcher," 147–67
   "The Rival," 157
   "A Secret," 158

"Sheep in Fog," 159
"Stings," 160
"The Swarm," 157, 160
"Thalidomide," 159
"Wintering," 157, 160
"Words," 158, 160
Pietsch, Michael, 169
Playboy (magazine), 192
Poirier, Richard, 5
Polk, Noel, 6–7, 128, 134–38, 140–41
   Children of the Dark House: Text and Context in Faulkner, 7
   Noel Polk Papers, 128
Pollack, Vivian, 117
   Dickinson: The Anxiety of Gender, 117
Pope, Alexander, 9, 16–17, 31–32, 34
Porter, Carolyn, 138
Post, Amy Kirby, 87–89, 103–8
Price, Reynolds, 176

Railton, Stephen, 136
   Digital Yoknapatawpha, 136
Rampersad, Arnold, 192–93
Remnick, David, 192
The Riddle of Emily Dickinson (Patterson), 116
Rose, Jacqueline, 147, 153–56
   The Haunting of Sylvia Plath, 153, 155–56
Rosenberg, Edgar, 61, 72–73, 75, 78, 80, 84
Rosenstein, Harriet, 156

Sadrin, Anny, 74–74, 82
Sartre, Jean-Paul, 138
Sawyer, Samuel Tredwell, 107
Scribner, Charles, Jr., 169
Scribner's Magazine, 171
Sewall, Richard B., 110, 112–13, 115, 117–18
   The Life of Emily Dickinson, 113
Shakespeare, William, 1, 9, 11, 13–35
   All's Well that Ends Well, 29
   King Lear (Oxford World's Classics), 17
   The Life of Henry the Fifth, 2
   Love's Labours Lost, 29
   Measure for Measure, 26
   A Midsummer Night's Dream, 21
   Much Ado About Nothing, 26
   The Norton Shakespeare, 2, 15–16, 18

Oxford Shakespeare, 16
Pericles, 16
The Tempest, 21
The Tragedy of Hamlet, 21, 29, 30
The Tragedy of "King Lear" (New Cambridge Shakespeare), 17
The Tragedy of King Lear: A Conflated Text (The Norton Shakespeare), 3, 9, 12, 13–35
Troilus and Cressida, 25–26
The Two Noble Kinsmen, 16
Shattuck, Charles H., 14
Shaw, George Bernard, 61–62, 78
Shore, Jane, 36
Slocum, Joshua, 86
Smith, Harrison, 130–33
Smith, Martha Nell, 112, 117–20, 122, 125
   Dickinson Electronic Archives, 122
   Open Me Carefully: Emily Dickinson's Intimate Correspondence to Susan Huntington Dickinson, 118–19
   Rowing in Eden: Rereading Emily Dickinson, 117, 125
Soares, Lota de Macedo, 118
Socrates, 26
Spaulding, Timothy, 114
Spectator (magazine), 65
Spenser, Edmund, 27
Stanton, Elizabeth Cady, 100
Stepto, Robert B., 90, 93–94
   "Distrust of the Reader in Afro-American Narratives," 93–94
Sterling, Dorothy, 104–5
   We Are Your Sisters: Black Women in the Nineteenth Century, 104–5
Stevenson, Anne, 150, 153, 155–56
   Bitter Fame: A Life of Sylvia Plath, 155–56
Stillinger, Jack, 53
Stimpson, Catherine, 117
Stowe, Harriet Beecher, 6, 87–88, 100, 105, 107
   The Key to Uncle Tom's Cabin, 88, 105
   Uncle Tom's Cabin, 87, 100
Summers, Jill, 134–35
Sundquist, Eric J., 133, 140

Taggard, Genevieve, 116
Tanselle, G. Thomas, 5

A Rationale of Textual Criticism, 5
Tate, Nahum, 13–14
Taylor, Gary, 16
Teller, Walter Magnes, 101–2
Theobold, Lewis, 2
Todd, David Peck, 113–14
Todd, Mabel Loomis, 109–15, 119, 124–25
   Bolts of Melody: New Poems of Emily Dickinson (Todd and Binghan), 115
   Letters of Emily Dickinson (Todd), 111
   Poems by Emily Dickinson (Todd and Higginson), 111
   Poems, Second Series (Higginson and Todd), 111
   Poems, Third Series (Todd), 111
The True Chronicle History of King Leir and His Three Daughters, 27
Truth, Sojourner, 100, 103
Tubman, Harriet, 100
Twain, Mark, 3–4, 94–95, 195
   Adventures of Huckleberry Finn, 94–95, 108, 195
Tyler, Julia, 88, 105
Tyndale, William, 210

Urkovitz, Steven, 24–25
   Shakespeare's Revision of "King Lear," 24–25

Vallon, Annette, 47–49, 53, 55
Vendler, Helen, 119, 124, 167

Wadsworth, Charles, 116
Walsh, Ernest, 173
Wasson, Ben, 130–33, 136
Weiskel, Thomas, 43–44
Wells, Stanley, 14, 16–17, 23
Werner, Marta L., 117, 120
   Emily Dickinson: The Gorgeous Nothings, 117, 122
   Emily Dickinson's Open Folios: Scenes of Reading, Surfaces of Writing, 120
"Western Wind" (poem), 173
Wevill, Assia, 149, 153
Wevill, David, 153

Whitman, Walt, 4, 6
Whittier, John Greenleaf, 87
Williams, Bernard, 145
   Shame and Necessity, 145
Williams, George Walton, 15
Willis, Bailey, 106
Willis, Cornelia, 88–89, 106
Willis, Nathaniel Parker, 104, 107
Wilson, Edmund, 4–6
   "The Fruits of the MLA I: 'Their Wedding Journey,'" 4
Wilson, Frances, 48, 50–51, 55
   The Ballad of Dorothy Wordsworth: A Life, 48
Wolfe, Thomas, 89
Wordsworth, Ann, 51
Wordsworth, Anne-Caroline, 47–48
Wordsworth, Dora, 38
Wordsworth, Dorothy, 38, 45–54
Wordsworth, John, 45–46
Wordsworth, Jonathan, 38–39, 43, 53
Wordsworth, Mary, 37–38, 45–56
Wordsworth, William, 9, 11, 36–57
—editions of *The Prelude*:
   The Prelude (ed. de Selincourt), 38
   The Prelude: The Four Texts (1798, 1799, 1805, 1850), 36–56
   "The Two-Part Prelude," 38, 39–41, 44, 49, 51–52
—poems and introductions:
   "Preface to Lyrical Ballads," 49
   "Resolution and Independence," 45
   "The Ruined Cottage," 55
   "Tintern Abbey," 49, 52–53
   "Vaudracour and Julia," 48–49
   "Yarrow Revisited," 45
Wyclif, John, 210

Yellin, Jean Fagan, 90, 97, 100–101, 103–8
   Harriet Jacobs: A Life, 97, 100
   "The Intricate Knot: Black Figures in American Literature," 103

Zak, William F., 32
   Sovereign Shame: A Study of "King Lear", 32

www.ingramcontent.com/pod-product-compliance
Lightning Source LLC
Chambersburg PA
CBHW020328240426
43665CB00044B/894